Brahms and His World

THE BARD MUSICAL FESTIVAL

*Other Princeton University Press volumes
published in conjuction with The Bard
Music Festival*

Brahms and His World
   edited by Walter Frisch (1990)

Mendelssohn and His World
   edited by R. Larry Todd (1991)

Richard Strauss and His World
   edited by Bryan Gilliam (1992)

Dvořák and His World
   edited by Michael Beckerman (1993)

Schumann and His World
   edited by R. Larry Todd (1994)

Bartók and His World
   edited by Peter Laki (1995)

Charles Ives and His World
   edited by J. Peter Burkholder (1996)

Brahms

Edited by Walter Frisch

and
His
World

Princeton University Press
Princeton, New Jersey

Copyright © 1990 by
Princeton University Press
Published by
Princeton University Press
41 William Street,
Princeton, New Jersey 08540
In the United Kingdom:
Princeton University Press,
Chichester, West Sussex

All Rights Reserved

Library of Congress
Cataloging-in-Publication Data

Brahms and His World
edited by Walter Frisch
p.   cm.
Includes bibliographical references
and index
Partial Contents:
Essays, Reception, Analysis
and Memoirs.
ISBN 0-691-09139-0 (cloth)
ISBN 0-691-02713-7 (paper)
    1. Brahms, Johannes, 1833–1897
    I. Frisch, Walter
    ML410.B8B65   1990
    780' .92—dc20   90-8623
                          CIP
    7 6 5 4 3   MN

Princeton University Press books are
printed on acid-free paper and meet
the guidelines for permanence and
durability of the Committee on
Production Guidelines for Book
Longevity of the Council on Library
Resources

Contents

Preface and Acknowledgments

This volume was conceived as a companion to a music festival entitled "Rediscovering Brahms," held at Bard College in Annandale-on-Hudson, New York, in August 1990. The festival placed Brahms in the context of his own time by programming his works alongside those of such figures as Joseph Joachim, Karl Goldmark, Clara Schumann, Johann Strauss, Alexander Zemlinsky, Eugen d'Albert, and Robert Fuchs.

The book seeks a complementary contextualization by means of a three-part design. In Part 1, six scholars probe aspects of Brahms's relationship to his world. The kinds of relationship treated might be categorized roughly as personal (Ostwald, Reich), cultural-aesthetic (Botstein), compositional (Brodbeck, Frisch), and piano-technical (Bozarth and Brady).

Part 2 comprises substantial selections from contemporary or near-contemporary analyses and reviews. The commentaries by Schubring, Kretschmar, Hanslick, and Tovey all form part of a characteristic nineteenth-century tradition whose verbal language and imagery reveal much about the way Brahms's music (and that of other composers) was understood in its day. The excerpts by German commentators appear here in English for the first time.

In Part 3, important memoirs of Brahms are presented in translation, also for the first time. The excerpt from Gustav Jenner contains invaluable testimony from Brahms's only private pupil in composition. The Hanslick segment is notable for its avoidance of sentimentality (unlike many Brahms memoirs) and for its wealth of information about Brahms's views on such topics as Beethoven's compositional development and contemporary art and politics. The brief memoirs by Zemlinsky and Weigl suggest how much Brahms was revered by a younger generation of Viennese composers that had only a brief opportunity to know him as a living figure.

Many dexterous hands and sharp minds helped bring this book into being in a remarkably short time. Elizabeth Powers of Princeton University Press displayed quiet and firm faith in the project when it was only fractionally baked. Dan Schillaci and Cynthia Saniewski have guided the book smoothly through the production process. Leon Botstein generously and enthusiastically shared his encyclopedic knowledge of Viennese culture; he contributed the introductions to the Kretschmar and Hanslick selections and provided many helpful annotations for parts 2 and 3. Susan Gillespie deserves mountains of gratitude for translating large chunks of difficult German prose with extraordinary speed and elegance. I am grateful to the Wiener Stadtbibliothek for permission to make use of Brahms's handwritten list of dedications, which forms the basis of the Appendix. Virginia

Hancock kindly provided me with a photocopy of this document and also helped transcribe the composer's occasionally problematic handwriting. Gregory Leet diligently tracked down vital information about many of those obscure composers who appear in the Appendix and who formed the interstellar dust in the nineteenth-century musical galaxy where Brahms shone brightly. The handsome musical examples for this book were prepared by Don Giller. Karen Painter prepared the Index. The editor of this volume and the organizers of "Rediscovering Brahms" also acknowledge the generous assistance of the Andrew W. Mellon Foundation.

Earlier, briefer versions of the articles by Nancy Reich, George Bozarth and Stephen Brady, and Walter Frisch appeared in the American Brahms Society News-letter, respectively in issues 3/2 (Autumn 1985), 6/2 (Autumn 1988), and 7/1 (Spring 1989). The article by Peter Ostwald appeared in a previous form in German as "Johannes Brahms: 'Frei aber (nicht immer) froh,'" in *Johannes Brahms: Leben, Werk, Interpretation, Rezeption. Kongreßbericht zum III. Gewandhaus Symposium* (Leipzig, 1983), pp. 52–55. A more expanded version will appear as "Johannes Brahms—Music, Loneliness, and Altruism," in *Psychoanalytic Explorations in Music,* ed. Stuart Feder, Richard Karmel, and George Pollock (Madison CT, forthcoming). The editor gratefully acknowledges the permission of Oxford University Press to reprint Donald F. Tovey's essay on the Joachim Hungarian Violin Concerto.

Walter Frisch
New York, May 1990

part

1

Essays

Leon Botstein

Time and Memory: Concert Life, Science, and Music in Brahms's Vienna

How can one grasp the nature and impact of Brahms's musical language and communication in his own time? In the first instance one has to guard against an uncritical sense of the stability of musical texts, their meaning and how they can be read and heard. The acoustic, cultural, and temporal habits of life of the late nineteenth century in which Brahms's music functioned demand reconsideration if the listener in the late twentieth century wishes to gain an historical perspective on Brahms's music and its significance. A biographical strategy and the history of critical reception themselves are insufficient.

Brahms's considerable success and notoriety, in Vienna and in German-speaking Europe as a whole, can be approached by a speculative effort to understand better the making of music, the thinking about music, and the listening to music during the latter half of the nineteenth century. In reconstructing the world in which Brahms worked and in trying to reimagine the exchange between Brahms the composer and the various publics to which his music was directed—the meaning of musical discourse in Brahms's era—one aspect of nineteenth-century life and culture on the periphery of musical life can be useful: science and the philosophical and psychological speculation related to it.[1]

Understanding Brahms, his ambitions as an artist, and his impact on his contemporaries requires a grasp of the centrality of science and technology in Brahms's world. His friend the Swiss writer J. V. Widmann described Brahms's own perspective: "Even the smallest discovery, every improvement in any sort of gadget for domestic use; in short, every sign of human reflection, if it was accompanied by practical success, delighted him thoroughly. Nothing escaped his notice . . . if it was something new, in which progress could be discerned." Except for the bicycle, Brahms "felt himself lucky that he lived in the age of great discoveries, and could not praise enough the electric light, Edison's phonograph, and the like."[2] For example, Brahms welcomed innovations in the design and manufacture of pianos.[3]

This widespread late nineteenth-century fascination with scientific progress was sufficiently pervasive to influence the conception of music and the musical experience. The enormous body of writing about the physics of sound, the psychology of hearing, the design of sound-producing instruments, and the aesthetics of music from the latter half of the nineteenth century mirror the intersection of the intense enthusiasms for both music and science. The application of varied scientific and

Leon Botstein, president of Bard College, is the author of *Music and its Public: Habits of Listening and the Crisis of Modernism in Vienna*, forthcoming from University of Chicago Press.

philosophic methods to the nagging questions of beauty, memory, time perception, the nature and meaning of music, consonance, and the historical evolution of musical communication illuminate habits of musical expectation, listening, and judgment.

Systematic thinking, talking, and writing about the lure and consequence of music in themselves were important aspects of the musical experience, particularly in Brahms's Vienna. The writings of such diverse individuals as Hermann Helmholtz, H. A. Koestlin, Heinrich Ehrlich (Brahms's colleague in the 1850s), Theodor Billroth, and other members of the university faculties of Vienna and Prague (e.g., L. A. Zellner, Richard Wallaschek, and the great Ernst Mach) provide evidence of conceptions of music that both mirrored and influenced the contemporary evaluation of the experience of music. In order to make this connection, however, dimensions of the musical world Brahms inhabited require clarification.

I. The Character of Viennese Musical Culture

The salient dimensions of Viennese musical life during Brahms's years were (1) the existence of an active amateur choral tradition; (2) the broadening, re-definition, and domination of music education (as well as the transformation of the ideal of musical sound) by the modern piano in the form it took after the late 1860s; (3) the evolution of musical connoisseurship through reading about music in newspapers, journals, and books; (4) the slow extension of concert life until the 1890s and the gradual formation of a canon in the repertoire; and (5) the professionalization of music history as an aspect of historicism in musical taste.

When one thinks of Brahms's public, particularly in Vienna between 1862 and 1897, one can distinguish among three discrete generations. The first was composed of those who had come of age before 1848: a cohort that included individuals of the ages of Franz Grillparzer (1791–1872), Felix Mendelssohn (1809–47), and Robert Schumann (1810–56). The second was made up of Brahms's exact contemporaries, those born between 1825 and 1848: individuals who had reached full maturity during Brahms's lifetime. The third and last group included those who were young in comparison to Brahms: the generation around Gustav Mahler, individuals born in the 1850s, 60s, and early 70s.

The first group witnessed the great expansion of musical culture. The piano, although the subject of steady technological change between 1820 and 1860, became the leading instrument of musical communication. The first great period of virtuosity and concert life occurred between the years 1815 and 1848. Central to this first generation, however, was the voice and singing. The piano still played a secondary role in music education, in the cultivation of a mode of musical expression that linked words and music. Furthermore, amateur proficiency on string instruments competed and held its own against keyboard amateurism. This was the generation

for whom Beethoven remained the towering presence. The rediscovery of the
musical past, beyond the occasional Handel oratorio, was begun by Mendelssohn
and his contemporaries. This generation fought the first battle for the attention of a
wider public on behalf of serious music, past and present, and for music as a
Romantic art expressive of the poetic and the spiritual. The fight was against the
philistine tendencies of theatricality evident in virtuosity and the puerile sentimentality of efforts to entertain a rapidly growing public for music.

It is instructive to speculate about the impression those Viennese from this first
musically informed generation might have had when Brahms arrived in Vienna in
1862. Apart from the legendary article Robert Schumann wrote about Brahms in
1853, an article on Brahms published in 1856 in perhaps the leading encyclopedic
musical lexicon of the era revealed the extent to which Brahms was regarded as
unformed and a radical new spirit, possibly and ironically at odds with a Classical
aesthetic. The author, Julius Schladebach (1810–72), a trained physician who wrote
church music but worked primarily as a journalist, wrote that apart from the
enthusiasts who agreed with Schumann's assessment, there were those

> *moderatos* who found certainly talent and much courage, but also much rawness,
> lack of skill, and complete immaturity. The courage was not attributed by them
> as deriving from Brahms's uncanny artistic powers but, to the contrary, from a
> lack of skill in formulation, and therefore courage appeared to them rather as
> presumption, one that overrides arrogantly the laws of beauty and perpetrates
> lawlessness, without having sufficiently understood and recognized rules and
> laws; in other words, without having climbed to that level of artistic training
> from which one can distinguish freedom from licentiousness. Which of the two
> camps is right cannot yet be decided today.[4]   4

This judgment possesses a dimension of irony, considering Brahms's later reputation as a conservative and a Classical master, a reputation best demonstrated by the
ceiling painting of the Zürich Tonhalle, which opened in 1895. Brahms was placed
next to Beethoven and on a par with Gluck, Haydn, Bach, Handel, and Mozart.
Wagner was also depicted, but in profile and slightly obscured.[5]   5

This early criticism is also significant in view of Brahms's severe self-criticism
regarding his command of musical form and materials. Brahms's drive to conquer
and extend classical procedures in his work may have been spurred by the awareness
of such criticism from an older established generation. Those contemporaries of
Schumann who did not share Schumann's enthusiasm did so not because they
followed the path set by Liszt, but because they maintained a sensibility far more
traditional than Schumann's. Historians have a tendency to overlook dominant
tastes and aesthetics that seem not to play themselves out through some progressive
and teleological historical narrative. Schumann, after all, generally was not viewed
by his contemporaries as a conservative.

It was in the second generation, however—that of Brahms's exact contemporaries—that the piano advanced substantially over all other mediums of
musical activity. Among amateurs, solo singing was overshadowed by the intense
interest in choral singing. In this generation the professional musician came to
dominate musical life. In Vienna, for example, only in the later 1850s did the
Gesellschaft der Musikfreunde place all activites under the direction of professionals
and systematically begin to eliminate all amateur instrumentalists from official
concerts open to the public at large.

In the mid-century, between 1860 and 1880, music education experienced an
explosive growth, fueled by the piano, a stable, cheaply produced item of modern
engineering and industry. The piano's growing eminence began to direct the mode
of musical education away from techniques of ear-training and pitch recognition to
rote methods for training dexterity so that individuals could play finished works.
But in this generation amateur musical literacy remained high by late twentieth-
century standards. Billroth, for example, possessed exemplary skills and was able
to play several instruments and read scores.[6] Brahms valued his judgment.   6
Amateur composers existed. But during the mid-century, musical education
increasingly depended on reading about music and the teaching of repertoire and
an historical canon, usually beginning with Bach and ending with contemporary composers.

Nevertheless, the overwhelming character of musical culture was one that
underscored musical communication as a mode of contemporary expression. New
works by living composers took central stage, making music publishing a thriving
business, fueled by new works for home and concert hall. The skills of professional
and amateur were directed at a vital art form. Perhaps the most important aspect of
these years was the phenomenal growth in numbers of individuals engaged in
music. This enagagement, however, was still tied to the conceit of active playing
and singing; to the conception of hearing as related to one's capacity to anticipate,
follow, recall, and reproduce what one heard. But it was also in this generation that
a tension was felt between the widening of the audience and future standards of taste.
Musicality and the appreciation of music were clearly understood to be matters of
education and training and superior discernment; emphasis was placed on a high
order of cultural development.

The last generation to encounter Brahms as a living composer experienced the
gradual decline of the choral tradition, the almost total domination of musical
culture by the piano, the erosion of amateur singing and instrumental playing as an
alternative, and the centrality of music journalism. Coincidentally, the change in the
mode of musical education away from the active command of musical skills toward
the training of mechanical facility to reproduce existing works strengthened a
perceptible shift in taste. The historical became defined through familiarity, through
the repetition of selected repertoire.

Concert life achieved some greater frequency. In 1890 in Vienna, for example, there were roughly 240 concerts among the Bösendorfer, Ehrbar, and Musikverein halls. This number included amateur choral groups and group recitals of students. There were only 17 professional concerts using large orchestral and choral forces.[7]   7
And tickets for these were spoken for by an elite. The access to live professional concerts was limited to a mere fraction of the public.

In the decade of the 1880s, a resident of Vienna lucky enough to possess a subscription to the Vienna Philharmonic (which began its tradition of a limited series of regular concerts only in the 1860s) had to wait for nearly a decade to hear all Beethoven symphonies performed by a professional orchestra. The Vienna Philharmonic gave only eight concerts a year, and the tradition of traveling orchestras began in earnest only in the 1890s.[8] Brahms was in his twenties when he first   8
heard Beethoven's Ninth Symphony in Cologne.[9] It was performed in Vienna only   9
13 times in the 34 years between 1863 and 1897. In the five seasons from 1890 to 1895, the great Classical composers, from Haydn to Schumann, occupied 35 percent of the repertoire; Brahms, Wagner, and Bruckner accounted for 12 percent.[10]   10
Musical literacy, therefore, depended on active skills, not merely the capacity for listening. When Brahms continually emphasized the need for "proper" learning, the value of hard work, and the essentials of the craft and technique of musical composition, in the sense of historical models as well as normative aesthetic imperatives; when later in life he complained bitterly about the level of contemporary musical education and training, he was expressing more than his legendary habits of being critical and self-critical. He was articulating a form of generational and cultural criticism.

The transition from the first generation in the musical public to the third generation included a weakening of the skills of literacy, the kind that made Elisabeth von Herzogenberg so alluring. These included the capacity to read a score and hear music, to write down what one heard as well as to play and sing new and old printed music. The shift to piano-based music education and the increasing opportunity, however limited, to be a mere listener only served to weaken the level of active literacy, much less thorough training.

Brahms articulated a widespread concern for the decline in standards that accompanied the extension of the audience during his lifetime. The newer generation became the consumers of lexica, concert guides, and journalistic accounts— genres that experienced enormous success in the 1880s and 1890s. Hermann Kretschmar's famous concert guide, which first appeared in 1887—and of which an excerpt appears elsewhere in this volume—gives a glimpse of the standard of education in the late nineteenth century. Kretschmar assumed sufficient training to hear key changes, melodic lines, and orchestral timbres. The Vienna Philharmonic first felt the need in the 1890s to introduce written descriptive program notes. In both these notes and Kretschmar's guide, narrative description functioned as a translating mechanism, designed to enable the hearer to follow and remember by offering a descriptive narration akin to prose fiction, travel guides, or journalistic reportage.

Part of the impetus behind the criticism of Wagner and Bruckner that came from Brahms's amateur partisans in Vienna (Theodor Billroth, for example) was the recognition that Wagner, through the use of leitmotivs and thematic repetition, and Bruckner, through his own reliance on repetitions and extended moments of exposition, pandered to the new habits of hearing. Their popularity, Billroth suspected, was the result of the public's ignorance and insufficient musical education.[11] Brahms demanded the true connoisseur: the musical *cognoscenti* of his and Hanslick's generation who understood the communicatory power and logic of music alone and could hear a dense, purely musical discourse. As a result of the shift in music education, the superficial, foreground habit of hearing, recognizable in program notes and guides, became the norm. It was against this norm that both Heinrich Schenker and Arnold Schoenberg—following explicitly a concept of form and technique derived from their understanding of Brahms, and mirroring Brahms's own critique of composition, his own and others'—would expend their unforgettable vitriol.

However, despite Brahms's suspicion that a decline in musical standards was occurring during his lifetime, the modern reader should not underestimate the extraordinary aura carried by live performances, the premium on memory, and the level of musical literacy the late nineteenth-century audience possessed. Arthur Schnitzler provides a reasonable example. The passion of his youth (his father Johann Schnitzler was a laryngologist who treated many singers) had been the theatre. Although Schnitzler was trained as a physician, he played the piano well, using the instrument in quite typical middle-class fashion, playing four-hand repertoire—with his mother and later with the music critic and theorist Viktor Zuckerkandl—often reading through orchestral music.[12] Schnitzler was literate enough to write a light waltz or two.

Likewise, the type of amateur choral singers with whom Brahms had worked in Hamburg and Vienna in the 1860s and 70s still existed at the turn of the century. But that tradition was under siege within the amateur world with the dramatic success of the operetta and the resultant popular song. In short, a dimension of Brahms's self-image as the last of a tradition, and the view of him as conservative and poised towards the past and not the future, was the consequence of his sense that a tradition within the musical public was dying; that the mode of musical communication he sought depended on a literacy in increasingly short supply. As he often commented, his critique of Wagner was hardly musical in the narrow sense, but was directed against his influence. Those who attacked Wagner as a musician were quite ignorant. At stake was not style but the survival of a language of expression and communication among people that had flourished between 1750 and 1850.

11

12

Rudolf Louis, writing in 1912 about the music of his time, observed that the natural tendency of "the young to underestimate the value of artistic form" had become extreme. Although Brahms's self-appointed successors were largely too academic, the composers who considered themselves followers of Wagner (and Brahms's true opposite Liszt) easily overlooked Brahms to their peril. Brahms's "masculine" character contained secrets, which could be unlocked. But the mechanism required a capacity to grasp his command of counterpoint and form—Brahms's "hard earned" and staggering command of the language of music. Not only to write music, but to hear it, remember it, and respond to it required a discipline and training Louis regarded as all too rare. The enemies of music were "artistic dilettantes" and "professional experts" (by which Louis meant music journalists and historians) who did not possess the skills of music-making but thought that writing about music was sufficient.[13]

Brahms, in all his work, wrote for an audience. The several genres he used all had a public. Often, as in the *Liebeslieder* and the later piano works, there was clearly a playing and listening audience. For both, comprehensibility was an overt goal. Brahms accepted that premise, but without concessions.

Brahms's often-quoted letter to Adolf Schubring regarding the imputed motivic unity of the *German Requiem* made clear that sophistication in compositional skill was not to be pursued at the expense of comprehensibility: "If I want to retain the same idea, then one should recognize it clearly in every transformation, augmentation, inversion. The opposite would be idle playing around and always a sign of impoverished inspiration." In discussing a particular set of variations, Brahms claimed that the bass line was the stable basis for his creativity. The elaboration of the melodic over a constant foundation achieved both comprehensibility as well as a proper avenue for original expression.[14]

If music was to be its own communicative medium, then subtlety in elaboration—the development over a long form of ideas and a new landscape of musical imagination and expression—had to carry the player and/or listener along. Therefore, from the start, a dimension of comprehensibility was required, although not through the linear sequences of Wagner. The comprehensibility was contingent on a deeper level of musical education. This conceit was only strengthened by the polemical example and perspective articulated in Schumann's critical writings. Brahms's ideal audience, whether in the short piano works, the *German Requiem,* the symphonies, the songs, or the chamber music, were individuals who could either play or follow him and, in Louis's words, "uncover the hidden soul of Brahms's world of sound".[15]

II. Music and Science

Without question, the most significant contribution to the relationship between science and music to occur in the second half of the nineteenth century was the publication of Hermann Helmholtz's *On the Sensations of Tone* in 1862. (A fourth edition appeared in 1877.) Helmholtz's subject included both the physics of sound and the physiology of perception. Helmholtz established the reigning definition of consonance (defined by equal temperament), and therefore dissonance. He dissected musical sound from the point of view of the source. He then analyzed the mechanism of perception and described what we hear and why. He spun a theory of the evolution of keys and tonality, and of the relationship between musical tones.

But Helmholtz drifted, despite his disclaimers, into the realm of aesthetics and the evolutionary history of musical systems. He took great pains to argue that the "modern" system of music was "not developed from a natural necessity, but from a freely chosen principle of style." Yet he regarded earlier historical periods as having less "perfect" systems, and concluded that "it has become possible to construct works of art, of much greater extent, and much richer in forms and parts, much more energetic in expression than any producible in past ages; and hence we are by no means inclined to quarrel with modern musicians for esteeming it the best of all."[16]   16

Helmholtz, in his conclusion to his work, avoided deriving aesthetics from empirical findings. But there was no doubt that the system of harmony of the nineteenth century had its justification in the physics of sound and the apparatus and process of perception. Helmholtz realized that art extended beyond nature. Two arenas were required to understand fully the links between art and nature: the psychology of perception and the philosophy of knowledge (epistemology), and philosophical psychology.

The power of Helmholtz's work was that on the one hand it lent justification to those who saw in it a scientific vindication of a set of aesthetic, formal, and, in particular, harmonic procedures.[17] At the same time, Helmholtz's genius and subtle   17 awareness of the limitation of his empirical analysis—the limitations of scientific argument in establishing cause and effect—as well as his acute awareness of the problem of understanding aural perception and the consciousness of hearing, inspired the development of theory and research that justified the fundamental relativity and culturally determined character of musical systems and aesthetic norms.

The tradition of speculation begun by Helmholtz generated quite opposing schools of inquiry. In the history of twentieth-century aesthetics, this resulted in the radically opposed theories of Schenker, who argued the natural scientific basis of tonality, and Schoenberg, for whom, in the theory of the emancipation of the dissonance, perceptions of consonance and dissonance had purely historical and environmental determinant causes. An entirely new system of harmonic musical combinations could be developed. Schoenberg, however, continued to adhere to normative notions of the way music functioned in time and could be perceived to be derived from tonal practice. That permitted him to defend canons of form and structure and standards of judgment regarding musical craft, *per se,* above and beyond the logic of any specific harmonic system.

The impact of Helmholtz's book was extraordinary. It had a direct influence on the design of instruments, primarily the piano, especially through the relationship between Helmholtz and C.F. Theodore Steinway. Helmholtz seemed to have helped to solve the problem of how to build a stable instrument that could be tuned, remain reasonably in tune, and possess a rich resonating sound. Steinway's famous duplex scale patent of the 1870s owed its origin to Helmholtz.

Helmholtz's work contributed significantly to the standardization of pitch and tuning in the late nineteenth century and to the establishment (or the effort to do so) of an international standard tuning system. Brahms's colleague in Vienna, L. A. Zellner (for whom Brahms had little use), who was the longtime secretary of the Gesellschaft der Musikfreunde, lectured on aesthetics at the conservatory and organized an international symposium in Vienna in 1885 to establish standard pitch levels.[18]

Brahms, despite his dislike for theorizing, particularly about music, was no doubt aware of the intense interest in acoustics, hearing, and aesthetics surrounding him among his medical, scientific, and musical colleagues. Zellner's lectures and his fanatical efforts on the issue of pitch standardization reflect Helmholtz's influence and the conviction that there were links between aesthetic judgment, physiology (and therefore nature), and ultimately between the education and cultivation of the physiological capacity to hear. Aesthetic judgment in music became closely tied to the cultivation of natural properties, giving subjective perception, when fully developed, an objective basis, particularly in the matter of musical form, the use of time, and the harmonic structure of a work.[19]

The sociological implication was equally clear. Those who could develop their natural potential for musical discrimination were a superior lot. Musical cultivation was learned, perhaps not at high levels for all. As such, that learned skill was the *sine qua non* for judgment. A physiological and scientific basis for the judgment of the well-trained few over the many was, in Zellner's judgment, self-evident.

But beyond the arena of manufacture and the regulation of pitch, Helmholtz's work spurred a whole field of acoustical research. This research, throughout the nineteenth century, kept its links with the aesthetics and history of music. Furthermore, Helmholtz sparked a series of intense anatomical and physiological investigations into the design and function of the ear. How do we hear? Was there a physiological basis for not only how we hear, but how we discriminate and sort out sounds, particularly consonant from dissonant ones? In modern terms, as Noam Chomsky has argued concerning the innate capacity to fashion and grasp grammar and therefore language, the researchers of the nineteenth century sought to test the hypothesis that modern notions of harmony and beauty were not only the result of a progressive historical evolution, but also the mirror of the natural physiological design and logic of the ear. Consequently, the field of psycho-acoustics was created.

In turn, the line of reasoning that asked questions about how we hear drifted into the more fundamental issue of what is being heard; about the relationship between object and subject, between perceiver and perceived. Particularly under the sharp scrutiny of Ernst Mach, who first wrote on Helmholtz in 1866 and who was an avid amateur musician (with a preference for the harmonium, one of the nineteenth century's most popular amateur domestic instruments), an entire episte-mological theory evolved regarding perception and reality.[20] The intense preoccu-pation with music and hearing might be said, not entirely facetiously, to have altered the direction of modern science and been an essential historical precondition for relativistic mechanics and modern physics. Albert Einstein's notorious love of music (despite his dubious skills as a violinist) culminated a decisive seventy-five years of symbiotic contact between science and music.

The impetus behind Helmholtz's book and its consequence for music in the nineteenth century, particularly the perception of music, its character and history, can be gleaned from two leading popular tracts of musical aesthetics: H.A Koestlin's *Die Tonkunst: Einführung in die Aesthetik der Musik* of 1879; and a book of 1882 by Brahms's friend Heinrich Ehrlich, *Die Musik-Aesthetik in ihrer Entwickelung von Kant bis auf die Gegenwart: Ein Grundriss.*[21]

Both Koestlin and Ehrlich began from the premise that their books, designed for the layperson, reflected the fact that, as Ehrlich wrote,

> music is, of all the arts, the favorite, perhaps the especially selected favorite of modern society. It constitutes the dearest ornament of domestic life . . . it is the most widespread and most practiced art. The greater public finds from it the most facile accessible distraction which possesses an elegant form; for the edu-cated society music is an effective means of connection; high society likes to acknowledge music as the most important ethical means of education, because music is the politically least dangerous art; many noble individuals consider music as the purest art.[22]

Ehrlich noted that the two schools of music in the nineteenth century—the absolutists and those who regarded music as connected to speech and the visual—placed extraordinary demands on the meaning of music. The formalists, the absolutists claimed for music a "meaning for the life of the soul" greater than in all other arts. Ehrlich wrote, "The phenomenon such as the following is not easy to explain: that today the majority of the public finds more pleasure in music than in all the other arts."[23] Yet music seemed to make fewer demands on thinking, making any serious evaluation of why this passion for music existed difficult. Ehrlich concluded:

> This phenomenon just referred to can be explained only in the context of the entire cultural life, out of the relationship of the work of art with ideas of the

time, and the reciprocal impact between artist and public, that today still is supported by other means than the pursuit of art alone.[24]

24

Ehrlich identified, among others, the recent research into the nervous system, starting with Helmholtz's theory of hearing. Ehrlich argued that it helped to explain the impact of music on the mind and "the legitimation of the historical development of particular nations, from which important works of music have emerged."[25] Ehrlich concluded that the scientific research of the recent past created an agenda for the aesthetics of music to use the knowledge of science to understand why people got excited about music. But in order to base aesthetics on a firm footing, enabling it to achieve sufficient clarity to forge a serious link between the development of aesthetic taste and the development of a moral sense, one had to create a science that could underpin aesthetic judgment. Having understood the science of subjective response, it was possible to build an independent but linked system of the rules of beauty, to define and link the beautiful with the good.[26]

25

26

Like Ehrlich, Koestlin was in search of answers, about not only the nature of music, but also its impact on its public. Like Ehrlich, Koestlin sought to reconcile the objective findings about hearing with the apparent subjectivity of aesthetic judgment. However, Koestlin sided more clearly with the idea that the Helmholtz studies and their impact through later work (that of von Oettingen and Riemann) could justify a formalist, Herbartian aesthetic. That aesthetic might justify the autonomy of music even though it could also explain the success of the Wagnerian synthesis of music, words, and images. Koestlin wrote:

> The effort will be justified to take into consideration the construction of musical aesthetics in the first instance, and the particular nature of the material out of which musical art makes its forms, instead of, as before, taking concepts and claims from some other arenas and imposing them on the face of music. So perhaps we are close to that time when a satisfactory aesthetics of music will be available to us; that is, a presentation of the unique character and unique laws of our art which derives from the nature of sound and the particular existential conditions of the musical work of art.[27]

27

The direct impact of this mix of science and aesthetics was the triumph of the idea that music was autonomous of the other arts, perceived differently and bereft of content in the ordinary way. Within the well-known nineteenth-century debate between the Wagnerians and the followers of Liszt and the formalists, Hanslick and others, in which Brahms somewhat reluctantly assumed the symbolic role of the "counter-pope," scientific speculation seemed to vindicate the anti-Wagnerians on two accounts. First, the evolution of music, by analogy with evolutionary theory, rendered instrumental music and the modern system of harmony the highest forms of development within an historical logic that was progressive and selective. The independence from the voice and speech was historical and reflected the increasing complexity of self-sufficiency of modes of sound production and modes of perception. In this sense, Wagner could be justified, if at all, only in so-called purely musical terms.

Second, the specific character of tones and their logic, as well as the receptivity of the human ear, as a triumph of evolution led to the judgment that music was the purest art form since it was the most abstract, the most spiritual in the sense that it was the most rational—divorced from raw daily experience. The formal compositional procedures that organized sound into art (e.g., harmonic relationships and rules of counterpoint) were located in the objective nature of music itself as well as in the selective evolutionary process which established a valid tradition.

Richard Wallaschek (1860–1917), a Viennese aesthetician and music historian who, after working in England, returned in 1895 and subsequently taught at the University and at the conservatory in Vienna, provided perhaps the best summary of the impact of scientific inquiry into hearing and musical sound on the aesthetic prejudices of the late nineteenth century when he wrote in 1886:

> A comparison with the remarks made here about the musical work of art with the general remarks about the beautiful will reveal, with spontaneous logic, that through music the highest beauty can be achieved, because the forms that music provides are tied to no comprehensible content, but at the same time permit access to all—because musical forms reproduce in tones the general form of all experience to which spiritual activity is connected. Music constitutes the spiritual progress of modernity in comparison to antiquity in terms of the forms of perception. Music is the algebra of the arts.[28]

28

This credo corresponded closely with Brahms's convictions about the normative character of musical form and language. Brahms's much-discussed concern with historical models was driven by an absolutist instinct: that music as an independent mode of human experience was at once tied to human experience *per se*—the emotions and thoughts that humans display and have expressed in all of history. That independent element of expression and perception experienced a gradual historical clarification. In this sense, progress in science was regarded on a par with progress in musical technique and aesthetics. The conceit of certainty was such, however, that the forms of musical art seemed clearly understood. The past had bequeathed objective standards on the way in which musical materials might be used, true rules of the grammar of musical language.

Originality and individuality expressed themselves within a normative framework in which a future was possible since the basic framework based on objective physical and physiological phenomena was well understood. As Brahms urged younger composers, serious training in the rules of that framework was indispensable if one wanted to write great music of the sort that Wagner and Schumann

luckily managed to write without the proper fundamental training.[29] The histori-   **29**
cism of Brahms's formal models and procedures—in sonata form and variation—was
justified as an act of building on the truth, much as a scientist of Brahms's generation might build on proven hypotheses and then modify, elaborate and revise that
truth. In the modification—as in the case of Wagner and the occasional new
discovery—the cumulative progress of knowledge and the expression of individuality could be reconciled.

When one fin de siècle critic compared a Brahms symphony to "a chemical
and mechanical structure," the metaphor was not off the mark.[30] Brahms's aesthetic   **30**
convictions and his self-image as a composer mirrored the culture of science in
which he lived and in particular a contemporary conception of music, musical form,
musical perception, and musical judgment widespread in German-speaking Europe.
This conception was profoundly influenced by scientific speculation about the
phenomena of music and their aesthetic implications. Brahms satisfied the widely
held opinions and expectations among the educated, cultivated audience of Vienna
and other major cities about what music was, and could do; about what was
required to appreciate it, and why it was so alluring. His music, more than Wagner's,
was self-consciously non-populist and reinforced the identification of cultivation
and learning with aesthetic taste. Brahms's work underscored views about the
nature of music and the necessity, if not exclusivity, of an education that empowered
the elite individual truly to comprehend the purest and most objective form of art.

III. Theories of Sensation, Time Consciousness, and Habits of Listening, 1885–1905

Helmholtz's work spurred a new set of questions about how and why we
perceive sounds, and how we conceive of the logic of time, and therefore retain and
remember sequences of sound which possess their logic in associations with words
or pictures. If Brahms's music, as has been suggested, played into the conceits of the
successful cultivation of the understanding of objective musical elements and their
combinations, then it was nearly inevitable that the fundamentals of that conceit of
understanding itself would undergo critical scrutiny. The centrality of musical
communication in the world of educated citizens in which Brahms lived was such
that this critical enterprise entered at the center of epistemological discourse.

The journey from physics to psychology and then to philosophy can be traced
in the work of Ernst Mach and Edmund Husserl. Both were citizens of the Habsburg
Empire, and both experienced the lure of music as a mode of communication, in
their social milieu and their own private lives. Through a look at their ideas, one
can generate a speculative model of how the audience for Brahms's music listened—
the player and listener alike—before access to mechanically reproduced music (i.e.,

before 1910) became widespread. The assumptions about perception, recall, judgment, and expectation with which Brahms worked as a composer can be revealed, albeit indirectly. The logic of his formal procedures can then be illuminated, if only from the outside.

In Ernst Mach's notebooks from the early 1880s, one finds the following fragment:

> The spatial is reversible. It must be contingent on time. Music as a special instance; Music. The spatially reversible. The temporally irreversible; The same melody in different registers. The Third. Numerous ways. The form of sound. Conflict of sensations; The form of sound with the form of time. A tone is already a composite sensation. A mixed sensation.[31]

Mach's ruminations about the character of the perception of space and time led him finally in 1886 to the radical conclusion that in its subsequent elaborations would provide an impetus for Einstein's theory of relativity.[32] Mach denied the absolute character of space and time:

> The physiology of the senses, however, demonstrates that spaces and times may just as appropriately be called sensations as colors and sounds. . . . Nothing will be changed in the actual facts or in the functional relations, whether we regard all the data as contents of consciousness, or as partially so, or as completely physical.[33]

Mach opened up the radical possibility that scientific fact, as such, derives from the frame of reference of the perceiver, from the act of sensation. He did so by also denying the existence of a metaphysical ego, the "I," and therefore ending up with a monistic standpoint.

The appeal to nature as an external physical phenomenon was undercut. The perception of form and time duration, therefore, required an analysis quite different from that of Helmholtz: an analysis of how we mentally construct a sense of time. The center of Mach's argument in 1886 dealt with "The Sensations of Tone." Mach had greatly enlarged the research on the physiology of the ear. But his conclusion was that the perception of music was exclusively "a collateral product of [his] education . . . what we call talent and achievement . . . constitute but a slight departure from normal endowments."[34]

What Mach concentrated on was the notion that in music there was no absolute symmetry. Music possessed the spatial association of high and low but not right and left. Furthermore, a sense of order derived from the creation of a series of sensations and their remembrance. The logic of a series could not be derived from nature. Mach denied any scientific ability to prefer objectively one interval over another and broke any residual link between external physical reality and the aesthetic priority of consonance.

Furthermore, Mach speculated on the attention span and capacity to order series of notes and intervals. He stressed the context of remembrance. For example, he cited the link between the interval of a fourth and the Overture to *Tannhäuser.* The hearing of the former could imply the latter, and *vice versa.* The aesthetic judgment of pleasure in sensation for Mach was based on the fact that "the harmonic or the melodic addition of one to another affects agreeably only when the added tone reproduces a part of the sensation which the first one excited."[35]

In the discrimination of musical beauty, apart from references to the Helmholtzian overtone series in terms of how tones might be perceived by the ear, Mach distinguished between visual and aural perception, between the perception of space and time. Why can we consider a melody the same when it is transposed to a key where there are not even common overtone partials? Furthermore, one can distinguish common rhythm despite differential pitches which make two separate melodies. Rhythm is easier to distinguish than elapsed time or even tempo. The answer lay, for Mach, in the process of self-consciousness about orientation, about the mechanisms of selective self-representation in time and space. Mach's work constituted an effort to rescue the efficacy of science as a universal construct by retreating, so to speak, to the exclusive legitimacy of the act of perception. He generated a kind of legitimate, functional scientific impressionism.[36]

The dramatic shift of emphasis from the work of art to the hearer mirrored the historical reality. Any given work of Brahms was contingent not only on intent, but on perceived meaning. Although Mach, in line with his social philosophy, sought to reduce the distance between the normal and the genius, Brahms sought to communicate with compositional procedures that could reach a highly developed discriminatory sensibility. The capacity to follow and recall long stretches of variation and thematic development required the capacity to orient oneself within the balances among formal integrity, the total duration of a work, and its larger harmonic structure. The relationship of detail to form, sequential logic to structure as recalled after an initial hearing—comprehending the irreversibility—became a challenge. So too was the capacity to perceive the distinctions between levels of form in a complex procedure which, as Schoenberg argued, eschewed evident aspects of musical symmetry (one thinks particularly of Brahms's playful use of rhythmic asymmetry). All this made demands on the listener's skill, given that mere "playing around" (*Spielerei*) was not at stake but deep inner communication through ordered musical sounds.

These Machian speculations show in the first instance the centrality of musical experience in the formation of scientific inquiry in the nineteenth century. But they indicate as well the self-consciousness in the nineteenth century of the extent to which a work of musical art was contingent on the hearer, on a symbiotic overlap between authorial intent and subjective perception. Brahms's adherence to known forms—Classical models and procedure—may have reflected the recognition that

35

36

17

innovation within expectations framed by cultivated habits constituted a more valid and desirable means to assure correspondence between intent and result. The Wagnerian strategy not only simplified demands on the hearer but imposed a speech-based narrative structure and logic, eliminating a musical mode of expression. The purely musical communication was, for Mach, free of association but located, as Mach conceded that Schopenhauer correctly suspected, in a profound inner sensibility not necessarily accessible through ordinary experience or an imagination stimulated by words or pictures.[37]   37

Edmund Husserl, at the turn of the century, in his critique of Mach's theory of knowledge went even further.[38] Beginning with Augustine, Husserl focused on the   38 process of internal time consciousness beyond the conscious act of perception. Mental reproduction, and recapitulative memory; the difference between hearing a sound and rehearing in one's mind; and the difference between memory and expectation were, in part, Husserl's subjects. Furthermore, the mental rehearing of sounds, the mental reconstruction of the present, and the difference between objective elapsed time and experienced time became troubling issues.[39] In Husserl's   39 critical extension of the Helmholtz-Mach analysis, the internal psychic construct predominated over an external stimulus or sensation. But at the same time, the power of the mental creation of time, the inner expanse of subjective experience, became not merely evident but primary.

The experience of music was then subject to redefinition. Its social dimension — the shared elapsed time experienced by following a musical narrative — was implicitly compared to the intimate definition of music as heard (i.e., playing at home or hearing at a concert): the manner in which music can trigger internal expansive rehearing, recollection and transformation, even in strictly musical terms. The music of Brahms, in its comprehensibility and also its complexity, lent itself to an elastic internal interpretation that, since the formalists of the early nineteenth century, had been one of the heralded dimensions of instrumental and so-called absolute music.[40]   40

One might be willing to speculate that the power of Brahms's innovative adaptation of expectancies from within his audience can be understood by looking at his use of time. Brahms, by eschewing speech-based narrative, created at least three levels of perceived time. The first was the time of the unfolding of the work, which proceeded in small units (not, like Bruckner, in large sections). The transformation of material began immediately, merging recollectable symmetries with evident alterations.

Second, there was the use of time divorced from the actual objective surface. This involved the clear units used by the composer (e.g., thematic material), the time of transformation (e.g., variation), the groupings of events (e.g., movements), which, extracted and reworked and compared by the listener, enabled radically different sensibilities of proportions and focal points — altered durations — within a work.[41]   41

Third, there was the perceived time, the experience of time by the listener, in performance and memory.[42] This dimension, created during hearing and primarily after, constituted a mixed accumulation of the three other elements. All of them were contingent on the assumed contact between Brahms and his audience, on Brahms's tacit assumption that either intended or novel inferences from the work of art, as experienced, would be generated that could, despite the necessary process of individual appropriation and variation, approximate the intended experience.

    Furthermore, by employing an evidently historicist framework, Brahms sparked the process George Kubler describes for art and architecture. By invoking fragments of the past, the recognition of discarded and retained elements from the past creates a dialectic of time perception; between a consciousness of the present with one of an imagination of the past. In the nearly archeological invocation of recognizable traditions, Brahms, in his music, far from creating a static temporal or emotional experience, assumed a musical memory for his real and ideal listeners, and created experiences of the historical in the present.

    This in turn provided a transformed and flexible reconstitution of the past for the listener. In the context of nineteenth-century Vienna, the musical experience interacted with at least the visual experience of historicism in art and architecture. The self-assertion of novelty on the part of Wagner, together with the historicist language of Wagner's poetry and the aesthetics of the scene painting, may have minimized Wagner's stimulation of inner time sensibilities within the audience despite the other forms of response he generated.

    The subjective time experience in Brahms's music became a means to sense a collective experience of historical time, recast and renewed in the present moment. The use of the historical in Brahms therefore can be understood to be a strategy not of "aesthetic fatigue" but of contextualizing to highlight innovation and change. In the microcosm of each work, the present is set apart by the transformation of the evidently traditional.[43] As Heinrich Koestlin wrote about Brahms's music shortly after the composer's death, "The Romantic wealth of ideas is bordered by the discipline of Classical training, and contained by a hardnosed formal structure. The latter is unique, new, and not a simple repetition or recreation, but rather an organic progressive evolution and an entirely modern new formation."[44] In terms of the issues of internal time consciousness and its constitution, the Brahmsian exchange with a contemporary audience mirrored, in an authentic historical exchange, the direction and complexity of Husserl's contemporaneous framing of the issues of subjective time perception.

    The density of temporal consciousness and the demands made on the powers of discrimination and remembrance by Brahms's music were severe, even by contemporary standards. In this sense, Brahms realized the ideology of absolute music by eschewing forms of musical realism and retaining the intimate communication associated with the prestige of chamber music. Likewise, Brahms sought to realize a strategy central to musical Romanticism, the cultivation of inner subjectivity. His success depended not only on the level of music education in his audience but also on the acoustic and temporal environment in which he operated.

We forget too readily the vast stretches of ambient silence (punctuated not by regular background noise but by more random interruptions) in which the Viennese urban dweller lived and the concomitant space for musical contemplation. The urban environment operated with different expectations of volume and sound color. The absence of live performances and anything approximating today's means of reproduction placed a premium on powers of recollection and rehearing, as well as rereading musical texts in which imaginary sounds were present. This was true too for the use of the piano for hearing orchestral works.

Apart from the silence and the aura of musical sound derived from its comparative rarity, the Brahmsian use of form and time, the micro-unit of change, and the larger coherences of which Schenker was fond of stressing, one must consider the reception of Brahms's music in terms of the clocks of everyday life in his time. The pace of life and communication, the periodicity of the day (night and day), and the seasons, as well as the perceived value of time ratios—hour, minute, day, year, lifetime, and generational—were significantly different to warrant discussion. Furthermore, the rarity of stable regular mechanical devices in the surroundings driven by constant power sources influenced time expectations (e.g., a motorcar as opposed to a horse-driven carriage, or a gas light in relation to an electric current source).

A reasonable hypothesis is that the sense of intensity of time, as well as the tolerance for objective elapsed time (often referred to, in the Viennese context, as *Gemütlichkeit*), suggest that Brahms may have been aware that the writing of music, as it was likely to be experienced, permitted a contemplative intensity (beyond the references accessible by a musically educated audience), bounded by silence and a slower, more irregular daily clock of life than we are accustomed to. The structure of society, as seen through the conception of time and its uses, was more discontinuous from our own than most musicological analysis has accounted for.[45]   45

Therefore the mode of perception and recollection, the comprehension of a Brahms work—given the clear hints of historical analogies provided by the composer—cannot be inferred exclusively from the text of music bequeathed to us. Neither can one infer the imputed meaning to the act of hearing and playing. The significance of the musical experience in the nineteenth century heightened the desire to understand the human constitution of time. Husserl's inquiry was an extension of a line of inquiry that had part of its source in issues of art and its perception.

Notes

1   For a parallel characterization of the milieu in which Brahms worked see Michael Musgrave, "The Cultural World of Brahms" in *Brahms: Biographical, Documentary and Analytical Studies*, ed. Robert

Pascall (Cambridge, 1983), pp. 1-26. For a comparable piece on painting and Brahms see my essay, "Brahms and Nineteenth-century Painting," in *19th-Century Music,* forthcoming Fall 1990.

2   J. V. Widmann, *Johannes Brahms in Erinnerungen* (Berlin, 1898), pp. 58-59.

3   George S. Bozarth and Stephen H. Brady, "The Pianos of Johannes Brahms," elsewhere in this volume.

4   *Neues Universal Lexicon der Tonkunst,* ed. Julius Schladebach and Eduard Bernsdorf (Dresden, 1856), I, 447.

5   See Werner G. Zimmerman, *Brahms in der Schweiz: Eine Dokumentation* (Zürich, 1983), pp. 102-12.

6   This is evident if one reads his correspondence in *Briefe von Theodor Billroth,* ed. Georg Fischer (Hannover, 1897).

7   Ludwig Eisenberg, *Künstler und Schriftsteller Lexikon: "Das geistige Wien"* (Vienna, 1891), pp. 646-50.

8   From Richard von Perger, *Denkschrift zur Feier des Fünfzigjahrigen ununterbrochenen Bestandes der Philharmonischen Konzerte in Wien 1869-1910* (Vienna, 1910).

9   Hans Gal, *Johannes Brahms: Leben und Werk* (Frankfurt, 1961), p. 93.

10   From the perspective of the modern reader and concert goer, this is an indication of both the rarity of live performances of orchestral works and the gradual acceleration in concert life. Vienna's leading impresario, Albert Gutmann, sponsored 16 concerts in 1890, 39 in 1896, and 86 in 1900. In the three-year period between 1894 and 1897, the end of Brahms's life, 37 percent were vocal recitals, 32 percent were piano recitals, 12 percent violin recitals, 15 percent chamber music ensembles, and 5 percent visiting orchestras. Seventeen percent of the recitalists played their own music. See Leon Botstein, *Music and its Public,* Appendix (forthcoming, University of Chicago Press).

11   See Theodor Billroth, *Wer ist musikalisch?* (Berlin, 1898).

12   See Arthur Schnitzler, *Tagebuch 1879-1892* (Vienna, 1987), pp. 27 and 128; and *Tagebuch 1917-1919* (Vienna, 1985), p. 417.

13   Rudolf Louis, *Die Deutsche Musik der Neuzeit* (Munich, 1912), pp. 159-62, 328-29.

14   Brahms to Schubring, February 1869, in *Brahms Briefwechsel* (Berlin, 1908-22), VIII, 216-17. See the use of the same letter in Walter Frisch, *Brahms and the Principle of Developing Variation* (Berkeley and Los Angeles, 1984), p. 32.

15   Louis, *Deutsche Musik,* p. 161.

16   Hermann Helmholtz, *On the Sensations of Tone,* trans. and ed. Alexander J. Ellis (New York, 1885, rpt. 1954), p. 249.

17   Ibid., pp. 365-71.

18   See Max Kalbeck, *Johannes Brahms* (Berlin, 1904-14), II, 27-34; 388-89; also R. Hirschfeld and R. von Perger, *Geschichte des K.K. Gesellschaft der Musikfreunde in Wien* (Vienna, 1912), pp. 191-94.

19   L. A. Zellner, *Vorträge uber Akustik: Gehalten am Conservatorium der Gesellschaft der Musikfreunde in Wien* (Vienna, 1892), II, 113-14.

20   See Ernst Mach, *Einleitung in die Helmholtz'sche Musiktheorie. Populär für Musiker dargestellt* (Graz, 1866), and Leo Koeningsberger, *Hermann von Helmholtz* (Braunschweig, 1911), pp. 182-87; and William M. Johnston, *The Austrian Mind: An Intellectual and Social History 1848-1938* (Berkeley and Los Angeles, 1972), p. 182.

21   On the relationship between Brahms and Ehrlich see *Kalbeck* I, 73-75.

22   Heinrich Ehrlich, *Die Musik-Aesthetik* (Leipzig, 1882), p. 124.

23   Ibid., p. 2.

24   Ibid., p. 3.

25   Ibid., p. 4.

26   Ibid., pp.134-37 and 173-76.

27   H. A. Koestlin, *Die Tonkunst: Einführung in die Aesthetik der Musik* (Stuttgart, 1879), pp. 260-61.

28   Richard Wallaschek, *Aesthetik der Tonkunst* (Stuttgart, 1886), p. 230.

29   See Hans Gal, *Brahms,* pp.147-48; and Imogen Fellinger "Brahms's 'Way': a composer's self view," in *Brahms 2,* ed. Michael Musgrave (Cambridge, 1986), pp. 49-58.

30   Philip H. Goepp, *Symphonies and Their Meaning: Second Series* (Philadelphia, 1902), p. 361.

31   Ernst Mach, "Auszüge aus den Notizbüchern 1871-1910," in *Ernst Mach: Werk und Wirkung,* ed. Rudolf Haller and Friedrich Stadler (Vienna, 1988), pp. 171-72, 182.

32   See Gerald Holton, *Thematic Origins of Scientific Thought: Kepler to Einstein* (Cambridge, Mass., 1973), pp. 223-25.

33   Ernst Mach, *Die Analyse der Empfindungen* (6th ed. Jena, 1911), pp. 6, 28-30.

34   Ibid., pp. 250-52.

35   Ibid., pp. 230-34; see also Ernst Mach, *Populär-Wissenschaftliche Vorlesungen* (4th ed. Leipzig, 1910), pp. 43-47.

36   See the interesting discussion of Ernst Mach in Katherine Arens, *Functionalism and Fin de Siècle: Fritz Mauthner's Critique of Language* (New York, 1984), pp. 183-222.

37   Mach, *Die Analyse,* p. 214.

38   On Mach and Husserl, see Manfred Sommer, "Denkökonomie und Empfindungstheorie bei Mach und Husserl—Zum Verhältnis von Positivismus und Phänomenologie" in Haller and Stadler, *Ernst Mach,* pp. 309-28.

39   Edmund Husserl, *The Phenomenology of Internal Time Consciousness,* ed. Martin Heidegger, trans. J. S. Churchill (Bloomington, 1964); the slightly different German text is *Texte zur Phänomenologie des inneren Zeitbewußtseins 1893-1917* (Hamburg, 1985).

40   See, for a comparison on this subject, Stephen Kern, *The Culture of Space and Time 1880-1918* (Cambridge, Mass., 1983).

41   See Jonathan D. Kramer, *The Time of Music* (New York, 1988), particularly Chapter 11.

42   See a comparable discussion for fiction in Paul Ricoeur, *Time and Narrative,* Vol. II (Chicago, 1985), pp. 77-81.

43   George Kubler, *The Shape of Time: Remarks on the History of Things* (New Haven, 1962), pp. 77-82.

44   H. A. Koestlin, *Geschichte der Musik im Umriss,* ed. E. Nagel (6th ed. Leipzig, 1910), p. 538.

45   See Norbert Elias, *Über die Zeit* (Frankfurt, 1988), pp. 42-43, 126-27, 144-47.

Peter F. Ostwald

Johannes Brahms, Solitary Altruist

Brahms was a Janus-like figure who looked backward, seeking inspiration from the older Baroque and Classical traditions, while at the same time he looked forward and seemed the embodiment of modernism. A man of many contrasts, Brahms was devoted to his homeland in north Germany, but chose to live in southern Europe. He adored his parents and enjoyed family life, but never married. He was a kind and generous man, but often adopted an extremely rude manner toward others. He was fiercely independent, yet would mourn bitterly the loss of friends and relatives. He amassed a small fortune, but always lived frugally and dressed like a poor man.

I became interested in Brahms while working on a psychobiography of Robert Schumann and trying to understand the role he played during the two and a half years Schumann was hospitalized and his wife could not, or would not, see him.[1] Brahms became a kind of human link between these two artists. He loved Clara and lived with her; he also loved Robert and visited him regularly in the hospital. He played the piano for both of them, spoke with one about the other, and conveyed messages back and forth. This linking function is beautifully symbolized in a composition Brahms wrote in 1854, his Variations on a Theme by Robert Schumann, op. 9, dedicated to Clara Schumann. This work begins with a Schumann melody for which Clara herself had once written variations; it continues with variations that sometimes resemble Schumann's musical style and at other times are uniquely Brahmsian.

It occurred to me that Brahms's way of interacting with and making music for the Schumanns may have had certain characteristics of what Winnicott, working with mothers and children, has called the "transitional object" and Volkan, observing states of bereavement, called a "linking phenomenon."[2] These technical psychoanalytic terms have come to denote such tangible physical items as clothing, dolls, toys, or other belongings which can carry personal meanings and thus are capable of temporarily allaying the anxieties produced by separation from a true love object. In terms of providing emotional gratification, transitional objects are less real than human objects but more real than fantasized objects. Art objects in that sense can become very powerful transitional or linking phenomena, valuable not only for individuals but for entire cultures.

Music, as I have suggested elsewhere, may be especially well-suited for use as a transitional or linking phenomenon.[3] It has a unique capacity for soothing and

Peter F. Ostwald, M. D., Director of the Health Program for Performing Artists and Professor of Psychiatry at the University of California, San Francisco, is the author of *Schumann: The Inner Voices of a Musical Genius* (Boston, 1985) and a forthcoming study of Nijinsky.

comforting. It has both the concreteness of real events and the abstractness of symbols. Some composers seem especially gifted in exploiting these transitional qualities of music, and I would like to suggest that Brahms is a good example of such an artist. Not only did he create effective musical links for future generations, but he also manifested certain qualities of personality that I would consider "transitional."

Despite the voluminous literature about him, Brahms remains somehow remote and unfathomable. Perhaps that is the way he wanted it to be. Brahms seems to have resisted most efforts to get close to him. Those who tried to do it were rebuffed. Even Clara Schumann had to confess that nearly fifty years of acquaintance with this musician had given her no insight into his character or ways of thinking. Here was someone who habitually kept his feelings to himself, and he deliberately destroyed many manuscripts and other personal documents that might have revealed how his mind functioned.

For the clinician, such behavior can be frustrating as well as tantalizing. Does Brahms's reserve indicate the desire to hide something? Or was this a way of trying to get people more interested in him. My impression is that despite his efforts at anonymity, Brahms wanted to be understood. He seems to have suffered greatly at times, and he probably had a number of depressive episodes. But the basic textbooks about illnesses of great composers are not helpful in this regard.[4] In my review of the literature, I have been able to find only four authors who focus directly on his emotional condition. Lange-Eichbaum cites observations that depict Brahms as "obstinately depressive (*ein trotziger Melancholiker*) . . . sexually inhibited, immature, [and] with advancing age crotchety, pedantic, and helpless in practical matters."[5] Schauffler calls him a "schizoid personality."[6] Hitschmann describes his "marriage inhibition."[7] Geiringer, in the keynote address at the 1983 Library of Congress Brahms Conference, calls him "ambivalent."[8]

Each of these diagnostic hunches has something of merit. In addition, I would suggest that Brahms had something of the "avoidant personality" described in our modern diagnostic nomenclature, viz. hypersensitivity to rejection, unwillingness to enter into relationships that did not guarantee uncritical acceptance, social distancing, and low self-esteem. But how are all of these descriptive criteria to be understood in the context of his developmental history, particularly his musical development? In brief: he appears to have been hypersensitive and moody beginning in childhood, but music helped him to to find ways of avoiding personal intimacy and thus prevent overstimulation throughout adolescence. Most of his adult life he was a loner, and he never married. Severe emotional crises were generally averted, and no serious breakdowns ever occurred. With Brahms there was also a very good fit between his personality, his talent, and his ambition—he never seriously attempted to compose an opera, for example—so that despite a number of career frustrations he always continued to work. Finally, to appreciate Brahms's generally favorable state of health, it should be pointed out that he had the advantage of a long-term relationship with an outstanding physician and surgeon, Theodor Billroth, who became his devoted admirer and undoubtedly exerted a therapeutic influence. Thus conditions that might well have become more overtly psychopathological seem to have been held in check, so that Brahms's depressive disorder and personality problems were muted, leaving residues of great music, loneliness, and altruism.

All his life Brahms had a way of avoiding intimate relationships with other people. Already as a child he was solitary and reclusive, preferring to be at the piano or to play with his favorite collection of toy soldiers, an interest that may have combined his need for order with sublimated aggression (as well as his love for his father, who belonged to a military band). Brahms's interest in military matters never subsided. All his life he was very patriotic. Enthusiastic about the Franco-Prussian War of 1870, he wanted to be sure "that the French [would] get a good beating,"[9] and he composed the *Triumphlied* for Chorus and Orchestra, op. 55, when they did. Brahms greatly admired Bismarck, and knew many of his speeches and much of his writing by heart.

    Solitary pursuits, in particular reading, occupied much of his time. One of his favorite books was the Bible, from which he also could quote at length. He was widely read in the classics, history, legends, Renaissance art, biographies of musicians, and poetry. Brahms resented bitterly any allusions to his lack of formal education, and he was proud of his ability to discuss literature and the arts with some of the leading German-speaking intellectuals.[10] He was an avid collector of rare books, musical manuscripts, and original autographs, including works by Mozart and Schumann. Over the years this came to be a valuable collection, over which he fussed like an orderly librarian, conscientiously keeping track of every sheet of music he ever lent out.

    Some of the negative impression Brahms made on others may be attributed to the difficulty he had in using words. He often acknowledged this fault in letters containing apologies for the rough or clumsy way he would express himself — "I can't write letters, also can't write diplomatically."[11] He was often angry and self-critical for saying the wrong thing, and he would mock himself cruelly. Those who came to know Brahms well gradually came to realize that, as Niemann said, "his mockery and anger and humour were nothing but a 'lightning conductor,' a protection against his own soft-heartedness, of which he was afraid."[12]

    A man of rigid habits, Brahms rose very early (at 5 a.m. in the summer), brewed many cups of strong, black coffee for himself, and worked without stopping until midday. He then went to a restaurant, always the same one for the last fourteen years of his life in Vienna, *Zum roten Igel* (The Red Hedgehog). Then he would go for a long walk, preferably in the country. Toward the evening, he prepared himself

Brahms at the villa of Johann Strauss in Ischl, 1894 or 1895.

to go to a concert or the opera. Afterwards he had supper, often with friends, and usually in an informal setting such as a beer hall. He could easily take a catnap and seldom seemed tired. It was difficult for others to keep up with Brahms; for example, while travelling he always had to be on the go, to walk faster, climb higher, and explore more places than anyone else. Like Beethoven, he moved around a great deal, frequently changing his residence until he finally settled down in 1872 at Karlsgasse 4, in a small furnished apartment. Yet his bags were always kept packed for a trip, and he would spend long stretches of time each year away from home. Brahms always preferred older houses, and when travelling he would stay in simple, modest inns where he could relax unobserved, mingle with the help rather than the guests, and not have to dress up. His tendency to wear ill-fitting clothes, to forget his tie and collar, and to look rumpled if not disheveled (but never dirty), was noticed already in his twenties, at the Detmold court, where Brahms sometimes appeared in public and even conducted concerts dressed in a way that would draw attention to his "bad manners" and thus offend his patrons. Later, in Vienna, he habitually wore trousers that were too short, and instead of an overcoat would drape a green blanket around his shoulders, held in place with an oversize safety pin.

To account for these character traits, and others yet to be described, I would like to suggest two possibilities, fully recognizing that proving or disproving such explanations will be impossible, considering that our subject cannot be brought into the laboratory for biological study or into the consultation room for a thorough psychological evaluation.

(1) *Bio-energetic factors:* I assume Brahms to have been afflicted with some type of mood disorder, possibly a bipolar or cyclothymic disturbance that he tried to control, more or less successfully, through strenuously compulsive musical activities, playing the piano, studying scores, composing, and conducting. We know this to be a not uncommon problem among exceptionally productive and creative individuals,[13] and I have described the pattern in several other nineteenth-century composers.[14] Such figures have unusually high levels of energy and are easily aroused. Unless contained through activity and work, their abundant vigor and interest can spill over into uncomfortable states of ("hypomanic") excitement, as it probably threatened to do when Brahms would become overly abrasive, jocular, and irritating. At the other extreme are states of exhaustion and fatigue, with which Brahms attempted to cope through caffeine and nicotine. A certain narrowing of interest may also conserve energy, and I suspect that after a long and exhausting day of struggling with musical problems, insufficient energy remained for him to attend to the "less important" matter of social conformance.

(2) *Psychological conflict:* Brahms may have been torn between disobedience and conformity. This polarization undoubtedly reflected the influence of his parents, who were so widely discrepant in age, social background, and cultural attitudes. In

regard to his habits of dress, one of my favorite anecdotes is about Brahms leaving home as a teen-ager. His mother gave him a sewing kit, with careful instructions on how to use it. He never did. Any holes in his clothes he would mend with sealing wax! This was his way of rebelling, through simultaneous protest and submission. Indeed, it has been noted that in contrast to the carelessness in his physical appearance, Brahms manifested the utmost scrupulosity in polishing his musical compositions. No gap was ever permitted in the fabric of a work; there were never any "loose threads." Furthermore, I would suggest as an explanation for Brahms's deportment some internalization of the life style and personal characteristics of Ludwig van Beethoven and Franz Schubert, two composers he tended to idealize.[15]   15 Brahms's early infatuation with Robert Schumann, and his life-long interest in Clara Schumann, may also have led to a degree of identification with these musicians. If that was the case, then the internalized influence of Schumann would probably have had a balancing effect, tending to neutralize Brahms's identification with the lonely, eccentric, unmarried "mad genius" prototype. And that Clara did not permit a closer union and in the long run would not let him step into Robert's shoes, reflects perhaps her good judgment in recognizing that such a move would have been destructive to Brahms's great talent, which had to be nurtured in solitude and seemed to require certain eccentricities.

Needless to say, regular employment proved to be impossible for this artist who valued freedom and needed independence to do his creative work. Brahms used to say that he wanted to be appointed as Director of the Hamburg Philharmonic Society, and he felt rebuffed and embittered when Julius Stockhausen (a singer and friend of Brahms) obtained the prestigious post instead. But every time an equivalent position in Berlin, Cologne, or another major city was offered to Brahms, he would find various reasons for turning it down, and when the Hamburg post finally was made available for him, he claimed lamely that it was now too late to accept it. Brahms did accept employment on a few occasions, but only briefly. At age thirty, he served as conductor of the Vienna Singakademie; ten years later he became artistic director of the Gesellschaft der Musikfreunde but resigned after three years. By that time he no longer needed a salary. Brahms was now earning sufficient income by giving concerts, and he gradually became fairly wealthy through the sale and publication of his compositions.

Self-imposed bachelorhood was another reason for his loneliness. Brahms would speak regretfully about this at times, and his song *Kein Haus, keine Heimat*, op. 94, no. 5, expresses very well the unhappiness of a lonesome man who, in the words of Friedrich Halm, has "no house, no home, no wife, no child. I'm like a straw blown by the wind." But there also were times when he tried to make a virtue of bachelorhood. For example, when offered the Directorship of the Music Society in Düsseldorf (a post held earlier by Mendelssohn and Schumann), Brahms declined. In explaining why, he wrote to Billroth:

My main objections are of a rather childish nature, and I must remain silent about them. Perhaps the good taverns and restaurants in Vienna, the disagreeable, rough Rhenish tone (generally in Düsseldorf), and—and—in Vienna one can remain a bachelor without any hindrance. In a smaller city an old bachelor is a caricature. Marriage is something I no longer want and—I do have some reasons to be afraid of the fair sex.[16]   16

No friendship did more to reduce Brahms's loneliness than that with Joseph Joachim, the violinist and composer who was two years his senior (and outlived him by a decade). "Free but lonely" (*Frei aber einsam*) was Joachim's personal motto; its initials *FAE* make a musical pattern which Schumann, Brahms, and Dietrich used in their jointly composed "F.A.E." Sonata for Violin and Piano. Brahms also employed the theme elsewhere, for example in the first movement of his String Quartet in A Minor, op. 51, no. 2.

Brahms and Joachim often gave concerts together, and they maintained a lively correspondence for more than forty-one years, commenting on many musical matters as well as personal ones, such as their mutual dislike of gossip and their concerns about mental illness. Brahms held Joachim in very high esteem as a composer; in his typically ambivalent fashion he would regularly ask for technical advice, but just as regularly reject it. One source of difficulty in the relationship, alluded to earlier, was Brahms's discomfort with the violinist's need for physical expressions of affection. Apparently Joachim would try to embrace him, and while lying in bed would shed tears and beg his "dear Johannes" to come over to show his love.[17] An unconscious homosexual element in the relationship is also suggested by   17
Joachim's delusion about his wife having an affair with Brahms's friend Simrock. Early in the course of the troubled Joachim marriage, Brahms had written a cradle song for the couple's son, who in his honor was named Johannes. This song Brahms later incorporated into his moving Songs for contralto, viola, and piano, op. 91. He had hoped that the music would bring about a reunion between Joachim and Amalie. It did not.

Sexuality clearly seems to have been a problem for Brahms. He was able to be affectionate with women, even demonstrative at times (as suggested by photographs, although these are mostly of the older Brahms and tend to show the women hugging him rather than vice versa). His habitual caution if not abhorrence in regard to physical intimacy may reflect traumatic childhood experiences, with parents who were unhappily married, often at cross-purposes, and perhaps abusive at times. His reserve toward women may also have been conditioned by the climate of sexual promiscuity in the Hamburg taverns where he had worked as teenager. Hitschmann described it this way:

Too early he came to know the active, frivolous, purchasable sexuality of the prostitute. He once told of scenes he had witnessed: of the sailors who rushed into the inn after a long voyage, greedy for drinks, gambling, and love of women, who, half-naked sang their obscene songs to his accompaniment, then took him on their laps and enjoyed awakening his first sexual feelings.[18]

One would have to assume that unconscious and even conscious fantasies have been incorporated into such reminiscences. Nevertheless, Hitschmann's imagery suggests that young Brahms may have been seduced into playing the role of an aphrodisiac puppet, a go-between whose physical androgeny might be stimulating to men as well as women. And at a very critical period in his life he entered into the sexually complicated relationship between Robert and Clara Schumann, trying to satisfy both partners, as well as himself, in a marriage that had failed. "I dream and think only about the marvellous time when I will be able to live with both of you," he wrote on 24 October 1854.[19] Two months later: "I wish the doctor would employ me as an attendant or male nurse. . . . I could write to you about him every day, and I could talk to him about you all day" (15 December 1854). And finally, as we know, he was in love with Clara: "I think I can no longer love an unmarried girl—at least, I have completely forgotten them; they only promise the skies, whereas Clara shows it to us open."[20]

Brahms did attract other women. Several members of a female choir he conducted in Hamburg adored him, and a singer from Vienna named Bertha Porubsky may even have encouraged him to move to that city. The relationship did not continue. However, when Bertha later married and had a child, Brahms composed his famous *Wiegenlied,* op. 49, no. 4, for her. A more substantial romance was with Agathe von Siebold, the daughter of a professor in Göttingen, introduced to him by Joachim. Brahms is said to have given her an engagement ring, and when Clara Schumann found out about this, she warned him not to marry Agathe. Brahms soon terminated this relationship, but not without considerable anguish, which he symbolized by means of an agitated theme spelling her name A-G-A-H-E in the first movement of his Sextet for Strings in G Major, op. 36.

Brahms often teased Clara about possibly marrying one of her daughters, but he found excuses: "If [Eugenie] retains only a tiny scar on her pretty face [from a minor injury], then surely I can't marry her, and nothing will tie me down" (15 January 1856). Julie Schumann, probably the prettiest of the girls, also interested Brahms for a while. When she got married in 1869 to the Italian Count Marmorito, he felt embittered and angry, unjustly, since he had never declared any intention to marry Julie. Brahms had recently composed his melancholic *Alto Rhapsody,* op. 53, and he now made a point of saying it was "a bridal song for the Countess Schumann, but with rage do I write such things — with anger!"[21]

Another attractive woman in his life was Elisabeth von Herzogenberg, and again Brahms's avoidance of physical intimacy is apparent. She had been his piano student, and he broke off the relationship after noticing himself to be uncomfortably sexually aroused in her presence. They remained on good terms, however, and he regularly sought to please Elisabeth by sending her his "trifles," as he mockingly called compositions like the "tiny little Piano Concerto [in B-flat Major], written with a small, delicate Scherzo."[22]

 He also befriended a couple of contraltos. One was the buxom Hermine Spies, whom Brahms referred to jokingly as "Hermione without an O." She premiered many of his most beautiful songs. The other was Alice Barbi, a friend in his old age. These must have been exceptional women to put up with his derisive, self-disparaging remarks to the effect that any woman who could find him appealing must be out of her mind! Brahms liked to pose for photographs as a presumably happy bachelor surrounded by attractive women. In unguarded moments, however, his eccentricities became only too apparent, and many of his casual remarks sound utterly disillusioned: "I have no friends! If anyone says he is a friend of mine, don't believe it."[23] It is often said that he frequented prostitutes. In Vienna Brahms was occasionally observed in the company of a streetwalker whom he seemed to know on a first-name basis. Whether such contacts actually led to physical intimacy is anyone's guess. I find myself in sympathy with the art historian Alessandra Comini's opinion (personal communication) that after pleasurably chatting and gossiping with these women for a while, Brahms probably went home to satisfy himself in private.

One of his most active defenses against isolation was a highly developed feeling of responsibility. The sense of obligation Brahms displayed toward his own family and in his relationship with Robert and Clara Schumann has already been mentioned. His generosity in financial matters knew no bounds. He supported his parents, his siblings, his step-mother, and her children. He gave money lavishly to anyone, friend or stranger, who so much as requested it or seemed to be in need. Ruthless as he was toward mediocrity, he never stinted praise or direct helpfulness when it came to other musicians. He was genuinely impressed with the talent of Antonín Dvořák, found ways to get his compositions published, and even went to the trouble of copying scores for him. In the case of Richard Wagner, who on several occasions had made scurrilous statements about Brahms, he always behaved with utmost decency. Not that he had any sympathy for Wagner's extremism. On the contrary, Brahms had taken an early public position against the Liszt-Wagner camp. (He was also one of the few German composers who at that time did not make anti-Semitic remarks.) It was simply that Brahms respected Wagner as a composer of operas, the only musical form in which he himself had made no progress. Despite Clara Schumann's condemnation of *Tristan und Isolde,* Brahms judged this to be a "magnificent work,"[24] and he even assisted Wagner in a practical way, by copying orchestral parts for the premiere of *Die Meistersinger* in Vienna.

In his thirty-year relationship with Theodor Billroth one also observes Brahms's altruism. These men had much in common: their background in northern Germany, their loyalty to their parents, their energy and creativity, as well as their abhorrence of emotional display. Billroth habitually condemned moodiness, which he thought was a form of stupidity. Like Brahms, he firmly believed that the best way to handle one's emotions was through disciplined work. But Billroth and Brahms also had their differences: the surgeon was a tall, stately man, eloquent in speech, socially tactful and gracious, as compared to the short, awkward composer with his shabby appearance and impossible manners.

Billroth was an accomplished pianist, a passable violist, and an amateur composer. He had written three trios, a string quartet, and a piano quartet, all of which he destroyed. To please his mother, Billroth had studied medicine instead of music. He was the most daring and innovative surgeon of his day, pioneering such operations as radical mastectomy, total thyroidectomy, and various gastrointestinal procedures. His marriage was not a happy one, however, and that may have been a factor in his sensitive understanding of the lonely, sexually inhibited Brahms. Both men adored children, and Billroth was heart-broken when his first son turned out to be a deaf, mute, and possibly autistic child. (The boy died when Billroth was thirty-seven; that was the year he befriended Brahms.) They took many vacation trips together and in Vienna saw as much of each other as the busy surgeon's schedule would permit. Brahms regularly invited Billroth to his rehearsals, and he offered him many new compositions to be premiered in his home. Needless to say, Billroth championed Brahms's music with utmost enthusiasm.

The friendship began to deteriorate after Brahms learned from an old letter that Billroth had made disparaging remarks about his lack of formal education—a touchy point. He then discovered that Billroth committed the unforgivable sin of applying his surgical technique to the manuscript of a string quartet Brahms had dedicated to him. (In his worshipful attitude, Billroth had cut Brahms's signature from the title page and glued it onto his portrait.) For someone who revered original manuscripts as much as Brahms did, this was a sacrilege that justified the end of a long friendship. (Their relationship would have ended soon enough anyway, for Billroth had become ill, and died in 1894. Brahms wanted to publish Billroth's musical compositions in a posthumous edition, but the surgeon's wife objected to this plan.)

Nowhere is Brahms's generosity more apparent than in his behavior toward the old Clara Schumann.

> It angers me [he wrote her on 24 July 1888] that [among other things] you have these [money worries] — while I swim in money without even noticing it and without having any pleasure because of it. I cannot live otherwise, don't want to, and will not . . . and where my heart demands it, I can be helpful . . . and do

good without being aware of it. After my death, however, I won't have any responsibilities or special wishes.

Thus Brahms offered to send Clara 10,000 Marks for the support of her children. "Just think what a great pleasure [it would] give me were you simply and nicely to say 'yes'." Clara, characteristically, said "no." But Brahms found a way to give her the money anyway, by making an anonymous contribution to the Schumann Memorial Fund. He also took endless pains in helping Clara to edit her husband's complete works. That project led to many pathetic disagreements, caused partly by Clara's wish to suppress, and in some instances even to destroy, compositions by Schumann which she considered to be unworthy. Brahms was able to rescue Schumann's D-Minor Symphony from such a fate by having the original score published alongside its later, more thickly orchestrated version (op. 120). That infuriated Clara, whose coldness toward Brahms made him feel utterly rejected: "It is hard, after 40 years of loyal service (or whatever you might wish to call my relationship to you) to be thought of as nothing more than a 'bad experience' (13 September 1892)."

They soon forgave each other, however, and agreed to remain friends. Clara's terminal illness following a stroke in 1896 was heartbreaking for Brahms, and her death left him totally bereft. He said that she was "the only person [he] had ever really loved."[25]

One cannot measure a man of genius with the same yardstick used for normal people. Brahms may have had a depressive disorder and an avoidant personality. He often displayed obsessive-compulsive habits and an irritability and impulsivity that was upsetting to people. He became more eccentric as he grew older, and in the homes of his friends he was pampered like an overgrown child. An involutional melancholia in his mid-fifties probably interfered with both his creativity and his well-being, but he recovered with the sounds of Mühlfeld's clarinet ringing in his ears, only to be stressed beyond endurance by the death of his one and only Clara Schumann.

In terms of the theory of "transitional objects" which is so useful in explaining the childhood origins of shared pleasure, I would propose that there may also be "transitional personalities," people who do not attach themselves firmly to anyone, but who allow themselves to be used for purposes of aesthetic gratification by everyone. These individuals are able to endure great loneliness and even isolation without becoming psychotic. They may seem to be dualistic, and their behavior is paradoxical. One notices, for example, their brittleness and their integrity, their ruthlessness and their amiability, their vulnerability and their security. The art (or science, or other original things) they produce is meant to create linkages, to establish new connections between people, even across generations and cultures.

Brahms may have been such a transitional figure. He rose from rags to riches but never outgrew the rags. He was complicated and intellectual, but also simple and boorish. While he remained a stranger to many people, he was also a friend, able to transcend his painful loneliness through altruistic acts. As a composer of difficult music that is easy to enjoy, Brahms seems to have mastered "the interplay between originality and the acceptance of tradition [that is] the basis for inventiveness."[26] He was the kind of person who immerses himself so fully in his creative work that there is little time or energy left over for intimacy and the formation of families. One thinks of other geniuses for whom the whole world became a family, Beethoven, for example, or Michelangelo. Such men can change civilization. They give us new sounds, new visions, and new meanings. They achieve truths that become eternal.

26

Notes

1   Ostwald, *Schumann: the Inner Voices of a Musical Genius* (Boston, 1985), pp. 283-93.

2   D. W. Winnicott, *Playing and Reality* (London, 1971); V. Volkan, *Linking Objects and Linking Phenomena* (New York, 1981).

3   Ostwald, "The Healing Power of Music: Some Observations on the Semiotic Function of Transitional Objects," in *The Semiotic Bridge: Trends from California,* ed. Irmengard Rauch and Gerald F. Carr (Berlin and New York, 1989), pp. 279-96.

4   There is scant consideration of such matters in the Brahms chapter in F. H. Franken, *Die Krankheiten Grosser Komponisten*, vol. II (Wilhelmshaven, 1989), and no chapter about Brahms in D. Kerner, *Krankheiten Grosser Musiker*, 2 vols. (New York, 1973).

5   W. Lange-Eichbaum, *Genie, Irrsinn und Ruhm: eine Pathographie des Genies*, ed. W. Kurth (Munich, 1961).

6   Robert Haven Schauffler, *The Unknown Brahms: His Life, Character, Works* (New York, 1933).

7   Edward Hitschmann, "Johannes Brahms and Women" (1949), rpt. in *Great Men: Psychoanalytic Studies,* ed. Sydney Margolin (New York, 1956), p. 200.

8   Karl Geiringer, "Brahms the Ambivalent," *American Brahms Society Newsletter* 1/2 (1983), 5-6.

9   *Johannes Brahms in seiner Familie: der Briefwechsel,* ed. Kurt Stephenson (Hamburg, 1973), p. 175.

10   See Michael Musgrave, "The Cultural World of Brahms," in *Brahms: Biographical, Documentary and Analytical Studies,* ed. Robert Pascall (Cambridge, 1983), pp. 1-26.

11   *Clara Schumann-Johannes Brahms: Briefe aus den Jahren 1853-96,* ed. Berthold Litzmann (Leipzig, 1927), I, 597.

12   Walter Niemann, *Brahms,* trans. Catherine Alison Phillips (New York, 1929), p. 178.

13   Ruth L. Richards, "Relationship between Creativity and Psychopathology: an Evaluation and Interpretation of the Evidence," *Genetic Psychology Monographs* 103 (1981), 261-324.

14   Ostwald, *Schumann;* idem, "Anton Bruckner: Musical Intelligence and Depressive Disorder," in *Kongressbericht zum V. Gewandhaus-Symposium* (Leipzig, 1987); and idem, "Gustav Mahler: Health and Creative Energy," in *Rondom Mahler VIII* (Amsterdam, 1988).

15   The identification with Beethoven was brought home to me by Alessandra Comini in "Anzichten von Brahms—Idole und Bilder," in *Kongressbericht zum III. Gewandhaus-Symposium* (Leipzig, 1983), pp. 58-65.

Beethoven's slovenliness, rudeness, and disregard of social convention have been discussed psychoanalytically by Maynard Solomon in *Beethoven* (New York, 1977). Schubert's fluctuating sociability and withdrawal, his incessant involvement in things musical, and his ambivalence regarding women are also well-known. See, most recently, Solomon, "Schubert and the Peacocks of Benvenuto Cellini," *19th-Century Music* 12 (1989), 193–206.

16   *Billroth und Brahms im Briefwechsel,* ed. Otto Gottlieb-Billroth (Berlin and Vienna, 1935), p. 222.

17   Private communication from Boris Schwarz at International Brahms Conference, Library of Congress, May 1983.

18   Hitschmann, *Great Men,* p. 212.

19   *Schumann-Brahms Briefe* I, 24.

20   Artur Holde, "Suppressed Passages in the Brahms-Joachim Correspondence," *Musical Quarterly* 45 (1959), 314. Translation adapted.

21   *Johannes Brahms Briefwechsel* (Berlin, 1908-22), IX, 77–78.

22   *Brahms Briefwechsel* I, 154.

23   Cited in Niemann, *Brahms,* p. 180.

24   *Brahms Briefwechsel* VII, 83.

25   Niemann, *Brahms,* p. 175.

26   Winnicott, "The Location of Cultural Experience," *International Journal of Psychoanalysis* 48 (1967), 370.

Nancy B. Reich

Clara Schumann and Johannes Brahms

"I have buried today the only person whom I truly loved."
Brahms speaking to friends on the day of
Clara Schumann's funeral, May 1896.[1]   1

The friendship between Johannes Brahms and Clara Schumann has always been the subject of much speculation. The published accounts which sensationalize the "passionate friendship" (the title of a popular book on the subject) neglect the deeper personal and artistic bonds between the pianist and the composer. Theirs was a many-layered relationship—a friendship which began in 1853 between a mature performing artist and a beardless young composer, and which endured for forty-three years. As with Robert Schumann, Clara Schumann was for Brahms both muse and musician: the inspiration for much of his music and the sharer of his genius.

Clara Schumann was a working woman and an artist, one of the first of her kind. She began studying piano at five, played in the Gewandhaus at nine, made her formal solo debut at eleven, and carried on a succcessful, professional career as a concert pianist for over sixty years. She composed a number of works which were published and performed throughout the nineteenth century. She married Robert Schumann after a legendary legal battle with her father who disapproved of her choice, had eight children in fourteen years, composed, concertized, and taught during her marriage. Her husband was hospitalized in 1854 after a suicide attempt and died two years later in July 1856. Widowed and alone with seven children, she resumed her work as a touring virtuosa.

Her concert career almost spanned the century—1828 to 1891. Hailed as the peer of such giants as Liszt, Thalberg, and Rubinstein, Clara Schumann toured from Moscow to Munich, from Liverpool to Lucerne, and was dubbed Europe's "Queen of Pianists."

The circumstances of her early life were both fortunate and tragic: fortunate in that she was born in Leipzig in 1819 at a time when cultural and mercantile life was renewing itself in a city with a tradition of middle-class enterprise and a glorious musical and literary history. Fortunate also was the family history of musicality: her own talents were largely inherited from her gifted mother, Marianne Tromlitz Wieck, daughter and grand-daughter of working musicians. Marianne also had musical training and a career. During the eight years she was married to Wieck, she performed professionally as a singer and a piano soloist, helped out in Wieck's

Nancy B. Reich is the author of *Clara Schumann: The Artist and the Woman* (Ithaca, 1985).

Brahms in Düsseldorf in the autumn of 1853, drawn by J. B. Laurens.

Clara Schumann in a photo taken in 1854 or 1855, after Robert Schumann's hospitalization.

business, taught piano, and gave birth to five children. Clara's father, Friedrich Wieck, a difficult person but an innovative and creative pedagogue, devised the extraordinary musical training which created the child prodigy and later virtuosa. A successful piano teacher, he was also a merchant of pianos and related materials. In his shop, he sold music, music books, and periodicals; he established a lending library of books and music; and he rented and repaired pianos. Clara was born in an apartment over the shop and reared to the accompaniment of piano music.

Wieck saw to it that Clara had an education second to none—daily piano lessons with him, theory and harmony with the cantor of the St. Thomas Church, composition, orchestration, voice with Miksch, and counterpoint and fugue. Beginning at the age of six, Clara attended orchestra concerts in the Leipzig Gewandhaus, and on her tours between 1830 and 1838 almost every ballet and opera performance on the boards in Leipzig, Dresden, Berlin, Hamburg, Paris, and Vienna. This was an unparalleled education and absolutely unique for a female.

The tragic circumstances which shaped the girl and later the woman were the family conflicts followed by a divorce in which custody of the five-year-old girl and her two younger brothers was given to her dominating, tyrannical father. Her marriage to Robert was shadowed by the conflicts with Wieck, the man who had been her sole teacher and to whom she believed she owed her artistry.

Because Clara was from a family of teachers and musicians who had to work to earn a living, money was an important incentive throughout her life. In her childhood, when she toured under the aegis of her father, it had the highest priority: Wieck personally collected, kept, and invested the fees she earned. Later, during the years of her marriage, her income was necessary to keep the family going, though it was not discussed publicly because of the tradition of male support of the family. Her husband had ambivalent feelings about her career: he loved and hated it at the same time, as we might expect. But Robert had no regular source of income until he was forty, and the family found that there were occasions on which it was necessary to dip into Clara's earnings for necessities like rent.

Clara Schumann supported her children and many grandchildren by her earnings as a concert pianist. She premiered almost all of Schumann's piano music, edited the Complete Works of her husband, and was sought out by students from all over the world. She knew well many of the great nineteenth-century musicians including Chopin, Mendelssohn, Liszt, Wagner, Joachim, and Pauline Viardot. Brahms was her closest friend from 1854 until her death at the age of seventy-six.

Johannes Brahms came into the lives of Robert and Clara Schumann when they had been married for thirteen years. In 1850 Robert was appointed Municipal Music Director in Düsseldorf—his first salaried musical appointment. Brahms, who had just completed his first tour as a pianist, was urged by Joachim to visit Robert Schumann before returning home. Even as Brahms was making his way to the

Rhenish city, however, Schumann's position as conductor was precarious; his mental illness, which was to culminate in a suicide attempt some five months later, was progressing alarmingly.

The coming of the young pianist-composer was a most significant event in the life of both Schumanns. In a biography of her father, Eugenie Schumann gives a description of the first visit:

One day — it was in the year 1853 — the bell rang toward noon; I ran out, as children do, and opened the door. There I saw a very young man, handsome as a picture, with long blond hair. He asked for my father. My parents went out, I said. He ventured to ask when he could come again. Tomorrow, at eleven, I said, my parents always go out at twelve. The next day at eleven o'clock — we were in school — he came again. Father received him; he brought his compositions with him and Father thought that as long as he was there, he could play the things for him then and there. The young man sat down at the piano. He had barely played a few measures when my father interrupted and ran out saying, "Please wait a moment, I must call my wife." The midday meal which followed was unforgettable. Both parents were in the most joyful excitement — again and again they began and could not speak of anything but the gifted young morning visitor, whose name was Johannes Brahms.[2]

The friendship between Frau Schumann and the "gifted morning visitor" which ensued has been the stuff of myths and movies, but it is important to remember that the meeting had an enormous impact on the lives of three artists: Clara Schumann, Robert Schumann, and Johannes Brahms. Although Robert knew Brahms for only a few months before being confined to a mental institution, an immediate sympathy with the musical ideals of the younger man led him to proclaim Brahms a "young eagle . . . a mighty Niagara . . . the true Apostle."[3] He urged the famed Leipzig music publishers Breitkopf & Härtel to take up the young man's work; he himself published an article about Brahms which was to have repercussions for both men. Hailing him in ecstatic language as "he who was destined to come" and "springing forth, fully armed, like Athena from the head of Zeus . . . a young man òver whose cradle Graces and Heroes have stood watch,"[4] Robert Schumann placed a heavy responsibility on the shoulders of the younger man.

The coming of Brahms gave Clara Schumann once again the opportunity to share the thinking and work of a creative genius. The importance of this particular element of their relationship cannot be overestimated. From her earliest years, Clara had participated in the elite circles of Leipzig musical life. At nine, she was her father's "right hand" — the performer for the musical circle that met at the Wieck home, a circle which included the leading music publishers, editors, composers, and musicians of the day. She was applauded by Paganini, Spohr, and Spontini; Chopin, Liszt, and Mendelssohn dedicated works to her; Goethe rhapsodized about her playing. Robert joined the Wieck music circle when Clara was eleven and from that time on, she was *his* "right hand" and the major interpreter of his works. He entrusted her with the responsibility of introducing his music first to cognoscenti in Leipzig, Dresden, Vienna, and Paris, and then to a wider public.

Just as she could understand and interpret Robert Schumann's genius before it was generally appreciated, so could she understand that of Brahms; her musical instincts and understanding encouraged and inspired the young man who was destined to be the leading instrumental composer of his age. Her friendship with Brahms followed a life-long pattern of close and reciprocal ties with the creative figures of her time.

For Brahms, the encounter with Clara Schumann was to affect the course of his life. The young composer arrived in Düsseldorf with a knapsack of manuscripts, an imagination stimulated by Romantic German writers and poets, but with a limited acquaintance with cultivated, educated women. Clara was not merely Robert's wife and mother of his children; she was a musical partner who had entered marriage as a world-famous figure and maintained her vocation. At thirty-four, she was still a slender young woman, and though not conventionally pretty, she had an unusual beauty and strength. Not surprisingly, the twenty-year-old Brahms fell in love with her. In June 1854, he wrote to Joachim:

> I believe that I do not have more concern and admiration for her than I love her and am under her spell. I often have to restrain myself forcibly from just quietly putting my arm around her and even—I don't know, it seems to me so natural that she could not misunderstand. I think I can no longer love an unmarried girl—at least I have quite forgotten about them. They but promise heaven while Clara shows it revealed to us.[5]

Brahms was attracted to a number of women during his lifetime but never married. There is no doubt that no other woman could live up to this early ideal.

The rapport between Clara Schumann and Johannes Brahms deepened soon after Schumann's hospitalization in March 1854. For comfort and moral support, she turned to a group of young musicians who were devoted to the music of her husband. Among them, Brahms was the youngest, by far the most gifted, and the most available. As soon as he heard of Schumann's suicide attempt, Brahms, who had no steady employment yet and was living with friends in a rather Bohemian life style, came to Düsseldorf. Declaring that he was prepared to dedicate himself to the Schumanns, he virtually sacrificed himself to the family for the next two years. On his arrival, he began to keep Robert's household books, following the example set by the meticulous husband and father. Beginning with the entries for February 1854 and continuing until 30 December 1854, he noted (as had Robert) the costs for everything that pertained to the Schumann family, including postage stamps, servants' wages (including the wet-nurse after the birth of Felix), rent, and school tuition for Marie, Elise, and Julie. In keeping such intimate records, he became a member of the family circle. With those entries, he stepped into the shoes of the husband, an awesome responsibilty for a young man of twenty-one.

Brahms lived nearby, gave a few lessons, but spent much of his time at the Schumann apartment, using their pianos and helping to care for the children when their mother was away on concert tours. Given the run of the Schumann library of books and music, he began to complete what had been a haphazard education. He and friends played for Clara when she was depressed; he visited Schumann in the mental institution and reported on his condition to Clara who had been forbidden by the doctors to come; he searched for another hospital when Clara began to feel her husband might benefit from a move. He, with Joachim, was with her at the tragic closing moments of Robert Schumann's life.

Over forty-three years, Clara Schumann and Johannes Brahms actually spent little time together but corresponded regularly. After 1856, they saw each other several times a year for short periods, often meeting while one or the other was on a concert tour or for brief periods during summer vacations. They lived in widely separated cities and were kept apart by Clara's dizzying schedule of concerts, teaching, editing, and family responsibilities.

There was always some fear on both their parts that their friendship might be misinterpreted. After Robert's death, Clara wrote a letter to her children in which she explained what Brahms had meant to her in the years from 1854 to 1856:

> Like a true friend, he came to share all my sorrow; he strengthened the heart
> that threatened to break, he uplifted my mind, brightened my spirits where he
> could. He was, in short, my friend in the fullest sense of the word.[6]   6

In May 1856, he asked her to safeguard their letters in some way so that they would not be read by others.[7] By 1886 he had achieved international renown and   7 guarded his privacy even more carefully. (His concern for privacy extended to his creative workshop as well: he regularly culled works and destroyed all sketches and drafts. He left orders—which were disregarded—that all letters found in his home after his death should be destroyed.) Fearing exposure and perhaps misunderstanding of his intimate feelings, he asked that each return the letters to the other and that the letters be destroyed, a suggestion to which Clara reluctantly agreed (II, 300–01, 315–16). (Fortunately, however, she held on to her favorite letters from him so that a goodly number of his early letters to her were saved.) When she began burning her own letters, her daughter Marie prevailed on her to stop; thus most of the correspondence was preserved. Brahms, with no one to stop him, proceeded with his part of the bargain and threw his letters into the Rhine. Some thirty years after his death the remaining letters, numbering 759, were published under Marie Schumann's supervision, and so the record of the friendship remains.

It is from this record that we know the depth of their feelings and the extent of their musical and personal interaction. Even in the family-authorized letters, the emotions of the young Brahms still burn up the pages. In 1855 he writes, for example:

> Deeply beloved Frau Clara, now the longed-for Sunday, for which I was so fervently waiting, is finally drawing near. If only it brings you with it! I am actually shivering with expectation. It is becoming harder and harder to get used to being separated from you. (I, 118)

Or, in May 1856: "I would like to be able to write to you as tenderly as I love you" (I, 188). About this same time, and after a brief debate over his daring, he began to write "Du," the intimate form in German, in his letters to her. She may already have been using that form (he was the younger person). They continued to use the "Du" to each other till the end of their lives. He was, it might be noted, the only man outside her immediate family circle whom she addressed in this way. Even with other close friends like Joachim, Clara always used the formal "Sie."

The correspondence shows that soon after Robert's death, the ardor with which Brahms wrote cooled, but the friendship—which had its share of generosity, anger, love, quarrels, and reconciliations—continued.

Among the significant ties between them were their common childhood experiences of enduring family tensions and financial insecurity. Like Clara, Johannes was subjected to angry quarrels when he was growing up, although his father did not leave the home until his children were adults. Clara could understand, as few others could, the extent of Brahms's suffering when his parents separated. The circumstances of Clara Schumann's childhood were somewhat more comfortable than those of Brahms, but she had had neither a formal education nor a normal childhood. As a girl she had to work and the need for her earnings continued throughout her marriage and widowhood. Her daughter Eugenie referred to this: "The thought that everything I needed had to be earned by Mama with the work of her hands often troubled me when I was a mere child, and it was always awful for me when I needed new clothes."[8]

Brahms lived with economic insecurity for many years; he too was sent out to work at an early age and played the piano at Hamburg restaurants and private fetes as soon as his musician-father realized his talents could be turned to financial profit. Clara Schumann and Johannes Brahms discussed money matters such as rents, investments, fees, and honoraria without embarrassment, as between family members.

There were other bonds between them: in the early years she was mother, sister, friend, financial adviser, and musical colleague to him. She introduced him to influential friends and musicians, wrote to publishers on his behalf, premiered his compositions, and joined him and Joachim on concert tours in northern Germany, lending her prestige to the two younger musicians. She helped Brahms find employment, advised him on financial and musical matters as well as personal problems; she comforted him in his disappointments, gloried in his triumphs.

As the years passed, the correspondence shows that the roles were reversed: she turned increasingly to him for help and counsel. Although Clara had a large family and many friends, she asked Johannes for advice about her children—especially her sons—and discussed her own health and personal problems without hesitation. She requested his opinion on her professional commitments such as concerts, programs, students, and teaching jobs. Although she was listed as the official editor of the Collected Works of Robert Schumann, a project on which she labored from 1879 to 1893, she made few editorial decisions until she had heard from Brahms. Busy as he was, he never failed her, listening and advising patiently.

Much as she loved the music of her husband, one suspects that Clara Schumann admired the music of Brahms even more. She felt that each work was a gift to her. Writing about his Violin Sonata in G Major, op. 78, which moved her deeply, she exclaimed, "Many others could perhaps understand it and speak about it better but no one could feel it more than I do" (II, 179).

When, in August 1882, she received a manuscript copy of his Piano Trio in C Major, op. 87, she was unable to play it on a decent piano but read through enough of it to write this enthusiastic response:

> What a Trio! That was indeed a real musical treat! . . . Once again, a glorious work! There is so much that delights me in it and I long to hear it performed properly. I love each movement; how glorious the development sections are, how wonderful the way in which each motive grows out of the one before, how each figure grows from the others! How charming the Scherzo is, and then the Andante with its graceful theme. . . . How fresh the final movement is and so interesting in all its artistic combinations! (II, 258)

He in turn confided to her his hopes, dreams, fears, doubts, and—above all— his compositions. He valued her professionalism, experience, and musical sensibilities, and respected her work both as performer and composer. In each letter, he described concerts he had attended or in which he had performed; the two exchanged frank opinions on music and musicians. Almost everything he composed was sent first to Clara for comments, criticism, and reassurance. In December 1858, for example, he wrote regarding several manuscripts he had sent:

> Don't show these things to anyone because there are some bad spots in the instrumentation [his op. 13] that should not be seen by any eye but yours. You can be really critical; tell me especially what seems ugly, dull, etc. to you. (I, 230)

This was written early in his career but even at the height of his fame Brahms had great self-doubts. In 1888, he explained that he had sent his new violin sonata (op. 108) first to Elisabeth von Herzogenberg (who had liked it very much indeed) because of a peculiar shyness. He wrote:

> I never really believe that a new piece of mine could please anyone and this is still true. I still have doubts as to whether you will agree with Frau Herzogenberg's letter. If you don't like the sonata as you read through it, don't play it with Joachim, but send it back to me. (II, 363)

Clara's generally ecstatic responses were often followed by the frank criticism and suggestions Johannes requested. Despite all her other obligations, the opportunity to comment on the music of the younger composer was a task she accepted gratefully. She never failed to study the manuscripts and respond, knowing well that he might not heed her suggestions but that he depended on her interest and involvement. She knew that other friends were recipients of his manuscripts: Brahms sent his works to a trusted circle which included Joachim, Hermann Levi, the Herzogenbergs, and Dr. Theodor Billroth, but this circle changed over the years. Sooner or later, each was alienated because of Brahms's famous lack of diplomacy, prickly sensitivity, or uncouth tactlessness. Only Clara Schumann remained a constant.

One of the possible causes for Brahms's rudeness and gruffness (of which all his friends and Clara often complained) was that he was—and yet was not—a member of her family. He longed to be taken into the Schumann family circle as a brother, husband, or son. Yet he was none of these. He expressed this succinctly in 1896 when he wrote, in a letter meant to comfort her after hearing of the illness of her son-in-law, Louis Sommerhoff:

> It is the greatest good fortune to have a family and to live in a close relationship with people who are not only related by the bond of blood but who are also dear to us and beloved for themselves. You have enjoyed this beautiful happiness in full measure throughout a long life, yet I know you have paid for it dearly with much anxiety and pain. . . . But yet you would not want to exchange places with a lonely one, one who can no longer experience these things. (II, 612)

The friendship between Clara Schumann and Johannes Brahms was unique. Despite the tiffs and disagreements that occurred over the years, it was a deep source of comfort and solace to both. There was a time in 1891 when a break seemed inevitable because of a misunderstanding that began as an argument over publication of a Robert Schumann work (the Fourth Symphony). It was resolved with these words Brahms wrote for her seventy-third birthday:

Permit a poor outsider to tell you today that he thinks of you with the same reverence he always did and from the bottom of his heart wishes you—the dearest of all persons to him—a long life, everything good, and much love. Alas, I am more of an outsider to you than to anyone else. . . . But today I must repeat to you once again that you and your husband gave me the most beautiful experience of my life and represent its greatest treasures and its noblest moments. (II, 476-77)

Clara Schumann's death came on 20 May 1896. Johannes Brahms followed her eleven months later.

Notes

1 Gustav Ophüls, *Erinnerungen an Johannes Brahms* (Berlin, 1921), p. 20.

2 Eugenie Schumann, *Ein Lebensbild meines Vaters* (Leipzig, 1931), p. 357.

3 Joseph Joachim, *Briefe von und an Joseph Joachim*, ed. Johannes Joachim and Andreas Moser, 3 vols. (Berlin, 1911-13), I, 84.

4 "Neue Bahnen," *Neue Zeitschrift für Musik* 39 (1853), 185-86. English version in Robert Schumann, *On Music and Musicians*, ed. Konrad Wolff, trans. Paul Rosenfeld (New York, 1969), pp. 252-54.

5 Artur Holde, "Suppressed Passages in the Brahms-Joachim Correspondence," *Musical Quarterly* 95 (1959), 314.

6 *Clara Schumann: Ein Künstlerleben nach Tagebüchern und Briefen*, ed. Berthold Litzmann, 3 vols. (Leipzig, 1902-08), II, 337. (All translations here my own.) Published in abridged English version as *Clara Schumann: an Artist's Life, Based on Material Found in Diaries and Letters*, trans. Grace E. Hadow, 2 vols. (London, 1913).

7 *Clara Schumann-Johannes Brahms, Briefe aus den Jahren 1853-1896*, ed. Berthold Litzmann, 2 vols. (Leipzig, 1927), I, 187. Abridged English version *Letters of Clara Schumann and Johannes Brahms*, trans. Grace E. Hadow (London, 1927). Further citations are from the German edition and are given in the text.

8 Eugenie Schumann, *Erinnerungen* (Stuttgart, 1925), p. 75. English version, *The Schumanns and Johannes Brahms: The Memoirs of Eugenie Schumann,* trans. Marie Busch (New York, 1927), and *The Memoirs of Eugenie Schumann* (London, 1927).

George S. Bozarth and
Stephen H. Brady

The Pianos of Johannes Brahms

The pianos which Johannes Brahms encountered in Hamburg during his youth would have been essentially the same as the early Romantic fortepianos of Beethoven and Schubert. By the time he wrote his final compositions half a century later, the piano had evolved to a state virtually identical with the modern instrument. The two grand pianos commonly associated with Brahms—an 1839 instrument presented by its Viennese builder Conrad Graf to Robert and Clara Schumann on the occasion of their marriage in 1840 and passed on to Brahms in 1856, and an 1868 piano by Johann Baptist Streicher presented to Brahms in 1872 for use in his apartment in Vienna and kept by him for the rest of his life—were both conservative for their times. Indeed, in light of the advances in piano technology made internationally during the 1850s and 1860s, Brahms's Streicher might be considered an anachronism and, by extension, the piano ideals of its owner old-fashioned. Yet Brahms's correspondence and other documentary materials reveal that the composer performed on a wide variety of instruments during his long career, many demonstrating the latest advances in piano building.

The type of piano Brahms grew up playing at home is unknown. Brahms's childhood friend Louise Japha recalled that the instrument was of poor quality—not surprising given the family's modest means—and that the young musician frequented the establishment of the Hamburg piano builders Baumgardten & Heins in order to practice on their instruments.[1] From Hamburg in October 1854 he wrote to Clara Schumann that the Baumgardten & Heins square piano (*tafelförmigen Instrument*) delighted him with its glorious sound: "I don't believe I've ever found such a songful tone."[2] A piano of this type is now on exhibit in the Brahms *Gedenkstätte* in Hamburg, and, although it is not in good working order, one can nevertheless confirm Brahms's observation. The instrument is fitted with heavy brass string-termination bars similar to the *capo tasto* bars found on most modern grand pianos. They provide a rigid termination for the speaking length of the string, reflecting the maximum amount of vibrational energy back into the string, thus prolonging the duration of the sound and producing a "songful tone."

On 24 March 1859 Brahms gave the Hamburg premiere of his First Piano Concerto on a Baumgardten & Heins grand piano.[3] In April of the following year

1

2

3

George S. Bozarth, who teaches music history at the University of Washington, Seattle, is completing an edition of the correspondence between Brahms and his music editor Robert Keller.
Stephen H. Brady, head piano technician and curator of early keyboard instruments at the University of Washington, is completing a study of Brahms's pianos and piano music.

he may again have performed this work on one of their instruments, as part of a concert in Hamburg conducted by G. D. Otten.[4] At that time Brahms offered advice to Joseph Joachim on the purchase of a Baumgardten & Heins square piano for a family in Hannover, noting that "the high price [of 340 Thaler] should not shock you; the instruments are really much nicer and more durable than others."[5]

During the 1850s and 1860s Brahms came into contact with grand pianos built by Erard in Paris, instruments which, with their double-escapement "repetition" action and beautiful tone, were preferred by most European concert artists, including Mendelssohn and Liszt, from the 1820s until mid-century.[6] Erard instruments were also distinctive for their range of tonal shadings or colors (which changed with dynamic level as well as with register) and for the unusual clarity of their tone, particularly in rapid passages.[7]

A brief explanation of the different types of piano actions might prove helpful at this point. Since the 1770s, two different technologies had existed. Pianos with "Viennese" actions were characterized by lightness of touch, bright tone quality, rapid repetition, and swift, efficient damping. This type of action was developed by Johann Andreas Stein in Augsburg and adopted by Anton Walter and other builders in Vienna. In contrast, John Broadwood and his colleagues in England perfected a piano that yielded a more powerful, sonorous, and resonant tone, but demanded a heavier touch and had a less reliable repetition. Sébastien Erard adopted the "English" action for his pianos, but, with his "double-escapement" action patented in 1808 (and with an improved version in 1821), he gave his instruments increased rapidity in repetition.[8]

In 1858 Brahms declined to premiere his First Piano Concerto in Hamburg because an Erard grand could not be secured for the performance;[9] in 1865 he reported to Clara Schumann that he had played on "a beautiful Erard" in a concert in Zurich.[10] Brahms may have come to know the Erard piano at the home of Frau Schumann. According to the English pianist and Brahms biographer Florence May, in the spring of 1856, at the end of Frau Schumann's London concert series, Erard had given her a grand piano which continued to be her favorite for private use until 1867, when she was presented with an instrument by John Broadwood and Sons. May recalled that when Brahms visited Clara Schumann in Baden-Baden in the 1870s, although he played duets with her on her Broadwood, it was on her Erard that he performed the third and fourth books of his as-yet-unpublished Hungarian Dances, "his eyes flashing fire the while."[11]

The sound of Brahms's music performed on a restored 1866 English Erard (from the Finchcocks Collection, Goudhurst, Kent) may be heard on a recording recently released by the English pianist Richard Burnett, assisted by Alan Hacker using a pair of Albert clarinets from the late nineteenth century and Jennifer Ward Clarke playing a "modernized" 1729 cello by Joseph Guarnerius of Cremona fitted out

Brahms at a Bösendorfer grand piano, 1860s.

mainly with gut strings.[12] Although the repertoire on this recording—the Clarinet   12
Trio, op. 114, and the two Clarinet Sonatas, op. 120—dates from thirty years after
the height of Brahms's involvement with Erards, and might better have been played
on an early 1890s Bösendorfer, Bechstein, or even Steinway (see below), this
experiment in the use of period instruments is nonetheless instructive. To begin
with, the sound of the Erard is considerably less massive than that of a modern
piano, with the result that dynamic balance between the piano and the other
instruments is never a problem, the piano never overbearing.[13] It must be said that   13
at moderate and softer dynamics the piano's middle and bass registers are a bit
lacking in focus, yielding a somewhat "old upright" sound that surely cannot be the
one desired by the piano's original builders (cf. the middle section of the second
movement of op. 120, no. 2). But at higher dynamic levels, and in the upper
register at all dynamics, the color brightens and clears, and the decay of the sound
becomes quicker, so that fast passages can be played with an agility and clarity of
articulation suggestive of Haydn and Mozart on period instruments. After hearing
the demonic performance Burnett and Hacker give the opening Allegro appassionato
of op. 120, no. 1, with the clarinet and piano perfectly matching each other's every
gesture, and their highly articulated rendition of the finale of the same work, it is
easy to understand why Brahms would have selected Frau Schumann's Erard to
show off the colorful piano writing of his Hungarian Dances.[14]   14

The piano traditionally associated with Brahms's early years is the 1839 Graf which
Clara Schumann gave him in 1856, not long after she acquired her Erard. As noted
earlier, the instrument had been a present from Conrad Graf on the occasion of the
Schumanns' marriage in 1840. The piano stood in Robert Schumann's workroom
and may well have been the instrument on which the twenty-year-old Brahms
introduced his early compositions to the Schumanns in the autumn of 1853. To
Robert, Brahms's sonatas were like "veiled symphonies"; his playing, "full of genius,
transformed the piano into an orchestra of lamenting and jubilant voices."[15]   15
A feature of Graf pianos, as well as many other earlier instruments, is variation in
tone color according to register. Brahms capitalized on this quality in his early
works (see, for instance, the beginning of the finale in the F-Minor Piano Sonata,
op. 5) and apparently made the most of these orchestral effects in performance.
    Yet, in comparison with Erards of the 1850s, the Schumann Graf was quite
old-fashioned, and it is likely that Brahms viewed it as such. The range of the
piano—six octaves and a fifth, $CC-g^4$—is sufficient for nearly all of Brahms's solo
piano music of the 1850s and 1860s, but barely so; his three piano sonatas of
1852–53, which fit comfortably on the seven-octave keyboard ($AAA-a^4$) typical of
this time, explore the very extreme registers of the Graf (see, for instance, the
opening theme of the F-Minor Sonata, op. 5, which employs both CC and f^4 at its
climax). In the First Piano Concerto, op. 15, and the Paganini Variations, op. 35,

the highest notes are a⁴, and the B-Major Piano Trio, op. 8 (1854 version), and
several of the early songs descend to BBB. Moreover, the technology of the Graf is,
except for a general increase in size and weight, virtually identical with that of
Beethoven's famous Graf—single-escapement "Viennese" action, all-wooden construction, and leather-covered hammers.[16] (Before the Graf left Düsseldorf, its   16
hammers were replaced; on the lowest of the current hammers, written in pencil,
are the date and name "30 / 9 [18]56. J. B. Klems [a piano builder in Düsseldorf]."
Although the replacement hammers are now entirely felt, traces of what appears to
be glue suggest that they too were initially covered with a thin strip of leather.)

Lacking permanent lodgings, Brahms at first entrusted the Schumann Graf to
the care of his parents in Hamburg.[17] Sometime during the years 1861–62, when he   17
took rooms with Frau Dr. Elisabeth Rösing in Hamm, a suburb of Hamburg, he
apparently moved the Graf to her home, where he left it after taking up residence
in Vienna in the autumn of 1862. In February 1868 he wrote from Hamburg to
Clara Schumann that Frau Rösing had been storing "Robert's grand piano" for a
long time, but in a few months she would be moving to Hannover:

> I cannot, of course, leave it here; space is money. Yet you also have no room in
> Baden for such a dear but bulky memento. Yes, selling it here is also nearly
> impossible, as Heins informs me, and one would hardly want to think about
> [doing] that. If I lived here, I would not think of giving it away, but now I
> must come to a decision—and you?[18]   18

While residing with Frau Rösing, Brahms would have made use of the Graf for
composing the Handel Variations, op. 24, the two Piano Quartets, opp. 25 and 26,
and the F-Minor Piano Quintet, op. 34, as well as part of the First Cello Sonata, op.
38, and several of the *Magelone* Romances, op. 33, but, as this letter suggests, its
value to him by this time was mainly sentimental.

The immediate solution to the problem of where to keep the Graf seems to have
been to store it with Baumgardten & Heins in Hamburg.[19] In 1871, Brahms's father   19
took a new flat on the Anscharplatz in Hamburg, where he lived until his death the
following year and where his widow, Brahms's stepmother, resided until 1883. At
some point the Graf was moved into this apartment.

In February 1873, Brahms wrote to his stepmother that he would soon be
sending for the piano, for it was to be displayed at the Vienna World Exhibition,
together with the pianos of Mozart, Beethoven, and others; and in October he
informed her that the instrument had arrived and was on display.[20] When the   20
Exhibition was concluded, Brahms gave the Graf to the Gesellschaft der Musikfreunde, where it took its proper place among the historic instruments in that
society's collection.

The Schumann Graf is now on loan to the Musikinstrumentsammlung of the
Kunsthistorisches Museum in Vienna.[21] Unfortunately, the instrument can no longer   21

The living room of Brahms's apartment at Karlsgasse 4, with his 1868 J. B. Streicher grand
piano.

be tuned, for the pinblock has cracked. In a recording of works by Clara and Robert Schumann performed on this piano by Jörg Demus in the early 1960s,[22] one already hears an instrument in distress: the sound is clangorous, filled with "false beats" (probably produced by irregularities in the worn-out strings) and poorly damped. (The echo caused by the room or added by the recording engineers does not help matters.) A fairer idea of how Brahms's Graf may have sounded can be gained from recordings by Demus on his own 1839 Graf, this one in excellent working order.[23] Here the sound is well-focused, resonant but transparent, and ranges from delicate and harp-like to robust. Differences in tonal color from one register to another are clearly in evidence and are put to particularly good use in "orchestral" works like Beethoven's Diabelli Variations. With leather-covered hammers and dampers, the attack is clean and the damping is efficient. This instrument is truly a joy to hear, and one can easily imagine how exciting Brahms's earliest works would sound on it.

The piano which Brahms chose for his apartment in Vienna in 1872 was an instrument built by Johann Baptist Streicher in 1868. Streicher was one of the major piano builders in mid-nineteenth-century Vienna, the descendent of an illustrious family of piano makers—at the turn of the century his mother, Nannette Streicher, had built pianos on her own and in partnership with her husband Johann Andreas Streicher that were highly regarded by Beethoven; the pianos of his grandfather, Johann Andreas Stein of Augsburg, were praised by Mozart in 1777.[24] Among Viennese piano builders, a generally conservative lot, Johann Baptist was one of the more innovative. In 1831 he had patented a piano action that was neither "Viennese" nor "English," but of his own design and sharing features of both types.[25] In the 1860s Streicher experimented with the latest advances coming from America, and at the Paris Exhibition of 1867 he won a gold medal for an over-strung piano with a one-piece cast-iron frame modelled on a Steinway that had been exhibited in London five years earlier.[26] He also built pianos with "English" actions; in 1870 Clara Schumann performed a concert in Vienna on an 1868 Streicher with an "English" mechanism.[27] Meanwhile, he continued to build instruments with "Viennese" actions that refined rather than revolted against tradition, and it was probably these more typical pianos that Brahms knew and admired.

The earliest documented instance of Brahms's performing on a Streicher dates from 12 April 1863, seven months after he first came to Vienna. The occasion was a Streicher *Soirée Musicale*, held in a recital hall maintained by the firm to display its instruments. (On this program Brahms played an unspecified piece for solo piano, the *Pensées fugitives* for violin and piano by Stephen Heller and Heinrich Wilhelm Ernst, and several of Beethoven's Scottish Lieder, with violin and cello.) At the time, Streicher's major rival was Ludwig Bösendorfer, and concert programs and other documents from Brahms's first season in Vienna show that he performed at least twice on Bösendorfer pianos—a chamber recital with the Hellmesberger Quartet on 16 November 1862 (the G-Minor Piano Quartet, op. 25), and his first solo recital on 29 November (including the Handel Variations, op. 24, and the A-Major Piano Quartet, op. 26).[28] By October 1864, however, if not sooner, Brahms seems to have gravitated toward Streicher instruments. At the end of that month he wrote to Clara Schumann: "I have a beautiful grand piano from Streicher. With it he wants to demonstrate [his] latest achievements to me, and I believe that if he made a similar one for you, you would be pleased [with it]."[29] A letter from Frau Schumann to Brahms three years later suggests that the Streichers were courting her favor as well as Brahms's: "Frau Streicher wrote to me again. . . . Are the new instruments really so beautiful? She writes to me about them in such enraptured terms."[30]

During the decade 1865–75, Brahms played Streicher pianos almost exclusively when in Vienna, and in 1872 Streicher loaned Brahms a grand piano, serial number 6713, for use in his new apartment at Karlsgasse 4. This instrument remained with the composer until his death in 1897. Brahms's friends hoped to keep his apartment unaltered as a memorial, but in 1906 the building was torn down. Brahms's furnishings, most of which had belonged to his landlady, were first kept by the Gesellschaft der Musikfreunde, but eventually went to the Historisches Museum der Stadt Wien. During the Second World War most of the furniture was destroyed and Brahms's Streicher was severely damaged. All that now remain are one leg and the music desk.[31]

Judging from photographs of Brahms's living room, his Streicher was a small piano, measuring approximately 6′9″. Another 1868 Streicher, serial number 6668, a full-sized grand, but otherwise quite similar in appearance to Brahms's instrument and typical of the pianos Streicher built in the late 1860s, is now in the possession of Edmund Michael Frederick in Ashburnham, Massachusetts. Writing about this piano, Gregory Hayes has noted:

> With leather-covered hammers, Viennese single-escapement action, and parallel-stringing, it presents a velvety but astonishingly clear and variegated sound. At low dynamic, it is as mellow as a modern instrument, but without the aural fog; at higher levels a chiff in the attack of each note allows for the possibility of *sforzando* without *fortissimo*. The aural gratification . . . is complemented on the technical side as well; simply put, it is easy to play. . . . its action is lighter, faster, and a good deal shallower than that of a modern instrument. Lesser physical gestures—a snap of the wrist instead of an application of arm weight, for instance—beget more subtle musical gestures. Especially in mid-range (C to c¹) at low volume, the piano's own timbral characteristics reduce matters of voicing to a nuance rather than a preoccupation.[32]

Frederick and Lynn Edwards provide further details:

This 1868 piano, while a modernized version of [Streicher's] earlier pianos, still has a wooden frame and parallel stringing. Its soundboard is larger, and the treble scaling is longer, than in earlier pianos, and it is fitted with two iron bars and a *capo tasto*. . . . This late instrument retains other features of the Viennese piano as well, including leather-capped hammers and Viennese action. Its range of AAA–a⁴ (seven octaves) and its length of 7'11″ are both typical for late nineteenth-century Viennese pianos.

Like early Viennese [parallel-strung] pianos, the 1868 Streicher has a relatively transparent tone which begins with a distinct articulation from the rather soft-surfaced hammers hitting the strings. The tone is more sustained and mellow than that of Viennese pianos of forty years earlier, the more lush, full sound having been gained, however, at the sacrifice of some clarity, delicacy, and lightness of touch. There is a distinct contrast in tone color between soft and loud which makes it relatively easy to separate a melody from its accompaniment, a capability which makes the Streicher particularly well-suited to Brahms's combination of melody and polyphony. . . . The sound is generally sweet and gentle. It is not loud, but can sound thunderous in its fortissimo because it can so readily be played softly.[33]

Seth Carlin, who performed the Handel Variations, op. 24, and a group of short Brahms pieces on this instrument in a concert for the Westfield Center for Early Keyboard Studies in 1985, has described its tone as having "a grainy, woody quality—somehow more human or organic" than the modern piano. The treble he termed "angelic, sweet, bell-like," so that, for example, the "music-box" variation in op. 24 (variation 22) has a "celestial" quality not heard on modern instruments. Indeed, this Streicher, like other early pianos, has "a whole palette of timbres" that can be exploited in order to render most effectively the "orchestral" aspects of Brahms's piano writing.[34] This instrument can be heard on a recording of Michael Boriskin playing excerpts from the Handel Variations, released as an insert to the Summer 1985 issue of *The Piano Quarterly.*

It is clear from Brahms's correspondence that he considered there to be important differences between Viennese and English action pianos and between various sizes of Viennese instruments at this time. In April 1873 he wrote to his friend Adolf Schubring: "Today . . . I went to Streicher and tried all their grand pianos. I consider Streicher to be good and reliable. . . . You are accustomed to another [type of] piano, and the German [i.e. "Viennese"] action will seem strange to you. I have one in my room that I like very much, and yet I still cannot get used to the local grand pianos in the concert hall."[35] In November of the following year he wrote to Joseph Joachim regarding an upcoming concert by Heinrich Barth: "Bösendorfer was recently [at the Musikvereinssaal] and reminded me that his hall stands at our disposal at no charge. (I don't like such things at all.) But Herr Barth must be allowed to choose the piano for himself! He will sigh about it enough [anyway], but he must not be bound to Bösendorfer."[36]

To judge from these remarks, Brahms admired the smaller Streicher grands, like the one he owned, and in general considered Streicher's instruments dependable, but was not fond of the large, concert-size Viennese grands, including both Streichers and Bösendorfers. The Kunsthistorisches Museum houses concert grands by Bösendorfer (1877) and Streicher (1868 — the one Clara Schumann used) which employ a modified "English" action. Both companies experimented with such actions — enhanced with a device for improving repetition — on some of their concert instruments, while in their smaller grands, under eight feet, they continued to use "Viennese" actions. The larger actions of the concert instruments may have necessitated this change, for it was characteristic of "Viennese" actions to become unwieldy as they became larger. More than likely, it was concert grands with oversized, bulky "Viennese" actions to which Brahms objected. Such an interpretation of his remarks is also consistent with his predilection for Clara Schumann's Erard, with its double-escapement English-type action, and his subsequent admiration for Bechstein and Steinway concert grands, both of which employed actions similar to that built by Erard.

After the mid-1870s Brahms played most of his concerts in Vienna on Bösendorfers. The last time he performed on a Streicher in public, according to available documents, was at a quartet evening in November 1880 presented by Joseph Hellmesberger and at which Brahms and Hellmesberger played the G-Major Violin Sonata, op. 78. This shift in loyalty may have had as much to do with the decline of the Streicher firm as with any other factor. Johann Baptist Streicher had died in 1871. His son Emil continued the business as his illustrious forebears had, producing approximately 150 well-crafted instruments each year in a small shop.[37] While this strategy had worked well enough to earn the Streicher firm a formidable reputation during the first half of the nineteenth century, and to retain that reputation well into the latter half of the century, it proved not to be the best way to compete on the international scene with highly industrialized firms like Broadwood, Pleyel, Steinway, and Chickering, which were producing ten to fifteen times that number of pianos annually.[38] Nor could Streicher compete locally with Bösendorfer, which, in response to increasing demand, had moved to a factory in Wiener Neustadt in 1860 and by 1870 already found that facility too small.[39] Although some pianists, like the Austrian composer Karl Prohaska, continued to play Streicher pianos in their Viennese recitals, Bösendorfer and other makers came to the fore. Finally, in 1896, Emil Streicher had to liquidate his firm.[40]

On several occasions in the late 1870s and 1880s Brahms performed private concerts for small groups of friends on pianos manufactured by Friedrich Ehrbar. In each case the musical gatherings were held in the Ehrbar salon and designed as trial piano four-hand performances of large-scale orchestral works: the Second Symphony in 1877, the Second Piano Concerto in 1881, and the Fourth Symphony in 1885.[41]

At the time Ehrbar's pianos were slightly more progressive in design and technology than those of Streicher and Bösendorfer; the 1874 production model housed in the Kunsthistorisches Museum has a Viennese action and a composite iron framework similar to those in Streicher and Bösendorfer pianos, but employs an overstrung bass, a feature not yet found on Streicher and Bösendorfer production models, and a side-to-side grain orientation in the soundboard, a feature that even today would be viewed as experimental.[42] Ehrbar was also one of the first Viennese makers to adopt the full iron frame for all of his pianos.[43]

Brahms's concert tours exposed him to a wide variety of pianos, both European and American. As early as 1868 he played on a Bechstein in Berlin, the home of Carl Bechstein's factory, and by 1872 he had performed on Bechsteins in both Würzburg and Cologne.[44] Judging from concert programs, the pianos Brahms most frequently played when away from Vienna in the 1870s and 1880s were Bechsteins, Blüthners (which Hans von Bülow called bad imitations of Bechsteins[45]), and Th. Steinwegs. Other pianos he encountered on his tours included instruments built by Klems, Trau, Lipp, Knabe, Ibach, Bachman, Mand, Jacobi, and Steinway and Sons.

Brahms's fondness for Bechstein and Steinway pianos is well documented. Shortly after playing the premiere of his Second Piano Concerto on a Bösendorfer in Budapest in 1881, he wrote to Julius Otto Grimm about securing a piano for use in a performance of the concerto in Stuttgart:

> Would you be so good as to inquire in Cologne or wherever whether one cannot send for a Bechstein or a Steinway. I will gladly pay the transportation costs. But I will not play again [in Stuttgart] on some risky or questionable instrument.[46]

Brahms's willingness to accept a Bechstein or a Steinway virtually sight unseen suggests how reliable he considered these instruments to be.

At this time, Bechsteins were some of the finest and most popular instruments being produced. In many ways they were equivalent to the modern piano, utilizing an overstrung bass, a one-piece, cast-iron frame, and the Herrburger-Schwander version of Erard's double-escapement action. Bechsteins were noted for their strength and "velvety" tone.[47] In assessments sent to Carl Bechstein in 1868 and 1873, Hans von Bülow had noted that he found Bechstein instruments, "particularly in *piano* . . . less so in the *forte*," to be "splendidly equal and pleasing in tone and easy to play" and that they provided "the playing-fields that I need for my fine shades of touch and tone" (which von Bülow found wanting in Bösendorfers of the time). His only qualms were about their repetition: "incomparable as your pianofortes are in respect of nobility, fullness, and color of tone, not to speak of their splendid equalization and other advantages, they do leave much to be desired in their repeating mechanism . . ."[48] In the early 1870s Bechstein still used a single-escapement

English action; by the end of the decade he had remedied the problem of repetition by adopting Erard's double-escapement action.[49]

49

Two days after the Stuttgart engagement, Brahms arrived in Meiningen to perform his new concerto for Duke Georg II. The concert grand was a Bechstein. Hans von Bülow, who conducted on this occasion, reported to Carl Bechstein: "Maestro Brahms finds the new instrument quite excellent and very easy [to play]."[50] According to programs from his concerts, Brahms played Bechstein pianos more and more during the last fifteen years of his life.

50

Brahms's reference to "Steinway" in his letter to Grimm was to the pianos of Steinway and Sons, not "Th. Steinweg Nachfolger." When Heinrich Engelhard Steinweg and his family emigrated to New York in 1851 to found the Steinway and Sons dynasty, his eldest son Carl Friedrich Theodor remained in Germany to run his own piano factory. In 1865, however, he too moved to New York, selling his business to three of his workmen, who called the firm "Th. Steinweg Nachfolger." The following year one of these partners, Wilhelm Grotrian, assumed sole proprietorship.[51] At least as early as 1874 Brahms had played on one of Grotrian's instruments. Two years later, there is evidence of his trying a New York Steinway.[52] By 1881, the year of his letter to Grimm, Steinway and Sons had opened a branch factory in Hamburg, making their pianos even more readily available in Europe. The action in the instrument they produced then was, for all intents and purposes, technologically the same as the modern Steinway. Yet even here the sound may have varied significantly from modern instruments, due to differences in materials and voicing technology. Jon Finson has described the 1892 Steinway grand used by Ignaz Paderewski and now owned by the Smithsonian as having "great clarity of tone, penetration, and a soft overall sound" and being "more acoustically efficient, emphasizing the fundamental tone of each note, with less pronounced overtones than a modern Steinway." Finson continues, "As a result, the pianist was able to produce sound with a lighter touch, and the sound was not so massive as that of a modern instrument."[53]

51
52

53

In the mid-1880s Brahms became acquainted with the piano designer Richard Gertz, the son of a Hannover piano builder. According to Alfred Dolge, between 1886 and 1888 Gertz "often discussed the good or weak points of various pianos" with Brahms and von Bülow.[54] In 1895 the Boston firm of Mason & Hamlin engaged Gertz to design new scales (the layout and specifications for stringing, including string lengths, diameters, tensions, etc.) for their pianos,[55] and it is possible that Brahms's ideas found some expression in the instruments that resulted from this collaboration. Certainly the resonant, "singing" treble tone for which Mason & Hamlin pianos are renowned is consistent with the tastes of a man who prized Baumgardten & Heins square pianos for their "songful tone." The reliability of Mason & Hamlin instruments, the most ruggedly constructed of modern pianos,

54

55

weighing more than either Steinways or Bechsteins of similar sizes, would also have appealed to Brahms.

On at least two occasions, Brahms provided piano makers with written testimonials. After using a Bösendorfer piano during a summer vacation in Mürzzuschlag, Austria, he wrote to Ludwig Bösendorfer about "how excellent your piano was and how many rainy days it transformed into the sunniest days of summer for me."[56] 56
Similarly, after a summer stay in Thun, Switzerland, where he used a piano by the local manufacturer Jacobi, Brahms wrote to its builder: "Your piano has greatly beautified my summer sojourn here. It is an entirely excellent instrument and a model of its type."[57] 57

Like any other pianist, Brahms valued excellence in his instruments. Their action, whether "English" or "Viennese," had to be responsive, their tone beautiful and singing, their construction reliable. Available documents demonstrate that, given a choice, Brahms consistently favored the more technologically advanced instruments of his day. Although the Graf on which he composed keyboard music in the early 1860s was antiquated, the instruments he played in public kept up with the times. Likewise, while he had an 1868 Streicher in his apartment in Vienna for the last two-and-a-half decades of his life, the pianos on which he performed his concerts incorporated many of the latest innovations. During his professional lifetime, the piano underwent considerable change, but throughout his career, in his "ideal" in pianos, as in the style of his piano music, Brahms remained "the progressive."

Notes

1   Max Kalbeck, *Johannes Brahms,* 4 vols., rev. edns. (Berlin, 1912-21; repr. Tutzing, 1976), I, 35.

2   "Solchen gesangvollen Ton glaube ich immer nie gefunden zu haben." Letter of 21 October 1854; *Clara Schumann-Johannes Brahms Briefe,* ed. Berthold Litzmann (Leipzig, 1927), I, 23. In November 1854 Frau Schumann performed several recitals in and near Hamburg. Brahms's comments were probably occasioned by an inquiry from her about the availability of pianos for these concerts. Brahms spoke of a square piano because at the time Baumgardten & Heins had no grand pianos on hand. His recommendation, though, was that she have J. B. Klems, a piano builder in Düsseldorf, ship an instrument to Hamburg.

3   Concert program, reproduced in Kurt Hofmann, *Johannes Brahms und Hamburg* (Reinbek, 1986), p. 31.

4   Concert of 20 April 1860, which also included three pieces from Schumann's *Kreisleriana,* op. 16; cf. *Johannes Brahms Briefwechsel,* 16 vols., rev. edns. (Berlin, 1912-22; rpt. Tutzing, 1974), V, 269, and Renate and Kurt Hofmann, *Johannes Brahms Zeittafel zu Leben und Werk* (Tutzing, 1983), p. 46.

5   "Der hohe Preis gar nicht abschrecken, die Instrumente sind wirklich weitaus schöner und dauerhafter als andere." Letter of 18 April 1860; *Brahms Briefwechsel* V, 269.

6   Cf. Cyril Ehrlich, *The Piano: A History* (London, 1976), p. 109, and Florence May, *The Life of Johannes Brahms,* 2nd edn., rev. (London, 1948; rpt. Neptune City, NJ, 1981), I, 208.

7   Cf. David Wainright, *Broadwood, by Appointment* (London, 1982), pp. 170-71.

8   For a detailed account of the history of piano actions, cf. Rosamond E. M. Harding, *The Piano-Forte: Its History traced to The Great Exhibition of 1851,* 2nd ed. (Old Woking, Surrey, 1978).

9   Letter from Brahms to Clara Schumann, 28 February 1858; *Schumann-Brahms Briefe* I, 218. This letter provides a glimpse of musical politics in Hamburg: "So my concerto will also not be given here! All truly Hamburgish. Cranz will not give me his Erard, but with the utmost amiability offers useless small ones [*unbrauchbare Stutze*]. Aloys Schmidt and Alfred Jaëll were the last ones [to use Cranz's Erard?]. Otherwise there is no grand piano to be had."

10   "Ich hatte einen schönen Erard, der Hugs Privatbesitz war ..." Letter of 3 December 1865; *Schumann-Brahms Briefe* I, 518.

11   May, *Brahms* I, 208. As a young woman, Florence May studied piano with Clara Schumann and, during the summer of 1871, with Brahms. On numerous occasions, both public and private, she heard the composer perform his own works and those of his illustrious predecessors from Bach and Scarlatti on. In the "Personal Recollections" portion of her biography she provided accounts of Brahms as a pianist and teacher.

On Brahms's famous recording of an excerpt from his First Hungarian Dance and on performances by members of the Brahms-Clara Schumann circle, see Will Crut∶hfield, "Brahms, by Those Who Knew Him," *Opus* 2/5 (August 1987), 13-21, 60; Helmut Kowar, Franz Lechleitner, and Dietrich Schüller, "On the Re-issue of the Only Existing Sound Recording of Johannes Brahms by the Phonogrammarchiv," *Phonographic Bulletin* 39 (1984), 19-22; and George S. Bozarth, "Brahms on Record," *The American Brahms Society Newsletter* 5/1 (Spring 1987), [5-9].

12   Released by Amon Ra Records (CD-SAR 37; also on cassette, CSAR 37).

13   The engineers for this recording should be congratulated for producing a very "true" sound, with no added resonance and just enough sense of the room around the performers to bring the listener "into the hall." Unfortunately, the same cannot be said for the one other recording of a mid-century Erard available to the authors (a Parisian instrument of 1850, on Accent ACC 8330); for this recording of works by Schumann, Kalliwoda, and Pixis, sensitively performed by Paul Dombrecht, oboe, and Jos van Immerseel, piano, the engineers seem to have tried to compensate for a somewhat dull-sounding piano by allowing a considerable amount of "room echo."

14   Hacker's Albert clarinet, which he assures us in the liner notes is "very close to the design of Mühlfeld's Ottensteiner clarinets," is a delightfully multi-colored instrument, played to its fullest by Hacker in one of the finest performances of these late Brahms works available on record. The sound is not the plush Victorian one that many modern clarinetists try to produce, but seems to consist of a thinner central sound sheathed in resonance to make it rich, but not overly so. Hacker's pallet of sounds ranges from "inwardly melancholy" (to borrow one of his apt characterizations) to splendidly bright, even piercing. Some of the most beautiful passages in the Clarinet Trio are when the cello, taking advantage of the "reedier" sound possible with gut strings, joins with the clarinet in passages of parallel octaves or tenths, the two instruments merging into one.

15   Robert Schumann, "Neue Bahnen," *Neue Zeitschrift für Musik* 39 (1853), 185.

16   Detailed specifications for the Schumann Graf appear in an appendix to Deborah Wythe's article on Conrad Graf (*Early Music* 12 [1984], 458-59).

17   Cf. letter to Brahms from his mother, 20 November 1858; *Johannes Brahms in seiner Familie: Der Briefwechsel*, ed. Kurt Stephenson (Hamburg, 1973), p. 82.

18   "Ich weiß ihn hier natürlich nicht zu lassen, Platz ist Geld. Aber Du hast in Baden auch keinen Platz für ein so wertes, aber so umfängliches Andenken. Ja, auch das Verkaufen ist hier fast unmöglich, wie mir Heins sagt, und man denkt kaum gern daran. Schreibe mir doch ja und bald darüber. Lebte ich hier, so würde ich daran denken, ihn wegzugeben, aber jetzt muß ich mich ja entschließen—und Du?" Letter of 2 February 1868; *Schumann-Brahms Briefe* I, 576.

19   *Schumann-Brahms Briefe* I, 582. Frau Schumann thought to let her daughter Elise have the piano, but this apparently never came to pass.

20   Letters to Caroline Brahms of 23 February and 9 October 1873; Stephenson, *Johannes Brahms in seiner Familie*, pp. 204, 209.

21   Cf. Victor Luithlen, *Katalog der Sammlung alter Musikinstrumente, 1. Teil: Saitenklaviere* (Vienna, 1966), pp. 49-50.

22   Harmonia mundi 1C 151-99 773/5; also released as 30 475 K and as 30 662.

23 Beethoven's Diabelli Variations, on Archiv 2708 025; Schumann Lieder, with Elly Ameling, on Harmonia mundi 1C 065-99 631 (also released as 303 946 XK and, by BASF, as HB 29369); and selections from Schumann's *Fantasiestücke,* op. 12, on Harmonia mundi 1C 065-99 797 (also released as HMS 17 064, as 29 29069/7, and as 30 485K).

24 Letter from Mozart to his father, 17 October 1777; Emily Anderson, *The Letters of Mozart and his Family,* 2 vols., 2nd edn., rev., ed. A. Hyatt King and Monica Carolan (London and New York, 1966), pp. 328-29.

25 Harding, *The Piano-Forte,* p. 319. An 1848 J. B. Streicher piano with this hybrid type of action has been available to the authors for study. Harding termed this action "Anglo-German."

26 Edwin Good, *Giraffes, Black Dragons, and Other Pianos* (Stanford, 1982), p. 200.

27 This instrument is now in the Kunsthistorisches Museum, Vienna; cf. Luithlen, *Katalog,* pp. 54-55.

28 We would like to thank Dr. Otto Biba, director of the Archive of the Gesellschaft der Musikfreunde in Vienna, for placing at our disposal the large collection of nineteenth-century concert programs in the possession of his archive.

29 "Ich habe einen schönen Flügel von Streicher. Er hat mir eben neue Errungenschaften dadurch mitteilen wollen, und ich glaube, wenn er Dir ähnliche schafft, wirst Du zufrieden sein." Brahms informed Frau Schumann that in eight days (on 3 November; cf. Hofmann, *Brahms Zeittafel,* p. 66) he would be trying out one of these "improved" Streichers in a public concert in Vienna with the violinist Ferdinand Laube playing Schumann's D-Minor Violin Sonata, op. 121. Letter dated *ca.* 26 October 1864; *Schumann-Brahms Briefe* I, 471.

30 "Frau Streicher schrieb mir neulich . . . Sind die neuen Instrumente wirklich so schön? Sie schreibt mir ganz entzückt darüber." Letter of 11 January 1867; *Schumann-Brahms Briefe* I, 553. Friederike Streicher's letters to Clara Schumann have not been located, but seven letters from Frau Schumann to Frau Streicher, spanning the years 1856 to 1895, are owned by the Library of Congress and will soon be published.

31 We thank Dr. Otto Biba for kindly providing this information.

32 Gregory Hayes, "How Many Pianos Does It Take to Fill a House?: The Frederick Collection," *Early Keyboard Studies Newsletter* 1/2 (1985), 4-5.

33 Lynn Edwards and E. Michael Frederick, "Two Nineteenth-Century Grand Pianos," *Early Keyboard Studies Newsletter* 1/4 (1985), 4-5.

34 Seth Carlin's observations were made in an interview with Virginia Hancock in 1985.

35 "Heute bin ich . . . zu Streicher gegangen und habe alle Flügel probiert. Ich halte Streicher für gut und zuverlässig. . . . Du bist an andere Flügel gewöhnt, und Dir wird die deutsche Mechanik sonderbar vorkommen. Ich habe sie im Zimmer recht gern und kann nur, bis jetzt noch, mich im Konzertsaal nicht an die hiesigen Flügel gewöhnen." *Brahms Briefwechsel* VIII, 224-25.

36 "Bösendorfer war neulich da und erinnerte mich, daß sein Saal uns unentgeltlich zur Verfügung stände. (Ich liebe solche Sachen überhaupt nicht.) Herr Barth muß aber sich den Flügel aussuchen dürfen! Er wird genug seufzen dabei, muß aber doch nicht an Bösendorfer gebunden sein." Letter from [end of] November 1874; *Brahms Briefwechsel* VI, 107.

37 A small group of letters from Brahms to Emil Streicher, preserved in the Oesterreichisches Nationalbibliothek, Vienna, and dealing mainly with the borrowing of instruments, was published by Felix von Lepel in 1936 ("Sieben unbekannte Briefe von Brahms," *Signale für die musikalische Welt* 94 [1936], 510-11).

38 The production figures given here are taken from Good, *Giraffes,* p. 203.

39 William Leslie Sumner, *The Pianoforte* (London, 1966), p. 127.

40 Good, *Giraffes,* p. 203.

41 Kalbeck, *Brahms* III, 178, 298, 451.

42 Cf. Luithlen, *Katalog,* p. 56-57.

43   Alfred Dolge, *Pianos and Their Makers* (Covina, CA, 1911; repr. New York, 1972), p. 222.

44   Camilla Cai, "Brahms's Short, Late Piano Pieces, Opus Numbers 116–119: A Source Study, an Analysis, and Performance Practice" (Ph.D. dissertation, Boston University, 1986), p. 409; and also her recent article "Brahms's Pianos and the Performance of the Late Piano Works," *Performance Practice Review* 2 (1989), 59.

45   Letter from Hans von Bülow to Carl Bechstein, 1/13 March 1874; *Letters of Hans von Bülow,* ed. Richard Count de Moulin Eckhart and Scott Goddard, trans. Hannah Walter (New York, 1931; repr. New York, 1972), p. 147.

46   "Sei doch so gut, Dich in Köln oder wo zu erkundigen, ob man uns nicht einen Bechstein oder Steinway schickt. Transportkosten will ich gern zahlen. Aber auf einem irgend bedenklichen oder fraglichen Instrument spiele ich nicht wieder." Letter postmarked 18 November 1881; *Brahms Briefwechsel* IV, 144.

47   Good, *Giraffes,* p. 213.

48   Letters of 1 March 1868, 15 September 1873, and 14 October 1873; *Letters of von Bülow,* pp. 80, 138, 140.

49   Letter from Hans von Bülow to Carl Bechstein, 24 August 1877; ibid., p. 166.

50   Ibid., p. 178.

51   Sumner, *The Pianoforte,* p. 124.

52   On 29 December 1874 and 19 February 1876, respectively; cf. Cai, "Brahms's Piano Pieces," p. 409.

53   Jon Finson, "Performing Practice in the Late Nineteenth Century, with Special Reference to the Music of Brahms," *Musical Quarterly* 70 (1984), 461–63. Finson introduces evidence about the changes in techniques for voicing felt hammers since the turn of the century. Study of the composition of the materials used in the felt hammers and the strings may also prove fruitful.

54   Dolge, *Pianos and Their Makers,* vol. 2 (Covina, CA, 1913); repr. as *Men Who Have Made Piano History* (Vestal, NY [ca. 1980]), pp. 138–39.

55   Ibid., p. 139.

56   ". . . wie vortrefflich Ihr Flügel war u[nd] wie manche Regentage er mir zu den schönsten Tagen des Sommers gemacht hat." This letter, owned by the L. Bösendorfer Klavierfabrik A.G., is undated, but was probably written in 1884 or 1885. According to Ronald Fuchs, in personal communications, local tradition in Mürzzuschlag holds that Brahms specifically ordered a Bösendorfer piano for his summer residences there; during these two summers he composed his Fourth Symphony.

57   "Ihr Piano hat mir den Sommeraufenthalt hier sehr verschönt. Es ist ein ganz vertreffliches Instrument und in seiner Art ein Muster. Die wohlverdiente Anerkennung wird Ihnen nicht ausbleiben." A copy of this endorsement was found inside a twentieth-century Berger-Jacobi piano in Seattle, WA.

David Brodbeck

Brahms, the Third Symphony, and the New German School

During the first week of May 1883 Leipzig played host to the twentieth
Tonkünstlerversammlung of the *Allgemeiner Deutscher Musikverein,* the organization
founded some years earlier by Franz Brendel for the purpose of furthering the cause
of the New German School. The opening of the jubilee was marked in the *Neue
Zeitschrift für Musik* with a reverential greeting, by its publisher C. F. Kahnt, of the
society's honorary president: "Welcome, thou most admirable master Franz Liszt, who,
though deeply mourning for having recently lost Pollux and having now like Castor
to pass through life's course alone, yet with thine presence honors this festivity, and
with thine appearance places upon it a golden crown!"[1] Liszt's deceased brother was   1
of course Wagner, who had died during the previous winter. The festival, predictably
enough, reflected the tone set in Kahnt's salute: throughout the proceedings the late
master of *Zukunftsmusik* was commemorated; the living one, celebrated.

Yet the presence of Brahms's work was by no means inconsiderable. Both the
Violin Concerto and the *Gesang der Parzen* were heard, and both in conjunction
with pieces by Wagner and Liszt. On 4 May Adolph Brodsky played the concerto
in a program that also saw performances of Wagner's *Faust* Overture, and the
Prelude, Transformation Music, and Temple Scene to Act I of *Parsifal,* as well as
Liszt's E-flat Piano Concerto. Two days later, the *Parzenlied* shared a billing with,
among other works, Wagner's *Kaisermarsch* (with concluding chorus) and Liszt's
symphonic poem *Prometheus,* together with his choruses to Herder's *Der entfesselte
Prometheus.*

Brahms, with little taste for the *Musikverein* and its activities, declined to attend
these concerts; he remained in Vienna instead, where on 7 May he celebrated his
fiftieth birthday in the quiet company of his friends Eduard Hanslick, Theodor
Billroth, and Arthur Faber. (It was "a little small sad festival," as he put it to Billroth,
that he wished to make of his own jubilee, in what seems a cheeky reference to the
goings on in Leipzig.)[2] But from afar Brahms must have savored the ironic juxtapo-   2
sitions of his music with art of the New German School. This he ensured by means
of a delightful deceit. By prevailing upon Hanslick to publish a false report of his
imminent (and perhaps startling) departure for Leipzig, Brahms could look forward
to enjoying an irony of his own making: "It is not always necessary to be completely
truthful—in regard to the change!" he wrote to his friend, "but I have a strong
hidden reason to read in print the world-historic occasion of my departure—and to
have it read!"[3]   3

David Brodbeck, Assistant Professor of Music at the University of Pittsburgh, is the editor of a continuing
series of *Brahms Studies* and is presently working on a study of the sacred music of Mendelssohn.

The composer did soon enough head north—not for Leipzig, but Cologne, which he reached on 13 May; here at last he celebrated his recent anniversary in public with performances of the Second Symphony and Second Piano Concerto at the rather more congenial Lower Rhine Music Festival. The Rhineland struck a resonant chord, and within a week's time the composer, whose plans for the forthcoming summer remained open when he departed Vienna, had settled into rooms in Wiesbaden, where in the months that followed he crafted his Third Symphony.[4]

To Max Kalbeck, the act of composing this great work within sight of the Rhine seemed momentous. The river, steeped in nationalistic lore, as also in memories of the composer's Romantic youth, provided the fifty-year-old Brahms a natural setting in which to take stock of himself and his place in history, even to compose a "justification for his artistic existence."[5] Now the symphony does make one significant, if indirect, allusion to the Rhine: Brahms took both the prevailing hemiola rhythm and the main theme of the first movement from the opening Allegro in Schumann's *Rhenish* Symphony. But echoes of Wagner and Liszt, the composers to whom Brahms had recently been joined in the Leipzig concerts, resound quite as distinctly. Indeed, as I shall suggest, these less likely references speak most directly to the question of Brahms's musical *Anschauung* at age fifty; through them we can begin to take the measure of that "artistic justification" which Kalbeck sensed underlay the whole.

When Brahms set to work on the Third Symphony he was probably still smarting from certain barbed comments made in Wagner's "Open Letter to Friedrich Schön," published in the *Bayreuther Blätter* of July 1882:

> But as the Gospel has faded since the cross of the Redeemer has been hawked like merchandise on every street corner, so has the genius of German music grown silent ever since it has been hauled around the world-mart by the métier, and pseudo-professional gutter-witlessness celebrates its progress.[6]

This assessment was prompted by Hans von Bülow's recent championing of Brahms's music in touring concerts with his Meiningen Orchestra, the happy reception of which, Wagner bitterly continued, only went to show that the taste of the public had become so debased that posterity would choose to preserve nine symphonies by Brahms but at most only two by Beethoven.

Brahms's own poison pen was reserved for private communications. Thus the following remark to Bülow, written just after the appearance of Wagner's diatribe, wherein Brahms declined his friend's invitation to come to Bayreuth for the first performance of *Parsifal:* "Just from the 4th through 6th [of August] I have promised to be in Ischl and to pay a visit. What a pity, for I was planning nothing for the entire month apart from a pilgrimage to the Prophet, who has divined my future in so friendly a way."[7] Similar is a postcard sent to Billroth during the following summer, which shows that Wagner remained on Brahms's mind as he worked on the Third Symphony: "I live here [in Wiesbaden] quite charmingly, almost as if I were trying to imitate Wagner!"[8]

Michael Musgrave has lately speculated that Brahms sought to do just that. In his view, the importance that the composer places on the work's motto—his treatment of the notes F–A-flat–F as a *Leitmotiv,* so to speak—might imply that the Third was meant in part as an homage to Wagner (who was to be feared in the operatic arena but whose influence might safely be embraced on more familiar turf, the symphony).[9] The possibility of a Wagnerian background is suggestive, to be sure. The recent passing of the older composer was no mean event in the artistic and intellectual world, least of all to Brahms, who by the early 1880s was firmly entrenched as the symbolic leader of the anti-Wagnerians. Moreover, Brahms might well have been itching to requite Wagner's recent disparaging remarks about his place in music history, and to do so in his characteristic terms—through musical references that carry a point. But the role of the motto in this regard should not be overstated; Brahms had previously deployed such cells in the first two symphonies (C–C-sharp–D and D–C-sharp–D, respectively), as well as in other works. Wagner's influence instead touches upon features not surfacing elsewhere as a matter of course and is for that reason all the more powerful and significant.

The clearest echo comes early in the first movement, whose transition effects the modulation from the tonic to the second key by means of a real sequence: the model (mm. 15–22) moves from F to D-flat; the sequence (mm. 23–30) sets out in D-flat and thus comes around to the mediant, A. Since this eminently Wagnerian procedure is rarely encountered so openly in Brahms's oeuvre (least of all in his expositions), its unfolding here registers something of a surprise, especially as this follows on the heels of the theme derived from Schumann. Yet Brahms makes this sudden and unexpected orientation toward Wagner unmistakable in the conclusion of this section (mm. 31–35), wherein the general reference yields to a specific one (ex. 1a). As J. A. Fuller-Maitland noticed in his early monograph on the composer, these bars resonate with "the harmonies and melodic phrase" of a passage in the Venusberg music of the so-called Paris *Tannhäuser* of 1861 (ex. 1b).[10]

Fuller-Maitland, who was a true child of the nineteenth century, hastened to explain away what he feared might be taken as an unseemly lack of originality on Brahms's part and so dismissed the similarity as "nothing but the merest coincidence." But can it really be only coincidental that the source of Brahms's echo is, of all the Wagner operas, *Tannhäuser* (or, more properly, *Tannhäuser und die Sängerkrieg auf Wartburg*), whose famed vocal contest debates the issue of the true nature of love? After all, Brahms could scarcely have failed to see how the opera's contest between two *Minnesänger* of the thirteenth century parallels the real-life struggle over aesthetic matters waged in the music of nineteenth-century Germany's two greatest composers.[11]

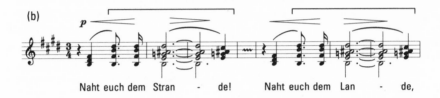

Naht euch dem Stran - de! Naht euch dem Lan - de,

Example 1: (a) Brahms, Symphony no. 3, I,
31-35; (b) Wagner, *Tannhäuser*, "Chorus of the
Sirens" (beginning).

The source of Brahms's recollection, the "Chorus of the Sirens," at once concludes the famous Bacchanale, which in its Parisian version shows a chromatic style
more in keeping with *Tristan* than the operas of the 1840s, and presents the first
verses of the opera:

> Naht euch dem Strande!
> Naht euch dem Lande,
> wo in den Armen
> glühender Liebe
> selig Erwarmen
> still eure Triebe!

[Approach the strand! Approach the land, where, in the arms of glowing
love, let blissful warmth content your desires!]

Brahms did not idly choose this passage to echo. This seductive song of the sirens,
this invitation to enter into the Venusberg realm, may well be emblematic of the

temptations which Wagner's musical language must periodically have exerted on Brahms.[12] In Brahms's hands the borrowed material, transposed down a whole step into the key of A, is woven into an even richer chromatic tapestry; the passage acquires an additional chromatic note, the lowered sixth scale-degree, and with that, in m. 31, unfolds an aching augmented triad. Yet this harmonic luxuriance did not blind the composer to formal exigencies; by repeating the material in mm. 33–35 in a lower register and with a written-out ritardando, Brahms created an air of expectancy that is clearly in keeping with the nature of a sonata-form transition (as also with the dramaturgical situation occuring at the end of the Bacchanale, with its gradually enveloping rosy light which slowly obscures from view all but Tannhäuser and Venus).

12

Example 2.: Brahms, Symphony no. 3, I, 36–39.

This Wagnerian context for the transition suggests an explanation for the unusually strong arrival in A major well before the appearance of the secondary theme (mm. 31 and 35, respectively). If the final four bars of the transition are an invitation to delve into Wagnerian waters, then the ensuing idyllic secondary theme (mm. 35–42) may be read as Brahms's reply (ex. 2). This only increases the significance of the drone bass underpinning the new melody: it is not merely an easy means of evoking a pastoral atmosphere, but a pointed one by which Brahms demonstrated the continuing viability, even in the post-Wagnerian world, of diatonic harmony, made sumptuous here by the many beautiful dissonant clashes which the tune creates against the pedal point (and by the characteristically supple phrase rhythm of the passage). In other words, by juxtaposing chromatic and diatonic treatments of the same key, Brahms was able to demonstrate all the more effectively the rich possibilities remaining to be explored within the confines of traditional tonality.

A similar commentary issues from the second movement, wherein a pointedly diatonic primary group—in C major, of all keys—yields to frankly experimental material. The transition (mm. 24ff) focuses on not one tonality but two (the dominant and submediant), which, astonishingly, are superimposed in the secondary group (mm. 41ff). The melody, in the clarinet and bassoon, begins in A minor, but the accompaniment, in the strings, sets forth clearly in G (ex. 3). At m. 45 the matter seems to have been settled along conventional lines, as the two tonal planes converge on a coordinated half close in the dominant. That key is not sustained, however; the cadence is elided to a real sequential statement of the bitonal passage, transposed now by fourth into the keys of D minor and C major. Likewise, the lovely and characteristic idea that follows at m. 51, with its metric displacement,

Example 3: Brahms, Symphony no. 3, II, 41-45.

subtle alternation of diatonically third-related keys, and melodic inversion, offers but a temporary return to normative means. Indeed, the greatest jolt of all is still to come, in the odd series of chords unfolded in mm. 57–62 (ex. 4).

These celebrated harmonies make explicit what Brahms's earlier uses of real sequence and multiple tonal axes had only hinted at—that the remarkable secondary group of the Andante offers another response to Wagner's chromatic idiom. Typically, Brahms's succession is grounded in the key of the local tonic (G); its root progression of IV–II–V could scarcely be more conservative. Yet the tonal flavoring is enriched, even made exotic, by the presence of several *Tristan*-like extended

$$(=iv^7) — IV^7 \qquad (=Fr.^6) — II^7 \qquad (=Fr.^6) — V^7 \qquad V^9_7$$

Example 4: Brahms, Symphony no. 3, II, 57-62.

appoggiaturas, each of which contrives to form a lengthy altered chord. Thus the D-sharp in mm. 57–58, the D-sharp in mm. 58–59, and the G-sharp in mm. 60–61, effect, respectively, a C minor-minor seventh chord, a French-sixth built upon A, and another on D.

The tribute to Wagner seems genuine enough, but the idiom must have appeared to Brahms limited and uncongenial. And again it is the music into which the Wagner-like material passes that reveals the composer's ultimate sensibilities (mm. 63ff). This section restates the familiar primary theme, at last unequivocally in the dominant, but varied now in an entirely characteristic manner. The new tenor register of the tune, the accompaniment in parallel sixths, the tonic pedal point, the background figures in triplets—each is a part of Brahms's stock in trade. But the

Example 5: Brahms, Symphony no. 3, II. (a) 1-4; (b) 63-67.

really telling earmark seen in the varied form concerns the introduction of chromaticism. The melody does not recur in the naive guise presented in the exposition (ex. 5a); its head-motive is split apart and worked over separately, eventually coming round to a chromatic inflection that subsequently leaves its mark on the theme's remaining motives (ex. 5b). Chromaticism per se, then, is no longer the focal point; here, instead, it is reined in and sublimated to that most venerable (and truly Brahmsian) of compositional procedures, variation.

The echoings of Wagner that I have sketched above sit well within the range of Brahms's normal working habits; each offers a tribute to the style of a composer whom he generally admired, coupled with a forceful demonstration of a valid alternative. More startling is the evident influence on the symphony of that other leading light of the New German School, Liszt—the real target of the ill-fated "Manifesto" that Brahms and his friend Joseph Joachim circulated in the spring of 1860. Some background and context for this document is appropriate here. Although Brahms's irritation had been growing for years, the immediate provocation for his desire to make a public quarrel with Liszt was Brendel's inaugural address to the first *Tonkünstlerversammlung* of what later became the *Allgemeiner Deutscher Musikverein*, held in Leipzig in June 1859 and timed to commemorate the Silver Anniversary of the founding of the *Neue Zeitschrift*. In these remarks Brendel proposed replacing the then-fashionable term "Music of the Future" with the expression "New German School," which he held was led by Wagner, Liszt, and Berlioz, and represented "the entire post-Beethoven development." In Brendel's view, this New German School represented a kind of synthesis of earlier historical periods: "Protestant church music up to and including Bach and Handel has long been known as the Old German School. The Italian-influenced epoch of the Viennese masters is the period of Classicism, of the equal supremacy of idealism and realism. Beethoven once more clasps hands with the specifically Germanic North and inaugurates the Neo-German School."[13]

Brahms, who during the course of the 1850s had come to very different terms with the Baroque and Classical past, responded angrily. In August 1859 he reported to Joachim that "his fingers oftened itched to start a fight, to write something anti-Liszt,"[14] and by the following spring the two were working on a text and circulating drafts among musicians who might be expected to go public with their opposition to the party line of the *Neue Zeitschrift*. Of special interest is Brahms's determination that Wagner not be mentioned, indeed that only Liszt be singled out by name. Thus this passage from a letter to Joachim of May 1860: "Bei unsrer Abwehr kann niemand an Wagner denken. Jedenfalls müßte man für Berlioz und Franz ebenso sorgen. Abfertigen, wie wir, kann man nur Liszt." And on 9 May, in response to a proposed draft of Joachim's, he insisted that the clause "wie sie in den Werken von Dr. Fr. Liszt und anderen Führern und Jüngern der neudeutschen Schule vorkommen" be replaced by the more pointed phrase "daß sie die Produkte

des Dr. Fr. Liszt und der übrigen Führer und Schüler der sog[enannten] Neudeutschen
Schule."[15] Unfortunately, a version of the text was leaked to the Berliner Musik-
Zeitung Echo before it was ready for publication—and without the names of some
twenty willing signatories—and it appeared on 6 May 1860 with only the names of
Brahms, Joachim, and two others, found underneath (Appendix 1).

The circumstances leading to the premature publication of this imprudent
document have never been fully explicated. At all events, the Manifesto clearly had
fallen into the enemy hands of the composer and theorist Carl Friedrich Weitzmann,
whose scathing parody of it the *Neue Zeitschrift* ran anonymously on 4 May, two
days before the publication in Berlin of Brahms's text itself (Appendix 2). Could
not Brahms's subsequent request, in 1883, that Hanslick mislead the public about his
plans for attending the twentieth *Tonkünstlerversammlung* reflect a desire to extract
belated revenge for Weitzmann's parody?[16]

To return to the Third Symphony: when suggesting a Lisztian influence, I do
not have in mind A. Peter Brown's conclusion, drawn from the appearance of
certain "unifying" thematic and motivic recurrences, as well as the presentation in
the finale of several "characteristic styles," that the work might be heard "as an
extended symphonic poem."[17] After all, there is nothing unusual about Brahms's use
of intermovement links, and a reading of nominally absolute music in quasi-pro-
grammatic terms was a normal activity of the day, even for many "conservative"
commentators—as is borne out by the familiar responses to the work at hand by
Clara Schumann and Joseph Joachim.[18] No, the Lisztian influence is seen in a feature
of the Third that is truly extraordinary: the dispersal of the elements of a sonata
form across the course of a four-movement cycle.[19] In undertaking this conflation
Brahms took up the challenge of the symphony in distinctly Lisztian terms, essaying
a *Gesamtform* best known from the older composer's Piano Concerto in E-flat. Here,
however, Brahms offers no homage or even a respectful airing of artistic differences,
but rather a "correction"—and, as we might expect, a none too gentle one.[20]

Although Liszt's work does not unfold in accordance with the older norms of
concerto form, its larger sections can be understood readily enough; they virtually
demand to be reduced into the elements of the ossified sonata form described in
nineteenth-century textbooks.[21] Thus the opening Allegro Maestoso, in the tonic,
offers a masculine primary theme-group; the Quasi Adagio, in the submediant,
presents a feminine contrasting theme; the Allegretto vivace stands as a scherzo but
culminates in a grand retransition that restates the primary material; and the finale
brings about the rest of the "recapitulation," focusing on a march-like transformation of the secondary material, but embracing other themes as well.

"The first realization of cyclic sonata form" was how Bartók characterized this
work, noting elsewhere that "what was formally perfect in Liszt was usually so
revolutionary that in the eyes of the apostle of traditional forms [Brahms], it was
anarchy."[22] Bartók's observations may have been skewed by his sense of national

pride (and in any case overstate Brahms's conservatism), but still they do not fall so wide of the mark. Indeed, the Third Symphony may be profitably viewed as a work which imposes compelling logic upon what must have seemed an offensive and even ludicrous realization of a "sacred form."[23]

[23]

Brahms does achieve a remarkable continuity across the entire span of the work. Conventionally enough, the motto of the opening Allegro appears more or less openly in subsequent movements, and the main theme of the first movement and the subsidiary theme of the second both recur in the finale. Less typical is the circumscription of the four movements to the sphere of the tonic and dominant keys (I–V–v–i/I), which fosters the impression of a long-range secondary key center in the middle of the symphony. The composer's handling of both thematic material and the crucial pitch conflict between the notes A and A-flat, first joined in the violins' opening theme, likewise reveals the underpinnings of a large-scale sonata form. The secondary theme of the Andante is omitted from the recapitulation of that movement, only to make several significant appearances in the finale, the "recapitulation" of the entire piece, wherein the A/A-flat conflict is at last straightened out.

In principle, then, Liszt's concerto and Brahms's symphony reflect a fundamentally similar long-range form. But how differently they realize it. For all its nontraditional structure, Brahms's symphony is tempered by a pronounced conservatism. As we have seen, its "second group"—the Andante and Intermezzo—is in the "orthodox" dominant, not in any of the third-related keys that Brahms more commonly employed in such forms. Moreover, no less than three of the four movements are themselves in some version of sonata form. Liszt, by contrast, approaches sonata form in none of his four movements, and the sense of a larger whole is really achieved only by means of thematic transformation, not by anything like the long-range tonal and thematic processes that Brahms so artfully unfolds.

Not that Brahms eschewed the straightforward use of the technique of thematic transformation. On the contrary, he displayed it openly on one occasion, and so made a serious point. The celebrated reappearance of the opening theme at the end of the symphony at once clinches the Lisztian background of the work and clarifies a profound difference in the composers' attitude and approach. When we recognize that the march-like finale of Liszt's concerto is based upon the beautiful theme of his slow movement, we may be amused or offended—but not edified. In contrast stand the final pages of the Third Symphony, whose effect is dependent upon everything that has transpired in the work. The return there of the opening theme seems at last to bring resolution to the many issues that Brahms had pointedly left unresolved. This return, as Walter Frisch has cogently put it, "constitutes one of Brahms's most persuasive thematic transformations because it seems genuinely to embody all the thematic, harmonic, metrical, and formal processes that have spanned the symphony since the theme's initial appearance."[24]

[24]

The E-flat Concerto brings us back to the Leipzig festival of the *Allgemeiner Deutscher Musikverein*. Brahms, as we know, avoided the festivities, but his friends Heinrich and Elisabeth von Herzogenberg attended several of the rehearsals and concerts and kept him apprised through the mails. The conservative Elisabeth, a vociferous opponent of Liszt and the New German School, could not be expected to take much pleasure in the festival; her reports to Brahms, accordingly, betray more than a trace of smugness and sarcasm. Thus these remarks about the Liszt concerto:

> D'Albert [who on the previous night had performed the work] is in the hospital with measles. That is what comes of

oder ♭♩ ?

> "It is all the same to us—
> For what does it matter to us?
> It matters nothing to us!"[25]

25

The musical incipit is, of course, the beginning of Liszt's concerto; the underlying text comes from a Viennese street song ("Das ist uns alles eins, / denn was geht denn uns das an, / das geht uns gar nichts an"). Perhaps the latter was selected to make a play on the humorous lines that Hans von Bülow associated with the theme: "Das versteht ihr Alle nicht. Haha!"[26] At all events, in a work that Brahms wrote only a few weeks after he had received this report, he himself parodied Liszt. For when placed in its proper historical context, the Third Symphony may be read as a study in criticism, as Brahms's claim to "understand" better than Liszt how to fuse the sonata form and sonata cycle. More importantly, as Kalbeck suspected (if for the wrong reason), the work does appear to stand as an autumnal "artistic justification." It offers us a telling account of a composer who, though so often seeking to measure himself against the achievements of the past, seems for once determined to take the better of the New Germans at some of their own games.

26

Notes

1   [C. F. Kahnt], "Zur zwanzigsten Tonkünstlerversammlung des Allgemeinen Deutschen Musikvereins in Leipzig," *Neue Zeitschrift für Musik* 79 (1883), 209. Unless otherwise noted, all translations are mine.

2   *Johannes Brahms and Theodor Billroth: Letters from a Musical Friendship,* trans. and ed. Hans Barkan (Norman, Okla., 1957), p. 132.

3   Quoted in Max Kalbeck, *Johannes Brahms,* rev. edns., (Berlin, 1912-21), III, 380. Hanslick's untruthful report appeared on 3 May 1883 in the *Neue Freie Presse:* "Johannes Brahms reist Ende dieser

Woche zu den Musikfesten nach Leipzig und Köln ab. In Leipzig werden sein Violin-Concert und das Parzenlied, in Köln seine D-dur-Symphonie und das zweite Clavier-Concert aufgeführt." Toward the end of this essay, I shall suggest a reason for Brahms's "strong hidden desire" to see this misleading announcement in print.

4   There is no credible basis for the widely held belief that the beginnings of the symphony stemmed from an earlier time. The only documentary evidence that Max Kalbeck could adduce in support of this proposition was Brahms's reference to the symphony, in a letter of 15 September 1883 to his publisher Fritz Simrock, as some "Notenblätter aus Jugendzeit" (Kalbeck, *Brahms* III, 387n). But surely the biographer was misled here by another wholly typical display of Brahms's wit; it is difficult to imagine how he could have failed to see that Brahms's account parallels those that the composer had made to Simrock of the Second Symphony (a work so melancholy as to require publication with "black borders") and the Second Piano Concerto ("a pair of little piano pieces").

5   Ibid., pp. 379–80.

6   Richard Wagner, *Gesammelte Schriften und Dichtungen*, 3rd edn., 10 vols. (Leipzig, 1887-88), X, 292. For earlier invectives by Wagner against Brahms, see "About Conducting" (1869), and "On Poetry and Composition," "On Operatic Poetry and Composition in Particular," and "On the Application of Music to the Drama" (1879). The most thorough consideration of the complicated relationship that existed between Brahms and Wagner may be found in Karl Geiringer, "Wagner and Brahms, with Unpublished Letters," *Musical Quarterly* 22 (1936), 178-89; more recent studies include Klaus Kropfinger, "Wagner und Brahms," *Musica* 37 (1983), 11-17; Otto Biba, "Brahms, Wagner und Parteiungen in Wien," ibid., pp. 18-22; and Helmut Wirth, "Richard Wagner und Johannes Brahms," in *Brahms und seine Zeit: Symposion Hamburg 1983,* Hamburger Jahrbuch für Musikwissenschaft 7, ed. Constantin Floros, Hans Joachim Marx, and Peter Petersen (Laaber, 1984), pp. 147-57.

7   Quoted in Kalbeck, *Brahms* III, 346.

8   *Brahms and Billroth*, p. 132.

9   Michael Musgrave, *The Music of Brahms* (London, 1985), pp. 221-22; yet, as Carl Dahlhaus has observed, Brahms actually combines "the pregnant significance of the leitmotiv, which strictly speaking cannot develop, with the principle of developing variation." Although the motivic shape of the motto is always recognizable, it serves at the same time as a vehicle for "formal progress," since it "recurs in changing harmonizations wherever there is what could be called a 'hinge' in the form" ("Issues in Composition," in his *Between Romanticism and Modernism: Four Studies in the Music of the Later Nineteenth Century,* trans. Mary Whittall [Berkeley and Los Angeles, 1980], pp. 51-52).

10   J. A. Fuller-Maitland, *Brahms* (1911, rpt. Port Washington, N.Y., 1972), p. 149; for an earlier observation of this reference, see Hugo Riemann's analysis of the symphony in *Johannes Brahms: Erläuterung seiner bedeutendsten Werke* (Frankfurt am Main, [n.d.]), p. 101.

11   In light of the central conflict in *Die Meistersinger von Nürnberg* between musical progressivism and conservatism, it might be wondered why Brahms did not refer to that opera instead. Such a reference, in fact, would not have served his purpose as well. In the first place, the dramatic confrontation in *Tannhäuser* was mirrored in the real lives of the artists under question; as is well known, Wagner and Brahms carried on a protracted personal row over possession of the autograph of the "Paris" Venusberg scene, the very source of Brahms's recollection (see Kalbeck, *Brahms* II, 122-27). Moreover, Brahms surely would not have identified with the pedantic Beckmesser (who, after all, was Wagner's parody of Hanslick); it seems more likely that he would have felt a kinship toward the earlier opera's Wolfram, whose ambivalent feeling toward Tannhäuser mirrors that of Brahms toward Wagner's music: devotion mixed with repulsion.

12   As early as 1862 — and not for the last time — Brahms described himself as a *Wagnerianer,* in a letter to his friend Joseph Joachim written during his first visit to Vienna (*Johannes Brahms Briefwechsel* [Berlin, 1908-22], V, 332). During this stay in the Imperial City Brahms became friendly with the Wagnerians Karl Tausig and Peter Cornelius, whom he aided in preparing orchestral parts for use in Wagner's impending series of three Viennese concerts. As the younger composer attended each of these concerts (given on 26 December 1862 and 1 and 11 January 1863), so did the older composer appear at Brahms's solo recital of 6 January 1863. Significantly, among the pieces that Brahms played on this occasion was the Sonata in F Minor, op. 5, the coda of whose second movement Wagner seemed to recall

when, near the conclusion of Act II, scene 3, of *Die Meistersinger,* Hans Sachs sings "Dem Vogel, der heut' sang." Years later, in the main theme of his Sonata in A for Violin and Piano, op. 100, Brahms repaid the compliment by alluding to another memorable moment from the opera, Walther's *Preislied* "Morgenlich leuchtend." A more immediate musical consequence of the Wagnerian experiences of these months, however, may be heard in the cantata *Rinaldo,* which Brahms began in the summer of 1863. In certain passages of this piece, which of all Brahms's vocal works is the most dramatic in its conception, the composer not only echoes the chromatic language of *Tristan,* but even, as Michael Musgrave has observed, approaches a genuinely Wagnerian arioso texture, with the solo voice at times playing a contrapuntal role, leaving to the orchestra the task of providing the main melody (*Music of Brahms,* pp. 76–77).

13 Quoted in *Music in the Western World: A History in Documents,* ed. Piero Weiss and Richard Taruskin (New York, 1984), p. 384.

14 *Brahms Briefwechsel* V, 249.

15 Ibid., pp. 273–74, 280.

16 For a recent consideration of Brahms's attitudes toward Liszt and of the background to the Manifesto, see Imogen Fellinger, "Brahms und die Neudeutsche Schule," *Brahms und seine Zeit,* pp. 159–69. For a point of view on the whole matter that is distinctly sympathetic to Liszt, see Alan Walker, *Franz Liszt: The Weimar Years, 1848–1861* (New York, 1989), pp. 344–53.

17 A. Peter Brown, "Brahms' Third Symphony and the New German School," *Journal of Musicology* 2 (1983), 451–52.

18 See *The Letters of Clara Schumann and Johannes Brahms,* 2 vols. (New York, 1927), II, 88, and *Brahms Briefwechsel* VI, 212.

19 For an excellent account of Brahms's intriguing form (but without reference to any model that the composer may have had in mind), see Walter Frisch, *Brahms and the Principle of Developing Variation* (Berkeley and Los Angeles, 1984), pp. 129–42. See also Robert Bailey, "Musical Language and Structure in the Third Symphony," in *Brahms Studies: Analytical and Historical Perspectives,* ed. George S. Bozarth (Oxford, 1990).

20 In certain respects, the opening of Brahms's Second Piano Concerto (1881), with its dialogue presentation of the main theme by the horn and soloist, giving way to a lengthy solo passage, already stands as a "correction" of Liszt's concerto. To be sure, as Charles Rosen has observed, by beginning the work with a cadenza Brahms alludes plainly to the opening of Beethoven's "Emperor" Concerto, and by altering Beethoven's scheme so as to include an initial statement of the main theme by the orchestra he simultaneously makes the gesture his own ("Influence: Plagiarism and Inspiration," *19th-Century Music* 4 [1980], 94–95). Yet Brahms's reference is really better understood as a double reference, for in his own E-flat Concerto Liszt had already echoed the "Emperor" (and anticipated Brahms's Second) by beginning with the main theme and cadenza-like material played in alternation by the orchestra and soloist. Brahms's more thorough integration of the orchestra and soloist—his use of the soloist not only to provide a cadenza but also to take part in the presentation of the main theme—can be read as a "realization" that Liszt failed to achieve the potential suggested in the "Emperor" Concerto.

21 *Pace* Sharon Winklhofer, who holds that "there is no evidence to support the view that Liszt ever attempted to superimpose multiple movements over a large sonata form (*Liszt's Sonata in B Minor: A Study of Autograph Sources and Documents* [Ann Arbor, 1980], p. 127). Not only does the stylistic evidence, which I set out below, justify such an analysis, but so, too, do Liszt's own remarks about the work, found in a letter of 26 March 1857 to his nephew Eduard: "The fourth movement of the concerto, from the Allegro marziale, corresponds with the second movement Adagio; it is only a compressed recapitulation of the earlier subject matter [*Gebrachten*] with livelier, more animated rhythm and contains *no* new motive" (*Franz Liszt's Briefe,* ed. La Mara [Ida Marie Lipsius], 8 vols. [Leipzig, 1893–1905], I, 273).

22 Béla Bartók, "Liszt Problems" and "Liszt's Music and Today's Public," in *Essays,* ed. Benjamin Suchoff (London, 1976), pp. 503 and 453.

23 Admittedly, my characterization is not Brahms's own; it comes instead from his like-minded friend Joachim, found in a report to Clara Schumann on a concert of Liszt's given in late 1855: "I have not been so bitterly disillusioned for a long time as I was by Liszt's compositions [mostly symphonic poems]; I have to admit that a more vulgar misuse of sacred forms, a more repulsive coquetting with the noblest feelings for the sake of effect, had never been attempted" (*Letters to and from Joseph Joachim,* trans. Nora Binkley [1914; New York, 1972], pp. 112-13). It is safe to assume that Brahms would have concurred in this judgement. In 1859, for example, he complained to Joachim that Liszt's "compositions are getting worse and worse, e.g., [the] Dante [Symphony]!" (*Brahms Briefwechsel* V, 248); and many years later, recalling his first encounter with Liszt, in June 1853, Brahms described the symphonic poems as "rubbish" [*das Zeug*] (Richard Heuberger, *Erinnerungen an Johannes Brahms,* ed. Kurt Hofmann [Tutzing, 1971], pp. 60-61).

24   Frisch, *Brahms and Developing Variation,* p. 142.

25   Letter of 5 May 1883, in *Johannes Brahms: The Herzogenberg Correspondence,* ed. Max Kalbeck, trans. Hannah Bryant (1909; rpt. New York, 1987), p. 179.

26   Reported in August Göllerich, *Franz Liszt* (Berlin, 1908), p. 223.

Appendix 1
Brahms's and Joachim's "Manifesto"[a]

Circulating among local musicians is an address of Herrn Brahms, Joachim, and Grimm, in which they send to the party of the Music of the Future a letter of refusal, which they invite their artistic comrades to sign.

The manifesto reads:

The undersigned have long followed with regret the activities of a certain party whose organ is Brendel's *Zeitschrift für Musik*.

The said periodical constantly disseminates the opinion that seriously striving musicians are fundamentally in accord with the tendencies it champions and recognize the compositions of the leaders of this movement as works of artistic value; and that, in general, and especially in North Germany, the controversy for and against the so-called "Music of the Future" has already been fought out, and settled in its favor.

The undersigned consider it their duty to protest against such a distortion of the facts, and declare that, at least so far as they themselves are concerned, they do not recognize the principles which find expression in Brendel's *Zeitschrift,* and can only deplore or condemn as contrary to the most fundamental essence of music the productions of the leaders and disciples of the so-called "Neo-German" School, some of whom put these principles into practice, while others keep trying to impose the establishment of more and more novel and preposterous theories.

Johannes Brahms. Joseph Joachim. Julius Otto Grimm.
Bernhard Scholz.

Appendix 2
C. F. Weitzmann's Parody of the "Manifesto"[b]

Dreaded Herr Editor! Everything is out![c]

A coup d'état is to be delivered, the whole of new music rooted out lock, stock, and barrel, and Weimar and Leipzig, in particular, struck from the map of the musical world. To this end a wide-ranging epistle was prepared and sent to selected right-minded persons of all countries, protesting in detail and very aggressively the increasingly spreading epidemic of the Music of the Future. The Board of Directors of this select group includes many selfless persons, traces of whose names, however, the most recent art history was unable to find. Nevertheless, in case the avalanche of signatories should be able to enlarge itself greatly enough, the storm shall thereupon suddenly break out. Although the hatchers of this musico-tragic finishing stroke enjoined the selected ones to the strictest secrecy, I succeeded nonetheless in examining the original, and I am pleased to be able to pass on to you in the following, dreaded Herr Editor, this timely official document, all the while remaining

Your
most devoted,
Fegweg [Sweep-Away]

David Brodbeck

Public Protest

The undersigned would like just once to play first violin and for that reason protest against everything that lies in the way of their requisite rise in the world—in particular, therefore, against the growing influence of the musical direction that Dr. Brendel has designated as the New German School, as, in general, against every spirit in new music. After the destruction of these things, which are to them most unpleasant, they will in its place hold out to all like-minded well-disposed persons an immediate prospect for a Brotherhood for "Unstimulating and Boring Art."
Sympathizing spirits are urgently admonished to join.
"The Staff Editors of the Music of Intelligence"
[Undersigned:]
J. Geiger [Joachim]. Hans Neubahn [Brahms].
Pantoffelmann [Hen-pecked husband]. Packe [The mob].
Krethi und Plethi [Everyman and his wife].

Notes to Appendices

a   Published on 6 May 1860 in the *Berliner Musik-Zeitung Echo;* quoted in Fellinger, "Brahms und die Neudeutsche Schule," p. 164; translation after *Music in the Western World,* p. 385.

b   Published on 4 May 1860 in the *Neue Zeitschrift für Musik* 52 (1860), 179-80. That Weitzmann was the perpetrator of the parody can be determined from Hans von Bülow's letter of 6 May 1860 to Felix Draeseke: "Die Parodie in der letzten Brendel'schen ist von Weitzmann ausgegangen, der das hier mitgetheilte Original noch nicht kannte. Er hat selbige nach Weimar geschickt, und von dort aus ist sie mit einigen Abschwächungen nach Leipzig expedirt worden. Demnach ist selbige als officielles Aktenstück zu acceptiren. Dies Alles unter uns" (Hans von Bülow, *Briefe und Schriften,* ed. Marie von Bülow, 8 vols. [Leipzig, 1896-98], III, 313).

c   The text here is "Alles is aus!" Throughout the rest of the original, the author plays upon this prefix (viz., *ausgeführt, ausgerettet, ausholender, ausgearbeitet, ausgewählte, ausgeschickt, ausführlich, ausfallend, Ausschuß, Ausbundes, Außersichseiende, ausfindig, ausdehnen, ausbrechen, Aushecker, Auserwählten*).

Walter Frisch

The "Brahms Fog": On Analyzing Brahmsian Influences at Fin de Siècle

In a letter written in April 1894 to his friend Adalbert Lindner, the twenty-one-year-old Max Reger staunchly defended Brahms against his opponents. Although the music may at first be difficult to grasp, Reger noted, "Brahms has nevertheless come so far that all truly intelligent and sensitive musicians, unless they want to make fools of themselves, must acknowledge him as the greatest of living composers." Reger continued: "Even if Lessmann takes such pains to destroy Brahms and the Brahms fog (to use Tappert's term), the Brahms fog will survive. And I much prefer it to the white heat of Wagner and Strauss."[1]

Reger refers here to Otto Lessmann, editor of the *Allgemeine Musik-Zeitung* in Berlin from 1881 to 1907, and to Wilhelm Tappert, a prominent critic of Wagnerian sympathies. I have not located where Tappert coined the term "Brahms fog," or *Brahmsnebel.* Nor is it exactly clear what he, or Reger quoting him, meant by it. But the image is certainly an evocative one: the music of Brahms is seen as generating or being enveloped in a thick, dark mist; from the opposite camp comes the fiery glow of chromaticism and program music.

It is well known that during the last quarter of the nineteenth century much of Austro-German music was polarized between the Brahmsians and the Wagnerians, between the fog and the white heat. Most scholars and performers have been attracted more readily to the brighter glow, to the phenomenon of Wagnerism in European music. There has been less appreciation of how widely, and in what ways, Brahms's influence extended over the world of Lieder and piano and chamber music.

"Brahms is everywhere," remarked Walter Niemann in an article of 1912.[2] Niemann, a devoted follower of Brahms (later to become his biographer), went on to survey briefly no fewer than fifty European composers whose piano music he said bore the unmistakable traces of the master's influence. Writing in 1922, Hugo Leichtentritt observed similarly that "from about 1880 all chamber music in Germany is in some way indebted to Brahms."[3] The same could be said of many of the thousands of Lieder issued from the German publishing houses in the decades around 1900.[4]

There is no question that the Brahms idiom had tremendous prestige in these repertories. For one thing, as Niemann noted, some external elements of the style—the thick piano figuration, the rhythmic devices (two-against-three), the characteristic textures—were easily imitated. Indeed, to do so was apparently a

1

2

3

4

Walter Frisch, Associate Professor of Music at Columbia University, is the author of *Brahms and the Principle of Developing Variation* (Berkeley and Los Angeles, 1984) and editor of the journal *19th-Century Music.*

point of pride among young composers. Alexander Zemlinsky, one of the most talented pupils at the Vienna Conservatory in the early 1890s (when the teaching staff was composed of such Brahms cronies as Robert Fuchs, Julius Epstein, and Anton Door), remarked in later years that "it was considered especially praiseworthy to compose in as 'Brahmsian' a manner as possible."[5] In 1893 the young Reger could actually boast to Lindner, "The other day a personal friend of Brahms mistook the theme from the finale of my second violin sonata [op. 3] for a theme from one of Brahms's recent works. Even Riemann [Reger's teacher] told me that I know Brahms really through and through." Reger went on to say that "Brahms is the only composer of our time—I mean among living composers—from whom one can learn something."[6] Reger's latter point is significant: Brahms represented, until his death in 1897, the most powerful and most respectable living model for younger German composers.

    Just as one cannot easily measure the extent or scope of a fog, so would it be impossible and frustrating to tally all the composers who from the 1880s on fell under the sway of the Brahms idiom. (Some sense of the thickness of the fog can be gleaned by the number of musical works dedicated to Brahms. See the Appendix to the present volume.) Even beyond any direct impact on musical style and technique —on the way music sounds—Brahms may have had a still farther-reaching effect on the whole concept of serious concert music in the twentieth century. Such, at least, is the provocative argument of J. Peter Burkholder, who suggests that with his self-conscious and complex historicism Brahms was seeking a place beside Bach and Beethoven in the "museum" of great music. Burkholder suggests that this attitude toward composition—in which one writes music chiefly to assure one's place in history—lies at the basis of musical modernism and has carried over into the present century.[7]

    What I would like to trace in this essay is something more modest than Burkholder's bold picture: a vignette of some of the technical and expressive ways in which Brahms's music was appropriated by three of the most talented younger Austro-German composers coming to maturity in the 1890s: Alexander Zemlinsky, Arnold Schoenberg, and Max Reger. Even with such a restricted field, a comprehensive study of the phenomenon of Brahms's influence is not possible.[8]

Zemlinsky and Schoenberg present an intriguing contrast in Brahms reception. Although the former was the more impeccably trained and technically proficient composer—and as such can perhaps be seen as representative of many similar figures of his generation—it was in fact Schoenberg who probed more deeply into the essence of Brahms's music. Let us look first at Zemlinsky's song *Heilige Nacht,* which was published at the head of his first collection of Lieder, op. 2 in 1897 (ex. 1). The anonymous poem, a hymn of praise to the night, which cloaks everything in a cloak of tranquility—"even sorrow is sweet"—is of a type that attracted Brahms

Example 1: Alexander Zemlinsky, *Heilige Nacht,* op. 2, no. 1 (1897).

(continued)

strongly.[9] The more specifically musical characteristics of Zemlinsky's song that
derive from his study of Brahms can be itemized:

- —the descending, broad triadic melody (mm. 1–4)[10]
- —the strong stepwise bass line (especially mm. 1–6)[11]
- —the arpeggiated figuration in the right hand of the accompaniment, which is
  in diminution of vocal rhythm and motives (mm. 1–8)[12]
- —the dip toward the subdominant at the very beginning (mm. 1–2)[13]
- —the sudden move, by third, from a G to an E-flat harmony in $^6_4$ position
  (mm. 6–7)[14]
- —the extension or augmentation of "während der heiligen Nacht" to create an
  irregular three-measure phrase (mm. 24–26)[15]
- —the final plagal cadence of the song (mm. 29–30)[16]

Despite their distinguished pedigree, these techniques fail to add up to a success-
ful song. First, the phrase structure is too square: the rather rigid succession of
two-measure units in the opening section, through m. 8, is scarcely concealed by the
small modifications, such as in m. 6, where Zemlinsky repeats the words "dein
Kuss" in order to extend the phrase another half measure. A subtler grasp of
Brahmsian technique might have led to the kind of asymmetry and irregularity that
Schoenberg delighted in pointing out in Brahms songs in his essay "Brahms the
Progressive."[17] Brahms himself would never be guilty of undermining what is
clearly supposed to be a magical moment, the shift to the E-flat $^6_4$ chord in m. 7,
with an almost verbatim repetition of the opening theme. In Brahms such special

Allegro con fuoco

Example 2: Zemlinsky, String Quartet no. 1 in A Major, op. 4 (1898), I.

Example 3: Brahms, String Quartet no. 3 in B-flat Major, I.

harmonic expansions are almost always accompanied by—or coordinated with—a farther reaching melodic or thematic development.[18]

Despite its surface resemblance to Brahms, the harmonic syntax of *Heilige Nacht* also betrays an unBrahmsian awkwardness. The root-position IV chord in m. 2 is too emphatic; it virtually brings harmonic motion to a standstill. When Brahms employs a root-position subdominant near the beginning of a piece, it is more a harmonic inflection, imparting a delicate ambiguity.[19] Zemlinsky's actual cadence to F in mm. 8–9, though perhaps intended as a fulfillment of the opening gesture, is likewise unconvincing. The tonic has barely been reestablished in m. 7 when it is transformed into an augmented chord that is made to function as a dominant. The augmented sonority with an added major seventh sounds particularly bizarre in the prevailingly consonant context.

If I seem to have been too hard on what is in many respects an attractive song, it is because Zemlinsky seems to me to be very good at appropriating many of the stylistic traits of Brahms without really absorbing the fundamental compositional principles. This aspect of his art has been pointed out by Adorno, who in his excellent essay of 1959 suggested that Zemlinsky was a genuine eclectic, "someone who borrows all possible elements, especially stylistic ones, and combines them without any individual tone."[20] Adorno tries to strip the term eclectic of its pejorative connotation, arguing that Zemlinsky was in fact something of a genius in his "truly seismographic capacity to respond to all the temptations with which he let himself be inundated." I would argue here that his "seismographic" receptivity prevented him from really absorbing the essence of Brahms. He registered the aftershocks, so to speak, but failed to locate the source of the tremor.

This tendency can be seen in Zemlinsky's early chamber music as well, especially in the First Quartet, op. 4 in A Major, composed in 1896 and published by Simrock in 1898. The first group of the first movement (ex. 2) comprises a virtual encyclopedia—grab-bag might be a more appropriate term—of Brahmsian metrical devices. Nowhere in the first group is the notated $\frac{6}{8}$ meter presented unambiguously. At the outset the measure is divided as if in $\frac{3}{4}$ (mm. 1–2). In the next measure the two lower parts move in $\frac{6}{8}$, the second violin in $\frac{3}{4}$, and the first violin somewhere in between. At the climax in mm. 9–12, Zemlinsky presents (although he does not notate) a dizzying alternation of $\frac{3}{8}$ and $\frac{3}{4}$ according to the pattern: $\frac{3}{8}$–$\frac{3}{4}$–$\frac{3}{8}$–$\frac{3}{4}$–$\frac{3}{8}$–$\frac{3}{4}$–$\frac{3}{4}$. After the fermata, the metrical roller coaster resumes its course.

In his commentary on this movement Rudolf Stephan has suggested that "rhythmic complications of this kind point to the model of Brahms, who, however, does not employ them in this (almost) systematic fashion."[21] Stephan's parenthetical "almost" betrays an appropriate diffidence. In fact, it is Brahms who is the more systematic, as a comparative glance at his Third Quartet, op. 67 in B-flat, will show. Brahms, like his follower Zemlinsky, continually reinterprets the notated $\frac{6}{8}$ meter. But where Zemlinsky dives headlong into complexity and conflict, Brahms unfolds a gradual, subtle process (ex. 3a). In mm. 1–2 he places accent marks on the normally weak third and sixth beats of the measure. In m. 3 these accents are intensified by *forzandos.* Only in m. 8 does Brahms introduce an actual hemiola. This hemiola serves an important structural function: it marks the first arrival on the dominant and the beginning of the B section of the A B A′ design of the first group. The following transition unfolds unproblematically in $\frac{6}{8}$, but the conflict between duple and triple articulation of the measure finds new expression in the notated $\frac{2}{4}$ meter of the second group (ex. 3b). As in the first group, the meter is carefully coordinated with the thematic and formal procedures: the arrival of $\frac{2}{4}$ coincides with a new theme and the confirmation of the dominant key area.

The implication of the above discussion may seem self-evident: no one could compose Brahms as well as Brahms himself. Yet my point is that a highly talented composer like Zemlinsky could in fact master many of the most complicated Brahmsian skills without really using them sensitively. He could *sound* Brahmsian without really *composing* Brahmsian.

The Brahms reception of the young Arnold Schoenberg presents a somewhat different picture from that of his friend (and later brother-in-law) Zemlinsky. Schoenberg was almost completely self-taught until 1895 when he began to take private, informal lessons with Zemlinsky for about two years. Among his earliest surviving compositions are piano pieces, one completed work of chamber music, and thirty-two Lieder that clearly show a Brahmsian stamp.[22] The Three Piano Pieces of 1894, among the earliest firmly datable pieces, show him, somewhat like the Zemlinsky of the A-Major Quartet, exploiting Brahmsian metrical ambiguities with a vengeance. Although notated in $\frac{2}{4}$, the first piece unfolds from the beginning as if it were in $\frac{6}{8}$ (ex. 4). As with Zemlinsky, this procedure seems somewhat arbitrary, unmotivated, as if Schoenberg is trying on some of Brahms's clothes for size.

But as he matured, Schoenberg seemed to look more deeply into matters of Brahmsian technique and expression. The song *Mädchenlied,* set to a text by Paul Heyse (a favorite poet of the master), shows a different level of absorption of Brahms. The song, probably written in 1896–97 (the manuscript is undated), bears many of the outward aspects of Brahms's style (see the first strophe, ex. 5): a modified strophic form, a broad triadic melody, and a primarily diatonic harmonic framework. Also reminiscent of Brahms (and to some extent of Dvořák) is the quasi-pentatonic opening melody, with its particular emphasis in m. 2 on the melodic sixth degree, B, and the harmony of B minor.[23]

But it is in the more subtle relationships between voice and piano and in the fluid phrase structure that Schoenberg's song reveals a more genuine Brahmsian inheritance. In the first two phrases, mm. 1–5, the accompaniment repeats a brief three-note motive, marked x in ex. 5. In mm. 6–7 this motive migrates from the piano into the voice, at the words "süsse" and "kredenz dem." This motivic trans-

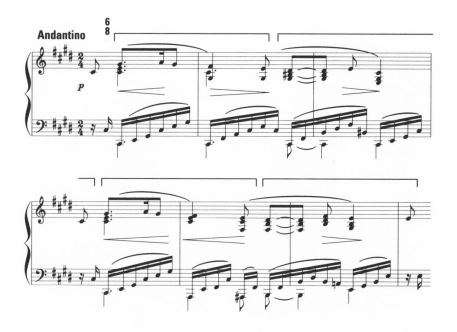

Example 4: Schoenberg, Piano Piece (1894).
Examples 4, 5, and 6, reproduced by permission of Belmont Music Publishers.

ference forms part of a still more sophisticated exchange of material between voice and piano. As the voice reaches a half-cadence on the dominant in m. 5, the piano begins a restatement of what was originally the vocal theme, now in the dominant. From the second half of m. 6, this restatement begins to deviate slightly from the original (an exact transposition of the vocal melody of m. 3 would bring an E in the right hand on beat 3 of m. 6), but the contour and rhythms are fully recognizable through m. 7.

This piano statement of the melody actually overlaps with the conclusion of the first vocal phrase in m. 5 and the beginning of the next one in m. 6. There is thus an asynchronous relationship between voice and accompaniment, perhaps intended by Schoenberg as a musical corollary of the drunken beggars outside the tavern door. The voice and piano get back into phase in m. 8, for the final phrase of the strophe.

Example 5: Schoenberg, *Mädchenlied* (ca. 1896–97).

In *Mädchenlied* Schoenberg seems to have assimilated basic compositional principles much more completely than the Zemlinsky of *Heilige Nacht*. The same can also be said of his own D-Major String Quartet of 1897 in comparison with Zemlinsky's quartet of the preceding year (with which Schoenberg was undoubtedly familiar). Especially impressive in the Schoenberg work is the motivic technique of developing variation, in which one thematic idea is drawn from the preceding in a fluid, almost continuous process.

Example 6a shows part of the ternary first group of Schoenberg's first movement. Already in its second two measures the main theme begins to develop, as mm. 3–4 take shape as a free but recognizable retrograde of mm. 1–2. Measures 1–4 function as an antecedent, mm. 5–12 as an expanded consequent deriving quite clearly from what has preceded. The rhythm of four slurred eighth notes in m. 5 (marked y) develops from the second half of m. 3. The rhythmic profile of m. 6 derives from the figure (marked x) spread across the barline between mm. 2–3, where the dotted quarter note has an accent. The consequent phrase develops the implications of that accent, as it were, by shifting it to the downbeats of mm. 6 and 8. In the brief B segment of the first group, beginning in m. 13, the eighth-note idea is further modified (x'). In pitch content the motive retains the neighbor-note motion of the consequent form (mm. 5, 7, and 9).

This developmental process continues well past the first group, as is shown in ex. 6b, which presents the climax of the transition and the beginning of the second group. Here y is presented *fortissimo,* then gradually "liquidated," as Schoenberg would later describe the process of reducing a theme or motive to its basic elements.[24] The motive is then immediately regenerated in the inner parts of the second theme, which begins in m. 39.

Schoenberg's strategy in this movement is clear: he seeks to saturate the texture with motive y in its various forms. Instead of using "filler" or empty figuration, he attempts to make all parts, and all moments, thematically significant. These are precisely the kind of techniques that he and his pupils would later admire and analyze in the music of Brahms. The D-Major Quartet and the song *Mädchenlied* both demonstrate how early and how well Schoenberg grasped these basic Brahmsian precepts.

In his later writings, Schoenberg would disparage the practice of composing "in the style" of a recognized master. He maintained that what most people call "style" is only an external "symptom": "To believe, when someone imitates symptoms, the style, that this is an artistic achievement—that is a mistake with dire consequences."[25] In his early works Schoenberg was himself somewhat guilty of adopting the symptoms of Brahms. But what is admirable, and what sets him apart even from technically more accomplished composers like Zemlinsky, is his concern with finding and appropriating underlying compositional principles, such as that of continuous motivic development. It is these principles to which he was to cling even as his "style" changed radically in the years after 1899.

(continued)

Example 6: Schoenberg, String Quartet in D Major (1897), I.

Perhaps the only other composer of whom this might also be said—even though he moved in different directions from Schoenberg—was Max Reger. Reger, as we have seen above, was a Brahms-*Verehrer* from very early on, and his devotion took extreme forms. In the summer of 1896, Reger, who up to that point had had no personal contact with Brahms, got up the courage to send the master a copy of his Suite for Organ, op. 16, a piece steeped in Bachian counterpoint and bearing the inscription, "Den Manen J. S. Bachs" (To the memory of J. S. Bach). Reger also asked Brahms to accept the dedication of a symphony in progress in B minor. Brahms replied: "Surely, permission is not necessary! I had to laugh, since you approach me about this matter, at the same time enclosing a piece with a startlingly bold dedication!"[26] Reger appears not to have finished the symphony. After Brahms's death the following year, he sought to pay homage in a different way. In the fall of 1897 he began work on a piano quintet in C minor that, although bearing a dedication to the critic Arthur Smolian, was, according to Lindner, "essentially dedicated to Brahms from the beginning."[27] Lindner suggests that woven into the main theme of the first movement is a motive containing the last three musical letters of Brahms's name, A–B-natural–E-flat.

More overt homage to Brahms is paid by two piano pieces composed around the same time. One, entitled *Rhapsodie* and subtitled "Den Manen Johannes Brahms," is a large, turbulent work modeled closely on Brahms's Rhapsodies, op. 79. It was published in 1899 as op. 24, no. 6. The other piano piece, the very opposite in mood, is entitled *Resignation* and subtitled "3. April 1897 — J. Brahms†," the date of Brahms's death (on, or shortly after, which it may have been composed). It was published in 1899 as op. 26, no. 5.

Resignation is a *tombeau* for a master whom Reger admired, and from whom virtually his entire oeuvre springs (the other main source is Bach). Although it can hardly be taken as typical of Reger's music, the intentionally exaggerated "Brahmsian"

(continued)

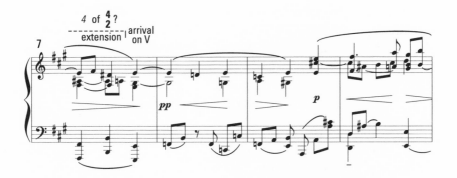

Example 7: Reger, *Resignation*, op. 26, no. 6 (1899).

spirit of the piece nevertheless makes it a wonderful specimen of Brahms assimilation by the younger generation of composers. In *Resignation* we can distinguish three levels of response to Brahms, which might be called quotation, allusion, and absorption. These can be considered not as exclusive categories, but as points on a spectrum of Brahms influence ranging from the very obvious to the almost indetectible or undocumentable.

The piece ends with an unmistakable quotation of the theme from the Andante of Brahms's Fourth Symphony (ex. 7a), which appears in its original key, E major, even though *Resignation* has been in A major up to that point. (It thus ends in the dominant!) Although the quotation in itself hardly represents a sophisticated degree of Brahmsian assimilation, Reger leads up to it by a wonderfully subtle process of allusion and absorption.

Example 7b presents the opening portion of the piece. (The piece as a whole has an A B A′ form, like many of Brahms's late piano works.) Needless to say, we find here many of the "symptoms" of Brahms's piano style, such as those described by Niemann in 1912: "passages in thirds and sixths, orchestral doublings, wide spacings, use of the deep bass register . . . [and] a tendency toward syncopated and triplet figures of all kinds."[28] But there is more as well, including allusions to at least three of Brahms's late Intermezzi: op. 116, nos. 4 and 6, both in E major; and op. 118, no. 2, in A major (ex. 8). Reger's bass octaves recall 8a; the distinctly polyphonic texture, with active middle voices, is a feature of both 8a and 8c. Reger also reinterprets the opening gesture characteristic of all three Intermezzi: *Resignation* begins on an upbeat with a root-position tonic chord, which moves on the subsequent downbeat to a ii⁶ (the chord is complete only when the middle-voice suspension resolves on beat 2). Brahms also has a tonic chord on the upbeat and

28

Example 8: Brahms Intermezzi.
a. Op. 116, no. 4.
b. Op. 116, no. 6
c. Op. 118, no. 2.

then moves to some kind of "pre-dominant" chord: in ex. 8a, vi⁶; in 8b, a passing chord over A, then ii; in 8c, a IV⁶₄. As in Reger, the precise formation of these downbeat chords is made initially unclear by appoggiaturas and suspensions.

In ex. 8b these procedures generate considerable metrical ambiguity. Our ear tends to hear the strong root-position chord as a downbeat, and the phrasing suggests a broad ³⁄₂ meter rather than the notated ³⁄₄. At the approach to the dominant in *Resignation,* mm. 6–9, Reger draws upon precisely these kinds of metrical ambiguity or conflict (as suggested in ex. 7). As we listen (at least for the first time) mm. 5–6 suggest a $\frac{3}{2}$ hemiola superimposed over the notated $\frac{3}{4}$. But the downbeat of m. 7 does not, as we might expect, restore the notated meter unequivocally. Instead, the implied $\frac{3}{2}$ measure is stretched, as it were, to accommodate the cadential approach to E through the circle of fifths, C-sharp–F-sharp–B–E. Reger now accelerates the harmonic rhythm, so that while the C-sharp lasts a half note, or a full beat in $\frac{3}{2}$, the F-sharp and B are only a quarter note each. The cadential goal, E, thus arrives on the notated last beat of m. 7. The two subsequent measures confirm E with the Phrygian approach through C-major and F-major triads. This cadence subtly foreshadows the actual quotation from Brahms's Fourth (ex. 7a), with its prominent C-naturals.

The Phrygian passage in the Reger prolongs the metrical ambiguity just long enough to bring the phrase to close on the notated second beat of m. 9, thus allowing for a varied restatement of the opening theme to begin in its proper place, on beat 3. The tonic now reappears modified by another Brahmsian gesture: the A enters half a beat too early, on the second half of beat of m. 9, sounding deep in the bass underneath the prevailing dominant harmony.[29]

The kind of procedures involving meter, harmony, and phrase structure that are manifested by mm. 6–9 of *Resignation* fall under the category of absorption discussed above. Reger is making no quotation of, or allusion to, any specific passage in Brahms. Rather, he seems fully to have internalized or absorbed a number of Brahms's most characteristic compositional techniques. This is the kind of influence that Charles Rosen has identified as the most profound, where the study of sources or models for a particular work "becomes indistinguishable from pure musical analysis."[30]

In an editorial in the *Allgemeine Musik-Zeitung* of January 1891, Otto Lessmann, already mentioned above as a willful "destroyer" of the "Brahms fog," attempted to summarize developments and trends in German music during the decade of the 1880s. He lamented at length the passing of Wagner and Liszt, and pointed presciently to the emergence of the young Richard Strauss, who at that time had to his credit only a few daring tone poems. About Brahms, Lessmann had this to say:

> As a self-assured personality, Brahms raised his head proudly among the many Mendelssohn-Schumann epigones and struck out on his own path, which wound around the noble palace in which Beethoven reigned. That this path did not lead into unknown areas, that Brahms opened no new perspectives—this should be conceded to his opponents without hesitation. But is it really such a misfortune that on the broad path along which art develops there should be resting places as well as signposts?[31]

Such a patronizing assessment can irritate us today as much as it did the young Reger at the time. Although some critics of the fin de siècle like Lessmann saw Brahms as a dead end or "resting place," younger composers felt differently. The most talented of these, including Schoenberg, Reger, and even Zemlinsky at his best, found plenty of "signposts" in Brahms's music. One merely needed the inclination and skill to intepret them. As these composers matured, they adapted and eventually sublimated Brahmsian principles and techniques to forge some of the most impressive musical achievements of the early modernist period.

Notes

1   Max Reger, *Briefe eines deutschen Meisters,* ed. Else von Hase Koehler (Leipzig, 1928), pp. 39–40.

2   "Johannes Brahms und die neuere Klaviermusik," *Die Musik* 12:1 (1912), 45.

3   Hugo Leichtentritt, "German Chamber Music," in *Cobbett's Cyclopedic Survey of Chamber Music,* ed. Walter W. Cobbett (London, 1929; rpt. 1963), p. 449.

4   The best bibliographic source for this enormous repertory is Ernst Challier, *Grosser Lieder Katalog* (Berlin, 1885), for which supplements (*Nachträge*) were published every two years well into the twentieth century.

5   Alexander Zemlinsky, "Brahms und die neuere Generation: persönliche Erinnerungen," *Musikblätter des Anbruch* 4 (1922), 70. See the translation of this excerpt elsewhere in this volume.

6   Reger, *Briefe,* p. 33. The resemblance noted is probably between the theme of Reger's finale and that from the finale of Brahms's Cello Sonata no. 2, op. 99 in F Major, published in 1887.

7   J. Peter Burkholder, "Brahms and Twentieth-Century Classical Music," *19th-Century Music* 8 (1984), 75–83.

8   There is a fairly extensive literature on Brahms followers, although much of it remains on the general life-and-works level. See the encyclopedic bibliography in Imogen Fellinger, "Zum Stand der Brahms-Forschung," *Acta Musicologica* 40 (1983), 131–201; and idem, "Das Brahms-Jahr 1983: Forschungsbericht," *Acta Musicologica* 41 (1984), 145–210. Especially valuable are the sections, in both articles, entitled "Brahms und seine Zeit" and "Brahms' Weiterwirken."

9   At least twelve of his works are set to such texts, including *Abenddämmerung,* op. 49, no. 5; *Abendregen,* op. 70, no. 4; *Der Abend,* op. 64, no. 2; *An den Mond,* op. 71, no. 2; *Dämmrung senkte sich von oben,* op. 59, no. 1; *Gestillte Sehnsucht,* op. 91, no. 1; *In stiller Nacht,* WoO 33, no. 42; *Die Mainacht,* op. 43, no. 2; *Mondenschein,* op. 85, no. 2; *Mondnacht,* WoO 21; *O schöne Nacht!,* op. 92, no. 1; and *Sommerabend,* op. 85, no. 1.

10   Cf. *Sehnsucht,* op. 49, no. 3, where the slow ascending arpeggios at the opening are inverted in the faster middle section. There are also ascending arpeggios at the opening of *Wie Melodien zieht es mir,* op. 105, no. 1, and *Maienkätzchen,* op. 107, no. 4; and a famous set of descending thirds in "O Tod," the third of the *Four Serious Songs,* op. 121.

11   Cf. *Dein blaues Auge,* op. 59, no. 8.

12   Cf. *Mein wundes Herz,* op. 59, no. 7.

13   Cf. *An ein Veilchen,* op. 49, no. 2, where, however, the tonic root remains in the bass. See also the examples discussed below from Brahms's late Intermezzi.

14   Like Schubert before him, Brahms frequently shifts to key areas or chords lying a major third below. In both "Wie bist du, meine Königin," op. 32, no. 9, and *Die Mainacht,* op. 43, no. 2, he moves from E-flat (via E-flat minor) to B major. In many instances he approaches the new area through its own $^6_4$ harmony, as in op. 57, no. 1 ("Von waldbekränzter Höhe"), m. 20.

15   Numerous examples of such phrase extension in Brahms songs were pointed out by Schoenberg in "Brahms the Progressive" (*Style and Idea,* ed. Leonard Stein [New York, 1975], pp. 416–22). See the augmentation of the phrase "tonreichen Schall" in *An die Nachtigall,* op. 46, no. 4, mm. 5–7.

16   See the end of *Die Mainacht,* op. 43, no. 2.

17   In his *Style and Idea,* pp. 418–22.

18   See, for example, the excellent analysis of the song *Feldeinsamkeit* in Christian M. Schmidt, *Johannes Brahms und seine Zeit* (Laaber, 1983), pp. 146–54.

19   See my discussion of this aspect of the Andante of the Third Symphony in *Brahms and the Principle of Developing Variation* (Berkeley and Los Angeles, 1984), p. 88. Normally, Brahms's inflections toward the subdominant take place over the initial tonic root, as in *An ein Veilchen,* op. 49, no. 2.

20   Theodor Adorno, "Zemlinsky," in *Gesammelte Schriften,* vol. XVI (Frankfurt, 1978), p. 351.

21   Rudolf Stephan, "Über Zemlinskys Streichquartette," in *Alexander Zemlinsky: Tradition im Umkreis der Wiener Schule,* ed. Otto Kolleritsch (Graz, 1976), p. 128.

22   There is no completely reliable inventory or catalogue of Schoenberg's early works. The best is Jan Maegaard, *Studien zur Entwicklung des dodekaphonen Satzes bei Arnold Schönberg* (Copenhagen, 1972), vol. I.

23   Indeed, Schoenberg clearly had a specific Brahms song in his ear: *Ständchen,* op. 106, no. 1, whose first phrase concludes with the same 6-3-5 melodic shape, harmonized by a vi-I progression.

24   See Schoenberg, *Fundamentals of Musical Composition* (New York, 1967), p. 58.

25   Schoenberg, "Why no Great American Music?" in his *Style and Idea,* p. 178.

26   Reger, *Briefe,* p. 55.

27   Adalbert Lindner, *Max Reger: ein Bild seines Jugendlebens und künstlerisches Werdens,* 3rd ed. (Regensburg, 1938), p. 146. Reger assigned the quintet the opus no. 21, but the work remained unpublished until 1922, six years after his death. It is printed in Max Reger, *Sämtliche Werke,* vol. XX, ed. Gunter Raphael (Wiesbaden [1960]).

28   Niemann, "Brahms und die neuere Klaviermusik," p. 39.

29   For a discussion of the overlapping of dominant and tonic at similar moments of return in Brahms's Third Symphony, see Frisch, *Brahms and the Principle of Developing Variation,* pp. 137–39.

30   Charles Rosen, "Influence: Plagiarism or Inspiration?" *19th-Century Music* 4 (1980), 100.

31   Otto Lessmann, "1881–91," *Allgemeine Musik-Zeitung 18* (1891), 2.

Adolf Schubring

Five Early Works by Brahms

Translated by Walter Frisch

In the spring of 1862 a series of substantial articles about the music of Brahms appeared in Germany's leading music periodical, the Neue Zeitschrift für Musik, *which had been founded by Robert Schumann in 1834 and was now edited by Franz Brendel. Written by Adolf Schubring (1817–93), a judge by profession and music critic by avocation, the articles formed part of a larger series entitled "Schumanniana," in which Schubring tried to argue that Schumann's legacy lived on in a small group of composers he dubbed the "Schumann school." Schubring's articles on Brahms, spread out over five issues, constituted the first full-scale assessment of the composer, who was then only 29 and had published only 18 works (through the B-flat Sextet). Schubring analyzed each opus with considerable perspicacity, often resorting to detailed musical examples. He did not hesitate to criticize, but also lavished praise where he felt it was due. Even if we today, with the hindsight of Brahms's complete works, cannot share all his judgments, we must admire the thoroughness and vitality of his commentary. His articles, conceived essentially as an elaboration and vindication of Schumann's "Neue Bahnen" of 1853, form a crucial part of the reception history of the early Brahms. Schubring refers to places in the scores by page number in the first editions; where possible I have, through consultation of editions, tried to provide the corresponding measure number. Some measure numbers have been added to the musical examples, where a few other editorial emendations have also been made tacitly.*

The excerpts are taken from "Schumanniana: Johannes Brahms," Neue Zeitschrift für Musik *56 (1862), 93–96, 101–04, 109–12, 117–19, 125–28.*[1]   1

Introduction

In his musical testament and swan song, entitled "Neue Bahnen," Robert Schumann wrote that he had always thought that, with music on the upturn in recent times,

> there inevitably must appear a musician called to give expression to his times in ideal fashion; a musician who would reveal his mastery not in a gradual evolution, but like Athene would spring fully armed from Zeus's head. And such a one *has* appeared; a young man over whose cradle Graces and Heroes have stood watch. His name is *Johannes Brahms,* and he comes from Hamburg, where he has been working in quiet obscurity, though instructed in the most difficult statutes of his art by an excellent and enthusiastically devoted teacher (Eduard Marxsen). A well-known and honored master recently recommended him to me. Even outwardly he bore the marks proclaiming: "This is a chosen one." Sitting at the piano he began to disclose wonderful regions to us. We were

drawn into even more enchanting spheres. Besides, he is a player of genius who can make of the piano an orchestra of lamenting and loudly jubilant voices. There were sonatas, veiled symphones rather; songs the poetry of which would be understood even without words, although a profound vocal melody runs through them all; single piano pieces, some of them turbulent in spirit while graceful in form; again sonatas for violin and piano, string quartets, every work so different from the others that it seemed to stream from its own individual source . . .

Should he direct his magic wand where the powers of the masses in chorus and orchestra may lend him their forces, we can look forward to even more wondrous glimpses of the secret world of spirits.[2]

Like a second John the Baptist, Schumann felt himself called, indeed impelled, to deliver this enthusiastic prophecy (of which only the main utterances are reported here) and joyous message. He then concluded by predicting that he himself was destined soon to give up his magic wand; he called together his little band of followers: "There exists a secret bond between kindred spirits in every period. You who belong together, close your ranks ever more tightly, that the Truth of Art may shine more clearly, diffusing joy and blessings over all things."

And how did people receive the new gospel of John?

The Schumann circle, at that time rather small, were surprised and elated; and they had faith. The rest of the musical public, both conservatives and progressives, laughed and shrugged their shoulders in disbelief. At the end of February 1854 the sad news came from Düsseldorf [of Schumann's suicide attempt]; and later, upon the publication of the seven Fughettas, op. 126, which showed traces of Schumann's mental illness, even many Schumannites shook their heads. Finally—it was about in the middle of 1854—the first works of Johannes Brahms were published. What astonishment, puzzlement, and bewilderment they generated: so difficult to perform, yet so clear in form, so new in content. At one moment they would be simply expansive, at another insanely colossal, at another demonically wild. At first people had difficulty making sense of the six cyclopean works forged by the young Vulcan (among them three sonatas), each one so different in character.

Scarcely had we taken these in when toward the end of the same year came a second smaller eruption. New bewilderment, for Brahms seemed to have entered another phase; he moved from ecstatic rejoicing to longing for the grave. But for some of us a *res severa* is true jubilation; we are accustomed to drill through the hard shell to get at the seed deep within. And so up to the work that has appeared most recently, the Sextet for Strings, op. 18, we continued to be amazed. We expected that each new work would be at least similar to the preceding one, yet were continually suprised by its complete novelty. We contemplated with increasing admiration the unusual path followed by this constellation newly risen to the musical heavens; it shone continually clearer and more splendidly.

Yes, these works are new, bold, large, and beautiful—but also very, very difficult to understand and to perform. The first sonata in particular is almost as difficult as the first movement of Beethoven's "Hammerklavier," whose main theme is in fact recalled by the opening. Yet the technical demands of Brahms's work go beyond even Beethoven. In his double counterpoint, his imitations in canon or contrary motion, Brahms does not restrict himself to two individual voices. When-ever possible he adds the third, fifth, or octave, and at the same time tries to charm us by adding a pedalpoint two octaves below. It is this uniting of the old contra-puntal art with the most modern technique that makes Brahms's two-hand piano works so difficult and prevents their wider dissemination. If Germany had a hun-dred musicians and music-lovers who could master the three sonatas and the Scherzo, then surely not even half of this small number would be able to perform it with genuine understanding; they would not feel inclined to penetrate with suffi-cient depth into music that is as demanding spiritually as it is technically.

And so it has happened that these treasures have remained up till now virtually unknown by the general public. The song collections certainly offer no difficulty for performers, but they demand a pianist of delicacy and a well-trained singer who can feel deeply—thus a duo that is not too frequently encountered. Nor have the recently published orchestral and choral works yet found the recognition due them, despite their melodic beauty, their consistently clear form and style, and their relative accessibility to performers. I can solve this riddle only by suggesting that the routine of official concert life has accustomed the majority of different groups of listeners to applaud only those works which they have come to understand through years of repeated performance.

I once attended a fiasco at the first performance of Schumann's *Manfred* and Joachim's Overture to *Henry IV.* In order to avoid such a calamity it is necessary to perform a work the *first* time as if it were the twentieth time. Moreover, it is certainly possible that the novelty of Brahms's music and the unfamiliarity of his name have worked against any sweeping success. (A concert public is never quick to applaud the work of a composer who is not yet famous; they could make fools of themselves!) And finally, we can also blame in part the unfortunate fragmentation of musical Germany. Here, Guelphs! Here, Ghibellines! The battle cry is sounding, and the Schumann banner, which stands between the two warring parties, gets dragged into the fray. May God protect them! But I, who have sworn allegiance to the Schumann banner, will in the meantime await the verdict of the ultimate judge, Time (if I err, at least I err in good company). I will not become polemical, but will rather be thankful that friend Brendel has granted a welcome spot in his journal for me occasionally to unburden my heart and to begin without further ado my cursory discussion of Brahms's works. If I seem to place undue stress on many passages in the early piano works that overstep the bounds of beauty, if I focus on various flaws of declamation in the songs, it is only to demonstrate that I, despite great admiration of the young master, have kept my eyes and ears open for his faults and excesses, for errors which Brahms himself will surely have noticed, since he already avoids them in his latest works.

When he wrote Brahms's letter of recommendation, Robert Schumann seems—on grounds which it would take too long to explore here—to have known only opp. 1–6 and perhaps individual pieces from opp. 7 and 10. He also makes passing reference to a few other works which have not yet appeared, such as string quartets and duos for piano and violin.

Even though the works published up to now are relatively small in number and very diverse in character, they nevertheless allow us to distinguish different phases and periods, or at least groups of related works. The most recent compositions, opp. 11 to 18, are like clear wine in comparison to the fermenting must of opp. 1–6. Between the two, opp. 7–10 appear as a kind of transitional group of less stable, more variable coloration.

Piano Sonata in C Major, op. 1

Of the works of the first period the C-Major Sonata is the boldest and stormiest. The construction of this sonata, and especially of its first movement (there is a first part which is repeated, then a development and a reprise of the first part, and a long coda) offers no obstacles to understanding. Less easy to grasp at first is the thematic work, which Brahms employs not merely in the development section, but almost without interruption from the beginning to the end.

Let us try to clarify Brahms's thematic work in the first movement of the C-Major Sonata, insofar as is possible without comprehensive musical examples.

From the brashly and boldly announced main theme *A,* in C major:

follows a gentle second one, *B,* in A minor:

Through two sequences this ascends to the high D and then from here descends again. The third main theme, C oscillates in sorrowful tones between Aeolian and Phrygian:

pp una corda

These three main themes are now split up into their component motives and each of these smaller motives or motivic particles leads to other combinations, which are treated mostly by sequence.

From theme *A* are derived the following motives, which are the most obvious because they are at the original pitches:

the inversions:

and the freer reformulations and variations:

From theme *B:*

and finally from theme *C:*

Sometimes a theme is hidden among other notes; it is only adumbrated, as is theme *B* in the phrase:

Of the many canonic and contrapuntal shapes we can present here the following in simplified form:

We see that Brahms is using the old thematic art of Haydn and Beethoven, and yet his work makes a very different impression from theirs. The use of imitation, increasing from the seventh, to the ninth, to the eleventh, gives the thematic work a strange character. When other voices are added as filler, the double counterpoint becomes ponderous and bloated, or at least loses that transparent simplicity which alone is suitable to the nature of arabesques. And since Brahms has already placed the most natural and pleasing of his thematic interweavings in the exposition, in order to bring about the necessary buildup in the development he must often have recourse to forced and harsh sonorities. Thus, especially in the development, he has repeatedly overstepped the limit of beauty. And thus it has happened that in his first sonata movement Brahms provides us with an image that is superb and original, yet overloaded with glaring contrast.

The following Andante (C minor, $\frac{2}{4}$) fully reconciles us with him again through its elevated simplicity. These are variations on the old German Minnelied "Blau, blau Blümelein." The first is distinguished by surprising harmonic progressions, while the second attracts us with its splendid double counterpoint, the third through a broad melody in the bass to which an intimate cantilena has been added, and the coda through graceful canonic imitation.

The third movement, scherzo (*Allegro molto e con fuoco,* E minor, $\frac{6}{8}$) and trio (*più mosso,* C major, $\frac{3}{4}$), is the most ferocious thing Brahms has written. The mood is broken only briefly in the middle of the scherzo with the insertion of a small secondary phrase of more gentle humor; otherwise Brahms storms forth in a hunt that is roaring, grisly, ever wilder, *feroce, strepitoso.* Though scarcely less stormy, the trio presents something of a contrast, since it is more melodic and less demonic than the scherzo.

(In this scherzo Brahms uses as a main motive the pitch sequence

which becomes a hallmark of his later melodies; a great number of these melodies, however different in character, have this progression or its inversion as a motivic element. In a similar fashion, Beethoven in his first sonatas liked to use the rising fourth as the beginning of his main and secondary themes.)

The rondolike finale (*Allegro con fuoco,* C major, ⅔ and ⅝) is once again truly human, but no less expressive. Here pulsates the irrepressible ardor of youth, his veins bursting with power and health. Particularly daring and audacious are the seventh and ninth chords [mm. 42–44] and the imitations on page 24 [mm. 51–57] which rise from the ninth to the thirteenth; also the defiant developments of the third (northern ?) main motive [m. 107]. (If I could eliminate anything, it would be the cheap double counterpoint on the third and fourth systems of the final page [mm. 269–80], unworthy of a contrapuntist like Brahms.)

Young must matures in its own particular fashion; and the more unique it is, the nobler and more fiery the vintage becomes.

Piano Sonata in F-sharp Minor, op. 2

The thematic work in Brahms's first sonata consists chiefly of taking a theme that appears fully formed right at the beginning, then splitting it up into particles and combining these particles into new shapes in the manner of a mosaic. The F-sharp-Minor Sonata adopts the opposite procedure.[3] Its principal and subsidiary melodies originate from mosaic particles before our very eyes. And what is most astonishing is that all these melodies, so diverse in character, are all derived from one and the same basic motive, which attains its broadest development and melodic unfolding only in the finale: 3

This rather unremarkable fifth motive had already been used by composers from Bach to Bargiel (the Introduction to the Trio, op. 8). Before Brahms, other composers, for example Berger, Loewe, and the Munich composer E. Leonhard, had composed sonatas in the older form on one theme.[4] But these pieces failed because 4 of the difficulty of combining diversity with unity; they became arid. Brahms has solved this tough problem in a truly ingenious way. He has managed to transform his basic motive more or less recognizably through rhythmic alteration, through displacement into other chordal inversions, and through exact or retrograde inversion, thereby creating themes and melodies of the most extreme contrast. It is impossible in this context to follow Brahms into all the hiding places of his creative workshop. But I cannot refrain from presenting at least the main motives of all four movements in simplified form and indicating with numbers the notes of the headmotive from which they derive:

First Movement:

Andante:

(inversion):

Scherzo, the same theme, rhythmically altered:

Trio, second inversion:

Finale, with an upbeat:

The same, varied:

likewise:

likewise the theme of the small fugato:

the retrograde:

Now, any musician can learn these truly clever tricks, which precisely for that reason become valuable only when they are employed in the creation of a soulful and poetic artwork. But in the case of the F-sharp-Minor Sonata, which certainly fulfills this condition, the listener and player would be convinced of the artistry even if they were unaware of the thematic unity of all the movements. The C-Major Sonata might be given the subtitle "Youth must sow wild oats." By contrast, the second is characterized by a depth and strength of passion; it bears itself with a more sober dignity. In the first movement we see a battle (an inner one), a struggle between opposing forces that are at once closely related yet contrasting. The Andante, written in variation form, contains the same struggle, now between two orchestras of lamenting and rejoicing voices. And in the third movement this opposition arises once again, now divided between a defiant scherzo and a peaceful trio which frequently breaks out in more boisterous jubilation. At last there is reconciliation in the elegiac, gentle finale.

Several particularly ingenious places in the score are: in the first movement, the *crescendo* on pages 2 and 8 [mm. 2–4 and 125–29] ("Wißt ihr, warum der Sarg?"),[5] the hammering triplets on page 10 [mm. 176–78], and above all the *fortissimo* coda [mm. 179–98], which begins so energetically and defiantly, but whose certainty of victory is then unexpectedly called into question by the two final chords, played *una corda*. In the Andante, we might point to the final variation [m. 68]; in the scherzo, the humorous transition from the trio to the reprise of the scherzo [mm. 64–72] and the Romantic sonorities on page 15, last system [mm. 42–47]; and in the finale, the grandiose chords on page 21 [mm. 119–42], which are spiritually allied with the description of Egypt in Schumann's *Paradies und Peri*.[6]

There are other bold moments, which tend to recall the wild spirit of the first sonata: in the middle of page 8 [mm. 131–38] (here [mm. 136–37] and in the parallel spot on page 2 [mm. 13–14], a ⁶⁄₈ time signature must be missing); the exceptionally difficult reprise of the scherzo on page 17 [m. 89]; some harsh passages in the middle of page 20 [finale, mm. 71ff.] and on page 23 [mm. 179ff.], which may, however, be due to printing errors; and finally the grating imitations on page 26 [mm. 253–57] together with the following theme, which is doubled at the octave and accompanied with chromatic chords [m. 258].

Piano Sonata in F Minor, op. 5

The third sonata, op. 5 in F Minor, consists of five movements of very diverse quality. The first movement (¾, *Allegro maestoso,* but better characterized merely as *Maestoso,* or simply *Moderato*) has the form of the four-part sonata movement and begins in truly splendid fashion with the motive:

The motives of all parts of the movement are derived from this basic motive, whose initial energy becomes dissipated when the subsidiary motives are extended, principally by means of augmentation. This is why Brahms has not succeeded in keeping us continuously spellbound in this movement. Although individual moments are outstanding, such as the *fortissimo* passages on pages 7 [m. 117], 8 [m. 137], and 11 [m. 200], the *misterioso* on page 8 [m. 131], the *pianissimo* on pages 4 [m. 37], 6 [m. 88], and 9 [m. 159], at others we are struck by a certain feebleness and stagnation. The more powerful the upward surge which has preceded, the more noticeable this impression becomes. The most important of the subsidiary motives derived from the basic motive shown above are as follows, arranged in the order of their appearance:

The second movement (*Andante espressivo,* A-flat major, $\frac{2}{4}$, alternating with two parts in D-flat major and in $\frac{4}{16}$ and $\frac{3}{4}$ time, and closing with a long coda in D-flat major, Andante molto, $\frac{3}{4}$, and Adagio, $\frac{4}{4}$, using a double pedal point on D-flat and A-flat) is headed by some lines from Sternau:

Der Abend dämmert, das Mondlicht scheint,
Da sind zwei Herzen in Liebe vereint
Und halten sich selig umfangen.

(The evening is coming, the moonlight shines,
Two hearts are united in love
And embrace each other blissfully.)

This is program music, one of the most beautiful moonlight poems ever created. Words cannot describe the blissful caresses of the two lovers in the still night, the sweet scent which wafts over the entire scene. One must hear the poem, hear it and experience it, as it is sung by Clara Schumann, who often plays it in her concerts. In the summer night's dream depicted in Robert Schumann's *Humoresque,* op. 20, the nocturnal love scene is interrupted in truly humorous fashion by simple Philistines, before whose silly chatter and foolish laughter the lovers withdraw into a secret corner (pages 17–20).[7] By contrast Brahms has *his* lovers embrace to their hearts' content, repeat their most tender farewells, and even call out the last goodbye from a distance (see the last two systems on page 17 [mm. 137–43]: in the upper voice "Ade, ade," in the lower voice retreating steps). One lover is left behind alone: "In darkest midnight, he stands alone on his quiet watch." Everything is silent; quietly he hums the *Schildwachtlied* by Hauff: "His heart beats warmly, he thinks of distant love," and loudly, ever more loudly, he rejoices in the night: "She loves me truly, she is faithful to me."[8]

7

8

Jetzt bei der Lampe Dämmerschein
Gehst Du wol in dein Kämmerlein
Und schickst Dein Nachgebet zum Herrn
Auch für den Liebsten in der Fern.

(Now by the faint light of the lamp
You go into your little room
And make your prayer to the Lord
Even for your loved one far away.)

The situation is now different from when his beloved came down to him; therefore the A-flat Andante closes with a pious Adagio in D-flat major.

I will leave self-proclaimed critics to cavil at details in this elevated song of love. To be sure, rules would forbid a melodic succession of five or six thirds (it is really a broken thirteenth chord); to be sure, the registral shift of the seventh chord from A-flat down to D-flat is somewhat peculiar (middle of page 15 [mm. 91–92]). But when something forbidden by the rules sounds good, and when the ear becomes accustomed to the unfamiliar, who wants to throw a stone? There was only one chord to which I could not become accustomed, the D-flat harmony at the beginning of the fourth bar on page 18 [m. 147]. Although I tell myself that the D-flat is nothing more than a pedalpoint, my ear still cannot tolerate it, because of the C that is sounded simultaneously in the tenor voice. Thus I now play the chord as:

Brahms may have felt it would be impossible to create anything more *poetic* than this solemn movement. Therefore in the following scherzo he aimed less at poetic force than at clever contrapuntal play. Both in the scherzo (*Allegro energico,* F minor) and in the trio (D-flat major) he resorts to contrary motion truly *ex professo.* The latter makes its effect through its ardent melody, the former chiefly through its lively rhythm and elegant counterpoint.

Between the scherzo and the finale Brahms has inserted a short Intermezzo which is subtitled "Rückblick." This is spun out of motives already heard and is full of poetry and dramatic life.

The rondolike finale is built in the following way: theme 1 [m. 1]; theme 2 [m. 39]; development of theme 1 [m. 71]; theme 1 [m. 104]; theme 3 [m. 140]; development of themes 3 and 1 [m. 195]; first coda, Presto, based on theme 3 [m. 249]; second coda, *grandioso,* derived from theme 1 [m. 349]. Both main themes, and especially the first half of theme 1, are used in a great variety of contrapuntal combinations:

In theme 3 diminution and stretto play a particularly large role, of which a few examples can be given here:

After the Andante and Intermezzo, the finale is the most beautiful part of this sonata, full of the most charming humor and, from the middle onward, full of increasing vitality. One could if necessary ease the difficulty of the stormy spot on the bottom of page 34 [m. 226] by playing broken chords (from bottom to top) in triplets, or by leaving out the upper octave—as on pages 27 and 31 [mm. 25, 126]—and playing sixths.

Piano Trio in B Major, op. 8 [1854 version]

The Trio for piano, violin, and cello, op. 8, belongs half to the transition period represented by opp. 7–10 and half to the earlier Sturm-und-Drang period.

No more than in his C-Major Piano Sonata is Brahms able to give the first movement of his first trio any unified shape. Here, as in the sonata, the same factors contribute to the failure: the padded counterpoint and the overloaded polyphony— and then chiefly the error that he draws from the main theme contrasting ideas that repel each other. Opposition within the theme is only appropriate in a humorous scherzo and trio; the rest of the sonata movements, on the other hand, require as themes merely *secondary* ideas, which do not conflict with the obligatory association and reduction of basic themes which culminate in the development section. This is also the reason why a scherzo and trio normally have no development section in common, but at most a coda which offers a truce or a kind of reconciliation between the two contrasting parts.

Brahms's first movement begins promisingly with a splendid cantilena in the piano, later given to the cello. But after a few measures the violin cannot resist throwing in a superfluous phrase like that of a canary—superfluous because it does not really belong to the theme and is not used in any later developments. The second group (page 4 [m. 63]) soon takes on a crabbed, grating quality, and still greater contrast is provided by the third (page 5 [m. 84]), which is more darkly brooding and unfolds mostly in canon. This is followed by the more idyllic, cheerful closing group. After this, brooding sextuplet figures return in the violin and cello; these are never used again and it is unclear whether the composer intended two or three accents. The sextuplets lead to the reprise of the first part, then to the development section, pages 7–12 [mm. 163–291]. Here it is principally the third and fourth themes which are developed in a humorous and ingenious way (only page 11 [mm. 262ff.] suffers from some rough spots and eccentricities); furthermore, the second theme is used as a principal accompaniment figure.

After the development section the glorious first theme resounds once again; but then up to the end of the movement Brahms bids farewell to beauty. Two new developments of the first and third themes surpass each other in bizarre eccentricities. First comes a four-voiced fugue on the third theme which we described above as brooding [m. 354]. From the initial imitation on, this fugue becomes virtually opaque as the different lines trip over their own feet. This opacity increases in the very cramped stretto which follows after only four (quite harsh) imitative entries [m. 384]. Soon it is no longer possible to govern the troops, who have tangled themselves up in a knot. The whole thing disintegrates into a frenzied rout (a canonically imitative episode [m. 396]), until the reserves of the first theme ride in to the rescue. But in the end they too are unable to resist the impact and are swept away in the general turmoil. Here passion and character celebrate their triumph, while beauty covers her face in sorrow.

The movement that follows is much more pleasing. It is really extraordinary how in the scherzo (B minor) demonic passion is kept so completely in check, held within appropriate limits by the powerful will of the master magician. And then in the trio (B major) a truly human geniality blossoms forth suddenly; in the second part it builds to the most blessed jubilation! After the repeat of the scherzo comes a gently flowing coda in B major, which resolves all the harsh contrasts.

The main theme of the Adagio suffers from the same rampant overabundance that we have already observed elsewhere. Two contrasting phrases, one gentler, one more robust, offer more solid support; yet their opposing qualities forbid any true unity or coherent overall impression, as happened in the first movement.

Beside the scherzo the most brilliant movement is the finale, in which driving restlessness alternates with sorrowful laments. The opening reveille sounds almost eerie:

Although the movement storms and charges forward in ever wilder fashion, the composer always remains master of his passion, and he never oversteps the boundaries of ideal art.

Piano Concerto No. 1 in D Minor, op. 15

In the Concerto for Piano and Orchestra, op. 15, Brahms draws himself up to his full height before our very eyes. In his last sonatas and quartets, and in his *Missa Solemnis* and Ninth Symphony, Beethoven had crowned his own earlier achievements in these genres, composed in his first and second periods; and he carried these musical forms so far beyond his time and ours that the general public will still need a long time to absorb these works. (Even today, as we say, the Tenth does not understand the Ninth.) Only in his concertos did Beethoven remain stuck in his middle period. In his third period he never wrote a concerto, in which orchestra and piano would have had to become entirely equal partners, even though such a path was laid in the first movements of his E-flat-Major Concerto, and in parts of the G-Major and Violin Concertos.

And this is the path followed by Brahms, who rightly recognized where necessity was leading. To be sure, he has reached his lofty goal only in the Adagio and in the last half of the finale. The first movement is even more ambitious than the other two and in certain parts even towers above them; yet it suffers here and there from a certain roughness and harshness, and from the thick counterpoint with which we have often found fault before. One would not be wrong in placing the conception and first version of this work in an earlier period.[9] Specifically, the solo entrance on page 7 [m. 123] is very rough and angular. The clash between A and A-sharp in the octaves played by bass and upper voice on page 14, system 2 [m. 282], does not sound good; it could have been easily avoided by means of another bass progression, for example B–F-sharp–A-sharp–B–D-sharp–G–B–B. The combining of the three themes on page 14 [m. 287] is not sufficiently transparent. At the beginning of the solo on pages 10 [m. 185] and 29 [slow movement, m. 87], orchestra and piano fall over each other's feet. Since in the piano reduction, the orchestral parts are not indicated at this place, I demonstrate the beginning here to make my point:

9

It is this kind of heel-treading, sometimes quite bizarre, that we often encounter in Schumann (e.g., in the Andante of the Piano Quartet, page 29 [mm. 95–101]; and in *Paradies und Peri,* no. 21, page 92 [m. 173]). Bargiel also has it in his first Fantasy, op. 5, page 4. In none of these places do I find the effect beautiful; it always arouses in me a feeling of distress. These sunspots on the old master Schumann, which we learned to overlook and even to appreciate in him, should never be imitated by his followers.

We are reminded of Brahms's hazy second period by the spots on page 4, system 4 [mm. 49–51], and page 7, final system [mm. 131–41]; only at the third return of the passage on page 13 [m. 255] does it emerge in a fashion that is clearer and less surprising and mechanical. This occurs chiefly through the aid of the thematic accompaniment in the violas, which is not indicated in the piano reduction and goes as follows:

With the exception of these small details, which virtually disappear in the splendor of the work as a whole, the first movement is more gigantic than that of any other concerto known to me. Gigantic movements demand gigantic dimensions; it is thus appropriate that the movement covers 23 pages in score and goes well beyond the sonata form in its construction. The movement begins with an orchestral introduction (filling three pages in the piano reduction), which presents the four main themes and begins to develop the first two. The piano now enters and develops the third and second themes after one another and then (page 8 [m. 157]) a new fifth main theme, and finally the fourth. The piano is frequently interrupted by the orchestra, which competes for the thematic development.

If we take what has just been described as the first part [exposition] of a symphony movement, preceded by an introduction, then what begins on page 12 [m. 226] would be the development section. The much-altered and partially truncated reprise of the first part begins on page 15 [m. 310]; it is followed on page 21 by a two-and-a-half page coda [m. 444].

I regret being unable to give here any comprehensive analysis of this magnificent movement, which is as great in its poetic conception as in its thematic development. I will restrict myself to pointing out that:

—Themes 2, 3, and 4 are conceived in double counterpoint to individual portions of the first main theme;

—Later on, both halves of theme 2 are also placed in double counterpoint with each other.

—Immediately upon its first appearance, the same theme appears in two variants (page 3, bottom system [m. 26]; page 4, system 3 [m. 46]), then later in various altered forms (perhaps least recognizable on page 18 [m. 372]). Its two parts also appear later in double counterpoint (beginning of page 14 [m. 278]; page 18 [m. 372]; middle of page 21 [m. 444]).

In this movement there is no main theme, no secondary motive that is not combined with all the rest in astonishing ways. (Compare, for example, the motive in the last measure of page 4, second system [m. 45], with its diminution on pages 14 and 21 [mm. 278, 444].) Nowhere does Brahms merely write a phrase or figuration for its own sake; never does he seek after effects. His only concern is a process that moves from within to without. Even underneath the cascading triplets of the coda, the orchestra is playing the second half of theme 3 (or, one might say, the final measure of theme 5, for both are rhythmically identical):

476 Violins

Unfortunately this is also not indicated in the piano reduction, although there is room for it.

This Allegro, which is, so to speak, as great and broad and deep as an ocean, is followed by a devout and solemn Andante, in which orchestra and piano compete to intone hymns in praise of the Highest, each one more ecstatic than the preceding. The score bears the inscription "Benedictus qui venis [*sic*] in nomine Domini." Moreover, Brahms uses for the most part motives from themes 2 and 5 of the first movement (more or less recognizable). These also appear in the rondo finale, which is livelier, and happier in its God, and in which the last third reaches truly dithyrambic energy. I give a few examples:

Andante   4

And I ask the reader to compare these main themes with the first two measures and the conclusion of theme 5 from the first movement (page 18 [m. 381]):

and with theme 2 as it appears on pages 4, 11, and 21:

At the end of the Andante, the G-major scale makes a very odd impression, especially the C-natural in the second bassoon against the tonic D pedalpoint (page 30, third system [m. 96]). It is all the more strange since the ear has accustomed itself to the C-sharp which has been heard repeatedly earlier on. (Can we explain the C-natural here as Mixolydian?)

In the first third of the rondo finale the piano part predominates; but in the last two thirds, and particularly from the end of the second cadenza on, the most intimate blending of piano and orchestra makes for a magnificent symphonic duo. Nowhere, even with all the novelty and meaning of the poetic content, is the beautiful balance of parts violated and the transparency of the web destroyed. Even the (forbidden?) fifths on the fourth bar of page 38 [m. 184], sound good because they are completely justified by the motion of the two lines.

I take this symphony-concerto for the most significant work that Brahms has published up to now. In it is realized almost completely the ideal that I have set for Brahms. The more immediately likeable opp. 16 and 18, which appeared later, may attract a circle of admirers more readily. But because of their very nature the Serenade and Sextet will not bear the least comparison with op. 15 as regards value, profundity, and grandeur.

Notes

1   On the context of Schubring's "Schumanniana" series, and on the personal relationship between the composer and the critic, see Walter Frisch, "Brahms and Schubring: Music and Politics at Mid-Century," *19th-Century Music* 7 (1984), 271–81. [Ed.]

2   Cited from Robert Schumann, *On Music and Musicians,* ed. Konrad Wolff, trans. Paul Rosenfeld (New York, 1946; rpt. 1969), pp. 253–54. [Ed.]

3   Schubring does not seem to be aware (or at least does not indicate awareness) that the F-sharp-Minor Sonata was actually composed before every part but the slow movement of the C-Major. Opus 2 was composed in November 1852. The slow movement of op. 1 was composed in April 1852, the rest in the spring of 1853. [Ed.]

4   I say specifically sonatas in the older form. Yet it would be inexcusable not to mention here the sonatas of the New German School, composed in a single movement and on a single theme, specifically the Liszt Sonata in B Minor, with its abundance of thematic transformations, and the Sonata op. 1 of Rudolf Viole. The latter also places the theme in retrograde. [Schubring's note.]

5   A reference to the final song of Schumann's *Dichterliebe,* mm. 44–45. [Ed.]

6   Schubring may mean No. 25 of the oratorio, Peri's aria "Es fällt ein Tropfen auf's Land Egypten." [Ed.]

7   Schubring refers here to the third piece of *Humoresque,* in G minor, marked "Einfach und zart." This piece is interrupted by a faster Intermezzo in B-flat. [Ed.]

8   Schubring quotes here from a poem, "Treue Liebe," by Wilhelm Hauff. In the mid-nineteenth century this poem was fitted to a folk melody which bears a strong resemblance to the melody of Brahms's coda. The song can be found in Friedrich Silcher, *100 Volkslieder für eine Singstimme mit Begleitung des Pianoforte,* rev. Alfred Dörffel (Leipzig, n.d.), p. 76. [Ed.]

9   Schubring is, of course, right. The concerto originated as a sonata for two pianos in 1854. All of Schubring's page references in this review are to the solo piano arrangement of the concerto, or *Clavierauszug,* published in 1861. This would have been the only printed source (apart from individual orchestral parts) available to him at the time; a full orchestral score was not published until 1873. It is clear from this review that Brahms gave Schubring access to the autograph manuscript of the concerto, which is the only source that contains the "Benedictus" inscription mentioned by Schubring in his discussion of the slow movement. [Ed.]

Hermann Kretzschmar

The Brahms Symphonies
Translated by Susan Gillespie

Hermann Kretzschmar (1848-1924) was among the most influential figures in late nineteenth-century music history and music journalism. After working in Rostock and Leipzig, in 1904 he succeeded Joachim as director of the Berlin Hochschule für Musik. He was a choral conductor and expert on church music and J.S. Bach, as well as a popular writer, and his education included training not only in music but also in classical languages. His view was that music and its history needed to be understood and interpreted from the perspective of cultural history. Beyond its history, musical culture possessed ethical significance for mankind. This latter view justified the task of spreading musical understanding through popular books and journalism. The following excerpt is taken from Kretzschmar's most successful effort, the leading German-language guidebook (from 1887 to the early 1930s) to the concert repertoire. Kretzschmar remained more sympathetic to modern music than Hugo Riemann, the other great contemporary German figure in the study of music. Kretzschmar's activity as a journalist began in 1874 when he published an article highly favorable to Brahms. Brahms in turn valued Kretzschmar's support and his scholarship; in 1877 Brahms asked the Herzogenbergs to pass on a copy of the First Symphony to Kretzschmar.

These analyses are translated from Führer durch den Concertsaal, I. Abtheilung: Sinfonie und Suite *(Leipzig, 1887), pp. 276-93.*

Brahms, who emerged from the circles of the Romantics, embodies the enduring principle of the Romantic tendency: the principle of mixed moods and rapid movement in the life of the emotions. But Brahms surpasses all previous representatives of musical Romanticism in the versatility of his spirit, acquired in the course of a wonderfully purposeful and energetic development, and in the objectivity, stringency, and diversity of his style. Among all the symphonic composers of our century, Brahms is the only one who equals Beethoven in the logic and economy of his structure, the unbroken expansiveness of his material and creations, and his lofty disdain for convention. Therefore, his works, and naturally his symphonies in particular, are not always easy to enjoy. Difficult, above all, is his First Symphony.

Symphony No. 1 in C Minor, op. 68

The First Symphony resembles the Beethoven Fifth in its character and in the progression of its ideas. It, too, leads the way from struggles and difficult times to clarification and joyful freedom of the soul.

The first movement begins with a slow introduction (*Un poco sostenuto*, C minor, §), which prefigures the following great Allegro in brief strokes. Like the latter, it flares up passionately, draws breath, and expresses hopes; in it, the thematic motives of the Allegro already begin to emerge. The underlying chromatic theme, in which the violins struggle up to the heights accompanied by the menacing bowing of the double-basses, is the same one that will have preeminent significance for the structure of the symphony as a whole:

This theme appears at the beginning of the symphony and provides the compositional basis for most of it. It reaches spiritually and bodily into the second and third movements; the first movement is built entirely on it. In the form

it appears now as the upper voice, now as the bass, functions within the fabric of the counterpoint as a secret *cantus firmus,* and serves as a loyal, guiding spirit in both good and bad moments. It sounds the warning signal and soothingly bids the storm of the passions to subside. The actual main theme of the Allegro is the following:

This theme supports the demonic scenes of the movement, which are expressed with great energy, power and rigor, but relatively briefly. More insistent, and almost more decisive as far as the overall effect of the Allegro is concerned, are those passages in which the despairing mood of struggle softens and gives way to milder, gentler sentiments. The transition to the second theme is wondrously beautiful—the gradual emergence of calmer movement, the appearance of plaintive motives, the tone of longing, in which the above-mentioned chromatic theme emerges to lead the imploring voices. The entire passage bears the stamp of authenticity. The second theme, whose first phrase

gives a good sense of the whole, concludes this peaceful turn of events. In a spiritual as well as a technical sense it, too, seems to derive from the chromatic leading motive of the symphony. A charming dialogue follows between the French horn and the clarinet, carried on almost entirely in the simplest, most natural tones; regrettably, it is of brief duration. The violas summon the chorus of instruments back into passionate action with a rough rhythm:

From this emerges the motive

which will play an important role in the development of the movement. In the development section, the two great *piano* passages stand out. In the sudden deathly stillness they introduce and in their quiet, half-hidden domination by somber thoughts, they have a transcendental quality. The first one is followed by a scene of strength and piety. The old motives of defiance come together as if joining in song:

The second *piano* entry leads into a passage that strikes the agitated tone of the introduction more strongly and emphatically than before, and makes the transition to the recapitulation with the most terrifying expression of inner outrage. This passage is one of the most powerful achievements in the pathetic style and is simultaneously a masterpiece in the art of making transitions. The recapitulation takes its normal course. But after leading the demonic forces of the movement to a still higher, unheard-of level at the end of the first group of themes, the music breaks off as if in natural exhaustion. The chromatic theme is expanded into touching melodies of lament, and the movement comes to an elegiac and melancholy close.

The second movement of the symphony (*Andante sostenuto,* E major, $\frac{3}{4}$) betrays the lingering oppressive influence of the first. However much it tries to avoid the previous Allegro in its key and in its purposeful search for consolation and peace, some of the terrifying elements of the former overtake it nonetheless. They find expression in the violent *crescendos,* in the abrupt modulations of individual themes; in fact, the Allegro even sends some of its motives literally into the slow movement. The chromatic passage of the fifth bar appears in the first theme:

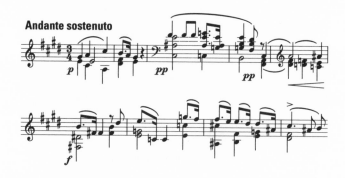

and the painfully reiterated

appears in the conclusion of the second group of themes.

In individual passages the tone of childlike trust comes through in an extraordinarily touching way, for example in the coda of the first theme:

It appears with even more engaging liveliness in the play of sixteenth-notes offered by oboe and clarinet as the second theme. The conclusion of the Andante, where the French horn and solo violin together take up the last-cited consoling theme, creates the effect of a true *musica sacra*.

The third movement of the symphony (*Un poco allegretto,* A-flat major, $\frac{2}{4}$) is far removed in its character from the Scherzo that is traditional in this position. It is conceived in strict accord with the spirit of the first movement; its cheerfulness is therefore muted, as it might be during a happy interlude that follows a series of sorrowful days. The sadness is evident in the second theme, in particular:

At the *forte* there is an accent of pain. The basic tone of this movement is childlike sincerity. This is expressed by the principal theme, particularly in its second half:

It is even more evident in the trio, a graceful alternation of woodwinds and violins on the theme:

There is much natural sound in the gentle bell-like tone of the winds, along with an original talent for instrumentation that in Brahms often finds expression in formulations of the utmost simplicity. The conclusion of the movement, quiet and half unexpected, is in complete accord with the discreet character of the composition.

The finale (*Adagio*, C minor–*Andante*–*Allegro*, C major, *alla breve*) begins with a return to the passionately sorrowful mood of the first movement of the symphony. The introductory Adagio commences with melancholy strains:

The violins try energetically and desperately to distract from the path of melancholy, in a phrase that is very sharply characterized by *pizzicato* and *stringendo* and that reappears at critical points in the Allegro. In vain! The imagination strays agitatedly in a dark circle; at the motive

the orchestra reaches a state of open revolt. The timpani give out a terrifying roll. Then the French horn appears, like a peaceful messenger from heaven, with the following melody:

We are in the Andante, the second part of the introduction. The mood softens, becomes more elevated, and prepares for the mighty, joyful hymn with which the principal section of the finale, the Allegro, begins:

Allegro non troppo

A long and folk-like melody develops out of this first section. This melody serves as the primary bearer of representation[1] in this movement. Among the other ideas that combine with this melody the most important is the wavering:

1

The energetically cheerful motives:

the fervent theme:

and the melancholy:

also take on passing significance.

The section gives a grandiose, dramatically spirited picture of a mood of victory that strides over all obstacles and swells to dithyrambic jubilation. This finale is as vivid[2] and lively in its cheerful moments as in its somber ones; it expresses a powerful quality. The most brilliant and moving passages in the Allegro are probably those in which the horn melody from the Andante reappears.

2

Symphony No. 2 in D Major, op. 73

Brahms's Second Symphony in D major, published at the end of 1877, is stylistically one of the author's most Romantic creations, in which pastoral motives and Anacreontic ideas occur in close proximity with ghostly strains. From the point of view of its musical composition, it is inferior to the First Symphony. Its outline is more deliberate, and at several points it reveals the junctures where additions and insertions have had to be made. In its content this symphony is related, in a distinguished modern form, to the imaginative world of the earlier Viennese School. Its basic tone is cheerful, and even in the melancholy portions of its Adagio, spiritual grace and a peaceful frame of mind hold sway.

The first movement of this symphony (*Allegro non troppo*, D major, ¾) resembles an agreeable landscape into which the setting sun casts its sublime and somber lights. It contains a far greater number of independent musical ideas than this scheme requires, and some of these numerous secondary ideas appeal strongly to the memory. The central theme of the movement consists of an amiably candid, warm-hearted dialogue between French horn and woodwinds:

The violins shadow the conclusion with soft triadic figuration; the trombones punctuate it with chords of dark solemnity. The transition section, whose middle part is based imposingly on fragments of the first theme, introduces two new motives, first a gay one:

and finally a teasing one:

The beginning of the second theme

betrays some influence of Mendelssohnian sentimentality. It is followed in the closing thematic group of the exposition section by a number of powerful ideas, among which the following two examples are noteworthy:

and

In the overall impression made by this symphony, the last theme stands out, intensified by vigorous imitations. The development section, which is relatively brief, is characterized by the use of contrast to create a fantastic effect. The recapitulation comes abruptly and with charming variations. The coda of the movement is among the most beautiful parts of the symphony. It is the product of immediate inspiration. The French horn leads with a peculiarly hesitant and searching melody, and the violins and woodwinds, aiding each other by turns, repeat in abbreviated form the most appealing and graceful things they have encountered on their previous long journey.

The second movement of the symphony (*Adagio non troppo,* B major, *alla breve*) is introduced by the cellos with a melody which begins as follows:

For a long time it seems to be seeking the key that will enable it to break out of a melancholy circle. Finally its sorrowful glances light upon a friendly image which seeks to lead the imagination back to youth, with its happy days of play and graceful dance:

A third part, dominated by the theme

deepens the gloomy mood with which the movement began, until a passionate climax is reached. The development, which is based on themes 1 and 3, is dominated by this tone of agitation. Nor does the conclusion permit the sweet melody of the $\frac{12}{8}$ rhythm to return; rather, it lets the sorrowing theme of the cellos vanish in a dreamily pleasant light.

The main part of the third movement (*Allegro grazioso,* G major, $\frac{2}{4}$; *Presto,* $\frac{2}{4}$; *Presto,* $\frac{3}{8}$) has the same naive character of melody and instrumentation as the original minuet of Brahms's D-Major Serenade. The principal theme of the movement begins as follows:

Allegretto grazioso

The harmonization and instrumentation of this modest, lovely melody are of equal simplicity. The second group is essentially nothing but a rhythmic reformulation of the main theme:

It is strengthened by the addition of a very weighty subsidiary theme:

In this theme, as in the $\frac{3}{8}$ bars

which take the place of the trio, the humor takes on the guise of Hungarian music.

The finale of the symphony (*Allegro con spirito,* D major, *alla breve*) recalls the shimmering colors of Cherubiniesque Romanticism. It is high-spirited and overflowing with life, like the Haydn symphonies. In the style of that master, even the fantastically lively principal theme

Allegro con spirito

begins with a suspenseful *piano,* which is followed, after a striking transition, by a ringing *forte.* The first subsidiary theme is the following:

The pleasantly familiar atmosphere of the second theme

is strongly supported by a series of subsidiary thoughts, some patriarchally strong, others, with their easy eighth-note figures, flirtatious. An intimate, enthusiastic episode based on the theme

provides the graceful centerpiece of its development section.

Symphony No. 3 in F Major, op. 90

The Third Symphony of Brahms, which was published in 1883, paints the picture of a powerful nature. It accomplishes this project in an unusual manner, inasmuch as the locus of its conflicts is at the end of the composition.

Stylistically, this symphony differs from its predecessors in its even greater clarity of articulation. It shows us the composer advancing steadily along the path of a noble popularity. The subjective aspect of development recedes more and more into the background; the ideas and their representation cleave to a sphere which is understandable and comprehensible to everyone. This Third Symphony of Brahms may perhaps represent the point of departure of a new epoch in the history of the symphonic art. For it seems to initiate the break with Beethoven's method of treating the movements, shifting the compositional emphasis from the development section to the themes, from elaboration and artful continuance to original invention. One stately theme follows on the heels of another. The majority of the melodies, it is true, are extended, and a practiced facility is required to grasp them— a task that is made easier by their extraordinary formal clarity.

The first movement, whose basic characteristic is a robustly spirited cheerfulness, is introduced by two bars whose melodic motive

Allegro con brio

takes an independent role in the development of the movement. It sets off the theme groups and expands at times into great, expressive melodies. The principal theme of the movement flares up combatively, now in major, now in minor, and develops an unusual energy by means of its quick succession of pauses and terse movement, its great strides and slow forward motion:

Allegro con brio

Winds

The subsidiary theme

p ‹ › ‹ *cresc.*

which follows immediately, is one of numerous episodes in this movement that seek to lull the powerful elements of the composition to sleep with gentle feelings. But to no avail: they are followed by yet bolder expressions of spiritual strength. The most seductive in this group of Delilah-figures is the second theme

Grazioso

p Cl.

pp

which proves to be extraordinarily rich in transformations. Elements derived from this theme can be found as leading voices in both the playful and the heroic scenes. In the development section it appears in minor and establishes the serious character of this section. A *sostenuto* in E-flat, based on the principal theme, provides the climax and at the same time completes and closes the development section. The coda takes the powerful phenomenon of the principal theme, raises it once more to a higher level, and then, with magical beauty, makes the transition to a state of rest. With a last soft quotation from its first bars, in a manner that recalls the opening movement of Beethoven's Eighth Symphony, the Allegro comes to an elegiac close.

The Andante of the symphony (C major, *alla breve*) is an unpretentious piece of poetry in a devout mode, a composition whose self-contained, unified, and dispassionate bearing finds scarcely any rival in the more recent symphony since Beethoven. The greater part of the movement is based on the theme

Andante

which is developed in a series of free variations that alter little in its character but offer the most glorious shifts of ornamentation. For just a moment a plaintive tone is struck:

But this melody, which formally plays the role of the second theme, is not further exploited. Only its consequent phrase, which ends in a mystical play of soft dissonances, returns at the end of the movement.

Beginning with the third movement (*Poco allegretto*, C minor, $\frac{3}{8}$), the character of the symphony becomes gloomier. Its principal theme rather resembles one of Spohr's melodies

Poco Allegretto

and presents the image of a graceful dance, like the reflection of a beautiful past. This is the passage in the principal section where the music displays its greatest charm. It is introduced by the cello-motive

and painted in the hues of recollection and dream. In place of the trio there is a middle section (in A-flat) that the winds fill with a tone of pleading and resignation:

It closes with a Beethovenesque phrase.

The fact that the third movement did not become a fiery scherzo results, as in Brahms's First Symphony, from the general poetic plan of the symphony. This third movement serves to prepare the way for the passionate and often darkly agitated finale (*Allegro*, F minor, *alla breve*). The latter is the focal point of the work. Here the heroic element of the symphony must prove itself in contest with harsh and unfriendly opponents. The movement begins in a darkly fantastic manner—scuttling figures, then a pause and complete standstill of rhythmic activity:

The tone becomes even eerier and more oppressive with the entrance of the trombones and the veiled theme that follows:

Immediately after this, the long drawn-out arc breaks off, and the situation takes on a definite aspect of struggle. Wild and defiant, the violins break in with:

The cellos sing in joyful victory:

In the development section there are several climaxes based on this passage of conflict. One of the most significant is the point at which theme *b* enters at full strength, in opposition to the fanatical figures of the violins. A notable and meaningful call from the bassoon calms the stormy waves. The composition moves into a *sostenuto*, which has all the beauty of a sky filled with rainbows. The dark themes *a* and *b* now exude quiet and peace, and as the conclusion of the symphony approaches, the heroic theme of its first movement reappears like an apparition transfigured.

Symphony No. 4 in E Minor, op. 98

Brahms's Fourth Symphony, published in 1885, has been described by many connoisseurs as the composer's most significant work in this genre—a judgment based largely on the conclusion of the work. Here, for the first time, Brahms expresses the most unique and powerful part of his individuality emphatically and in a clearly recognizable way in the sphere of the symphony—the singer of the *German Requiem* stands before us! Stylistically, this symphony follows the path of its predecessor. It even surpasses the Third in the simplicity and clarity of its basic musical ideas and in the disposition of its movements, which confine themselves to a few principal groups of themes. The symphony opens in a simple narrative tone, and the first movement, in particular, almost resembles a great stylized song.

The opening theme begins without preliminaries:

Allegro non assai

It is a long melody whose cloudy horizon brightens from time to time, only to assume a still gloomier character and an often painful accent. The accompanying theme (in the cellos) and the second theme

which proceeds by barely perceptible steps to its delicately fading conclusion, are close companions of the elegiac main figure which dominates this movement. They live on beside it in gentle diffidence, pose resigned questions, and rest, darkly brooding, on long chords. Immediately after the conclusion of the great E-minor melody comes a chivalrously gay countertheme, whose various transformations

give this movement its original stamp. Now powerful and commanding; now affectionate and gentle, teasing and secretive; now far; now near; now hurried; now peacefully expansive—its appearance is always surprising, always welcome, bringing joy and giving dramatic force to the progress of the movement. Here, too, as in the opening movement of the Third Symphony, the development section is kept very brief and is essentially content to express the elegiac elements of the poetry somewhat more forcefully. As simple as the whole structure of the movement seems, it is, however, extraordinarily rich and artful in its details. Each voice has an

independent melodic life. The principal choir of instruments and the accompanying
one relate to each other antiphonally throughout most of the movement, making
the effect fuller without being obtrusive.

The second movement (*Andante moderato,* E major, §) continues the elegiac ideas
of the first movement. Its relationship to the first is like someone recalling a story
from earlier days, in connection with a subject that has just been brought up. Its
principal theme

is introduced by several *unisono* bars and has the unvarying tone of old romances;
some of its cadences also include turns of phrase characteristic of medieval music. In
the middle of the movement, where the triplets begin, the music casts off its tone of
neutral narration, exhibits joyful involvement and enthusiasm, and breaks out in
heartfelt lamentations.

The third movement (*Presto [recte Allegro] giocoso,* C major, ²⁄₄) has the same
archaic ornamentation as the Andante. This is especially evident in the conclusion of
the countertheme, in minor

which is treated only fleetingly. This is a *presto* whose cheerfulness is not absolute. It
repeatedly touches on frightening elements. In the muffled and deeply penetrating
chords of the principal theme

in its hastening, restless rhythms, in its suddenly pulsing energy, in the predominant harshness of its character, the movement directly recalls the composer's demonic piano ballads (op. 10), which are among the most poetically significant of his early works.

The finale (*Allegro energico e patetico* [*recte passionato*], E minor, ¾) presents more obstacles to formal understanding than any other part of the symphony, due to the sheer volume of material that it contains. From the standpoint of idea content, it is one of the most serious and high-minded symphonic movements in existence.

It begins with a series of heavy chords, to which the trombones add threatening colors and accents. All the themes that are presented following this entrance have an anxious, alarmed, and searching character. Among them, the following

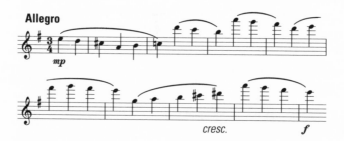

is to be regarded as the principal theme. It returns several times during the movement; however, it is not exploited in the usual manner of the development section. The leading element in this moody group of ideas is a long flute solo, which, true to its melodic and rhythmic nature, creates the image of an unstable frame of mind. After it comes the turning point: the harmony suddenly changes to E major; the rhythm becomes broad and peaceful; clarinet and oboe begin to sing consolingly and devoutly:

The trombones solemnly express the elevated ideas of a requiem:

The composition leads to the sphere where suffering and joy fall silent and that which is human bows before the eternal. In this natural sublimity of its conclusion, the Fourth Symphony of Brahms is one of the most magnificent and soul-stirring works of symphonic literature.

Notes

1   Kretzschmar uses the term *Darstellung,* literally "portrayal." This is only one of a number of terms which he borrows from the visual arts. Kretzschmar's use of the term *Bild* ("image" or "picture") in the following paragraph is another example. [Trans.]

2   The German term is *anschaulich* ("vivid") — another expression drawn from the realm of visual experience. Its root is *Schauen,* "to look." The use of the word *Anschauen* in a nineteenth-century German text would very likely have brought to mind the terminology of Goethe, who used *Anschauen* quite systematically to express the irreducible concreteness that he held to be common to scientific observation and artistic form. [Trans.]

Eduard Hanslick

Brahms's Newest Instrumental Compositions (1889)

Translated by Susan Gillespie

Despite the close friendship between Brahms and Hanslick, strengthened by their mutual friend Theodor Billroth (a fine amateur), Brahms did not quite trust Hanslick's critical capacities or judgment. Hanslick played the piano (but by all accounts quite coldly) and studied music from 1843 to 1847 with the great Bohemian composer Tomášek. Brahms was grateful for Hanslick's loyalty and admiration; he admired most the critic's gift for friendship and literary style. Hanslick's critical output was extensive. He began writing in 1846, before he completed his law degree. From the late 1850s until 1895 he was Vienna's most influential music critic. His critical stance derived from an idealized conception of Viennese Classicism, particularly Mozart. (Late Beethoven troubled him.) Hanslick admired Schumann, Mendelssohn, Schubert, Weber, and of course Brahms, even though Brahms and Billroth both thought that Hanslick, in his written criticism, often failed often to penetrate the surface of the music. Hanslick doubted the value of performing music written before 1750 and therefore did not share Brahms's enthusiasm for the Baroque and Renaissance. Hanslick's wide fame derived from two sources: his famous seminal 1854 tract On the Beautiful in Music, *which articulated the idea that music was an art uniquely autonomous, a language of forms set in motion by tones; and his persistent and stylish attacks on Wagner and Wagnerians. Hanslick regarded instrumental music, particularly chamber music, as the most elevated form of musical art.*

This excerpt appeared in Musikalisches und Litterarisches: Kritiken und Schilderungen. Die Moderne Oper, *Part V (Berlin, 1889), pp. 149–56.*

Making the acquaintance of two new, still unpublished sonatas by Brahms in a single season is in itself a stroke of luck. And the fact that we heard them both in such quick succession (in December 1886) made each of them all the more meaningful and valuable. The **Cello Sonata in F Major, op. 99**, and the **Violin Sonata in A Major, op. 100**, thus appeared as companion pieces that enhance and complement each other.[1]

In the Cello Sonata,[2] passion rules, fiery to the point of vehemence, now defiantly challenging, now painfully lamenting. How boldly the first Allegro theme begins, how stormily the Allegro flows! It is true that the passion subsides into quiet mourning in the Adagio and fades away, reconciled, in the finale. But the beating pulse of the earlier sections still reverberates, and pathos remains the determining psychological characteristic of the whole. When we then listen to the A-Major Violin Sonata, we feel more or less as if, following a thunderstorm that has gloriously discharged itself, we are drawn into the delicious stillness of an aromatic summer evening. A sublime sense of satisfaction fills the first movement, with its simple theme that rather too obviously recalls the "Preislied" from *Meistersinger*. The following movement is actually both Andante and scherzo at the same time. A slow song in D major seems to unfold itself and stretch contentedly; then it is interrupted by a joking Vivace in B minor. The Andante comes to the fore again, but only with a fragment, whereupon the tiniest little fragment of the scherzo, which seems to want to have the last word, laconically concludes the movement.

Just as this second movement flows harmoniously from the mood of the first, merely elaborating it further, so, too, does the Finale, whose characterization "Andante grazioso quasi Allegretto" already suggests its character. The whole movement is a nearly unbroken singing of the violin. I know of no other sonata that to such an extent foregoes the contrast of its various movements. The three movements form a pure triad of equally pleasant moods; a peaceful enjoyment of oneself and serene relaxation of mood. This distinguishes this composition markedly from the new cello sonata, which is so powerfully moving precisely because of its strong contrasts. Of these two, the violin sonata is the lighter, more popular; it sings its way into the heart of the listener more directly than the cello sonata, whose agitated and musically more complex essence conquers us more slowly, but just as surely and lastingly. We were not so uniformly fond of all of Brahms's things at first—but came to be fond of almost all of them. As works of art, both sonatas are offspring of the same strong, manly, and healthy spirit that, nicely mixed with intimate, not too tender-hearted feelings, characterizes and distinguishes all of the late works of Brahms. The unexpected nature of their phrases, combined with the strictly unified character of these new musical works, lends them an inexhaustible charm. Their brief form is noteworthy. May those young composers who no longer know the difference between a sonata and a symphony observe here that profound thoughts and passionate emotions can also be expressed in a condensed way, without verbosity. To attempt to describe this in words is admittedly quite useless. Even if we were to print the themes of the individual sonata movements of Brahms here, as the English concert programs do—what does one know of Brahms if one only knows his naked themes? The principal motive of the first and of the third movement of the new violin sonata, of the finale of the cello sonata—couldn't they, taken by themselves, almost be by Haydn?

Among Brahms's most perfect chamber music creations is the new (third) **Violin Sonata in D Minor, op. 108**, performed for the first time by Joachim and Brahms in February 1889.[3] Brahms's famous head peers unmistakably from every bar, and yet this third violin sonata has an entirely different visage than its two predecessors. It is mightier, more substantive, larger—outwardly larger too, as it consists of four movements, in contrast to the others' three. The first Allegro begins with a soft, long, drawn-out song of the violins in that seemingly composed, contemplative mood that characterizes most of the introductory movements of Brahms. But soon we hear half-suppressed sobs from the violins and mighty storms from the piano; passion has broken through the deceptive peacefulness and holds sway. The second section (the first is not repeated) climbs upward from a remarkable pedal point on A, which is held for the duration of forty-six bars, and above which there unfolds a wonderfully rich tapestry of modulations. At the conclusion of the section, in an apparent response to that pedal point on A, there is a somewhat shorter one on the tonic D. There follow chromatic piano passages in sixths and the gradually subsiding sighs of the violin, sinking deeper and deeper.

The Adagio (D major, $\frac{3}{8}$) is also initiated by the violin with a solemn song on the G-string that maintains its character of noble, composed lament to the very end, uninterrupted by any transitional material. The movement is beautiful, clear, and, in contrast to most of Brahms's Adagios, very brief. A charming detail is the chromatic ascending trill of the violin before the end.

More singular is the following Presto in F-sharp minor, one of Brahms's most ingenious inventions. It takes the place of the scherzo, but without the slightest inclination to jest. An uneasy, intermittent throbbing, like an anxiously beating heart, pulses throughout the principal motive and the entire mood of this thoroughly unified movement. This theme is the most original and remarkable one of the whole sonata; its rhythm does not let go of us, but pursues us persistently in memory.

The nervously agitated bitterness of the scherzo bursts into flaming passion in the finale (D minor, $\frac{6}{8}$). Here the composer brings two Presto movements in succession: the markings *Presto assai e con sentimento,* for the scherzo, and *Presto agitato,* for the finale, already give a general indication of the different mood of the two. The principal theme of the finale does not impress us with its novelty; it reminds us of related material elsewhere in Brahms. But just as the Adagio, about whose theme similar things might be said, develops more and more distinctively and richly with every bar, continually generating the unexpected from within its own strict organic unity, so, too, does the finale, but to a much greater degree. It is the longest movement and the most thoroughly developed. Beneath this flood of sound, pouring forth like hot lava, one will perceive on first hearing only a small number of the jewels of modulation and counterpoint that, on closer inspection, emerge to captivate us more and more; but the almost theatrical passion of the movement sweeps even the unprepared listener along in its wake. Admirable, once again, is the unified mood, which encloses the whole sonata as if in a golden ring. Each of the four movements tells a different story, but we nevertheless perceive each of the tales as belonging together and as inseparable from the personality of the narrator.

That the new violin sonata is larger, more passionate, richer in content than the first two was already noted. I would add that the virtuosity of the two soloists emerges more powerfully, more brilliantly, more in the style of a concerto. As far as the relative value of the three sonatas is concerned, we are never happy to be asked which of three beautiful but different things is the most beautiful. The second sonata, whose unassuming friendliness is so intimately appealing, is surely surpassed by the third. And the first (op. 78), in G major, the so-called *Regenlied* Sonata, is simpler and shorter than the new one—but whether it is therefore less significant? I feel that I am too biased to take sides. For me the *Regenlied* Sonata is like a dear and true friend whom I would never forsake for anyone else. In its soft, contemplatively dreaming feeling and its wondrously consoling strength, it is one of a kind. It moves me in more or less the same way as Goethe's poem "An den Mond," and like the poem it is incomparable, irreplaceable—rather like our own youth, which indeed seems to peer out at us from within it, as if from the mists of a faraway landscape.

The year 1889 brought us a new orchestral composition by Brahms, the **Concerto for Violin and Cello, op. 102**. Joseph Joachim, the master violinist, and the younger, scarcely less distinguished cello virtuoso Robert Hausmann had made the trip from Berlin expressly for the performance of this piece, and they played it with the sovereign mastery and perfect cultivation which we are accustomed to admire in them.[4] Both the composition and its execution were greeted with extraordinary acclaim. Brahms was called up after the Andante by stormy applause and had to be hunted for in vain for a long time before Hans Richter finally discovered him in a hiding place behind the double basses and persuaded him, with gentle insistence, to take a bow before the tirelessly applauding audience.

The actual success of this novelty in Vienna is thus beyond any doubt. I am sorry enough to have to admit that for me personally it did not provide as much pleasure as the earlier great works of Brahms. If I think back to his symphonies, his two piano concertos, his chamber music pieces, I am unable to place the "Double Concerto" among the first rank of Brahms's creations. The genre itself, from its very inception, has something rather dubious about it. Such a double concerto is like a play that instead of one hero possesses two, so that each has an equal claim on our sympathy and admiration, and they only get in each other's way. But if there is any musical form of which it may be said that its success depends on the ascendancy of one conquering hero, that form is the concerto. Isn't there a similar phenomenon in painting? The painters are hesitant to do double portraits; they do not like to immortalize man and wife on the same canvas. Two of the same instrument (violins, pianos) may be joined together in a single concerto more easily, as the older musical literature demonstrates, than two principal voices with such different pitch as the violin and the cello.

If it has already been remarked of Brahms's Violin Concerto that the solo violin is not accorded the sovereign place it deserves, this criticism applies all the more pointedly to the Double Concerto, in which both solo instruments are over-shadowed, not only by the orchestra, but by each other. The cello has been treated with a certain partiality compared to the violin; but here it seems to me that things are demanded of that instrument that, while they are capable of being performed by virtuosos, exceed the scope of the instrument's own natural character. Already in the first movement, the solo violin is overshadowed by the orchestral violin section, in three parts, cutting through the air like sheaves of fire. The two soloists do not have a decisive, leading role in this composition, which is handled just like a symphony. Only rarely do they clamber victoriously, for a moment, above the mighty waves of the orchestra, only to sink back again.

Thus the Double Concerto, with its virtuoso passages, bears more resemblance to a symphony that is embellished by a violin and a cello. It seems to me to be more the fruit of a spirit with a great gift for combinations than the work of an irresistible creative fantasy and sentiment. We feel that it is characterized by a lack of freshness and originality of feeling, of melodic and rhythmic magic. It is well known how cleverly Brahms is able to turn, to vary, to make use of every motive; and even in the Double Concerto we admire the artistry of its execution. But that which is executed, the thematic material, does not seem to me to be significant enough for such a great work. Thus, little by little, we gain the impression of a play, a drama in which all the characters are very clever and witty but there is never any action.

This applies above all to the first and last movements. The first movement, the most artful of all, does not break free from its half-defiant, half-depressed mood, or from its A-minor key. Its many suspensions, syncopations, and rhythmic displacements, its augmented and diminished intervals, only rarely allow the light of day to break through. We are almost reminded of Schumann's late manner. Nor does the theme of the last movement represent the height of Brahms's genius. A minor motive, floundering in a narrow net, it is more peevish than serene. The listener hopes, after this petty beginning, for a powerful, brilliant climax; but where it seems about to emerge (F major, *fortissimo*), the rhythm flags and moves forward only haltingly, dragged down by the lead bullets of heavy triplets. We are reminded of similar retardations in the first movement of the E-Minor Symphony.[5]   5

The Andante, in D major, is a refreshment between the other two movements. The theme, a graceful and simple melody sung *all' ottava* by the two solo instruments, exudes comfort and satisfaction for both players and listeners. The brief movement does not number among the most significant Andante movements of Brahms, but it is surely one of the most pleasing; it may be that it is generally responsible for the success of the whole piece. In Vienna this success has taken such a brilliant form that my modest dissenting opinion, which makes no claim to anything more than candor, already seems, in fact, to have been annulled.

Notes

1   The Cello Sonata was given its premiere in Vienna on 24 November 1886 by Brahms and Robert Hausmann; the Violin Sonata on 2 December by Brahms and Joseph Hellmesberger. [Ed.]

2   In the original German text Hanslick gives the opus number here as 108, which was eventually given to the D-Minor Violin Sonata. [Ed.]

3   This was the Viennese premiere, on 13 February. The actual premiere took place in Budapest on 21 December 1888, with Brahms and Jenö Hubay. [Ed.]

4   This concert seems actually to have taken place at Christmas 1888. See Max Kalbeck, *Johannes Brahms* (Berlin, 1904–14), IV, 120. [Ed.]

5   Hanslick actually writes "E-Major Symphony," which must be an error. [Ed.]

Donald F. Tovey

Joseph Joachim, Hungarian Concerto for Violin and Orchestra, op. 11

*In the 1880s and 90s Joseph Joachim (1831–1907), one of the most famous violinists of his day, became a mentor to the young Tovey (who as a child called him "Uncle Jo"). Their personal and professional relationship continued up to Joachim's death. Above all, Joachim represented, through his own relationship with Brahms, a direct link to the great Austro-German musical tradition about which Tovey would write so compellingly. The conductor Fritz Busch relates that Joachim, upon discovering the young Tovey's talents, had actually written to Brahms "how much he wished to bring him the little Donald" (*Pages from a Musician's Life [London, 1953], p. 96). No such letter is included in the published Brahms-Joachim correspondence; nor did any meeting take place. Nevertheless, Tovey's own writings about Brahms and Joachim, created close to the source, can lay claim to a certain historical authenticity. The program note about Joachim's Concerto (a work composed in 1861) is as significant for what it relates about the composer's relationship to Brahms and about the origins of Brahms's D-Minor Piano Concerto as for its analysis of the work itself.*

The essay, which was not included in the recent paperback reissue of Tovey's analytical writings (1989), originally appeared in his Essays in Musical Analysis: *Vol. III, Concertos (London, 1936), pp. 106–14.*

1 *Allegro un poco maestoso.* **2** Romanze. *Andante.* **3** *Allegro con spirito.*

The Hungarian Concerto illustrates nearly, but not quite, every aspect of Joachim's music. To the violinist it is a complete revelation of what Joachim's playing must have been when his physical powers were at their height. To students of composition and of musical history it is one of the most important documents of the middle of the nineteenth century. It is the second of three concertos that stand in direct line of descent, and that each cost their composer great efforts concerning fundamental matters of musical form. Joachim's model is Beethoven's Pianoforte Concerto in C-Minor, the work in which, without as yet perfectly solving his problem, Beethoven realized that his first and second concertos had misconceived the purpose of the long opening tutti. In the Hungarian Concerto Joachim begins by following Beethoven's C-Minor Concerto in organizing his first tutti on purely symphonic lines which give no hint that the work is going to submit to the dominance of a solo instrument at all. But Joachim finds a simpler way to explain the entry of the solo violin than the drastic stroke with which Beethoven diverted the course of his C-Minor tutti. He evidently did not trust himself to take Beethoven's later works as models: indeed to the end of his life he always had a smile of pity for the inexperienced composer who will not learn from any Beethoven earlier than the last quartets. And so the Hungarian Concerto accepts, as a definite principle, the element of conflict between symphony and concerto in the first movement. Within a few years of his meeting with Joachim, Brahms took up this problem with drastic power, and forced its extremest terms into a chemically indissoluble combination.

The process was accompanied, like many chemical experiments, with formidable eruptions of light and heat. Beethoven's Ninth Symphony and Wagner's *Tannhäuser* did not cost their creators greater agonies than Brahms's D-Minor Concerto. Joachim helped with advice and criticism at every stage of its growth, from its beginnings as a symphony drafted in an arrangement for two pianofortes, to its final perfection. When it was ready for orchestration, Joachim's relation to Brahms was practically that of master to pupil. In the handling of form Brahms was from the outset a bold and resourceful inventor who needed Joachim's criticism only as the painter needs to see his work reversed in a mirror. But in orchestration he was not only inexperienced but actually untaught. Moreover, orchestration had already come to be regarded as the special province of the progressive party in musical politics. Brilliant scoring was like brilliant playing; it was suspected of having a taint of virtuosity. Brahms would probably have worked out his own salvation even if he had not found a friend who believed in him. But in Joachim he found not only a believer, but a composer whose qualities were exactly fitted to complete his education. Joachim's artistic outlook was already becoming highly conservative, but his alienation from Liszt was a revolt, not a prejudice. At the outset Joachim had been as ready to revolutionize musical traditions as any of the groups who gathered round Liszt at Weimar. His objection to Liszt's compositions was based on no orthodoxies as to musical form, but was as fundamental and insurmountable as Wagner's objection to Meyerbeer. But he was in no danger of letting himself and Brahms miss the means to classical ideals because other composers used these means to purposes he did not approve. On his own instrument he was as great a player as Liszt; and Wagner alone had a greater command of orchestration. This estimate of Joachim's orchestration will surprise those who have never heard or read his scores, or whose judgement is at the mercy of ready-made effects such as harp-glissandos and prominent celesta passages, or, to use Brahms's gibe, "Tam-tam *divisi*." All competent judges of orchestration will agree with Stanford in regarding Joachim's mastery of this art as on a level with his mastery of the violin. Nothing more fortunate could have happened to Brahms than that his most whole-hearted admirer should possess not only an exceptionally fastidious ear, but also the most highly developed technique for satisfying that ear in composition as well as in playing.

And so the two composers worked together. Their motto was *"Frei aber einsam,"* and its initials, F, A, E, form several themes in Brahms's early works. They invert into the notes G-sharp, E, A, which may be read in a mixture of German and sol-fa terms, as Gis-e-la, the name of Joachim's beloved Gisela von Arnim, afterwards Gisela Grimm. Brahms pulled his mighty D-Minor Concerto into shape with the united strength of his own impulse and Joachim's advice. The orchestration did not get beyond the first page before Joachim showed Brahms that its whole basis of orchestral tone-production was wrong. Brahms was quick to learn, and it is no exaggeration to say that he learnt orchestration from Joachim. It would be a mistake to seek in the first two movements of his D-Minor Concerto for the influence of Joachim in matters of form and dramatic content. But Brahms's finale clearly shows the influence of the finale of the Hungarian Concerto. Both, indeed, are closely modelled on that of Beethoven's C-Minor Concerto; but it is from Joachim that Brahms has derived the main points in which his form differs from Beethoven's.

The great length of the Hungarian Concerto results mainly from the composer's determination to achieve clearness. Joachim told me that soon after he had finished the concerto he thought a certain passage too long; but that when he recast it the result came out longer. Few are the young composers who have escaped damage from well-meaning advice to shorten for shortness' sake. Horace knew better, and so did Joachim and Brahms. If a young composer is not a mere epigrammatist, he needs space in which to move freely. By the time he is nearer sixty than fifty he may be trusted to calculate rightly the force of the half-statement and to express in it the experience of a life-time. But when we advise young artists to move like old ones, we tell them not only to ape a sententiousness that is unnatural to them, but actually to say things which they do not believe. The young Joachim believed everything which Beethoven uttered in his last works; but the Hungarian Concerto represented Joachim's experience at twenty-three, not Beethoven's at fifty-six. The young Joachim's experience was extraordinarily rich, and he had had enough of his own efforts at what I have heard him call "psychological" music, such as his unpublished overture to Demetrius. The form of the classical concerto gave him exactly the opportunity he needed both to find himself and to learn how to help Brahms. Both to him and to Brahms the principal danger of their reaction against Liszt was that their music, in aiming at consistency, might become schematic. With Brahms one security against that danger was his constant preoccupation with the setting of words on a basis consistently lyric instead of loosely declamatory. He never accepted the dogma that sustained melody was contrary to the true declamation of words; and his instrumental melodies all show the freedom which comes only to composers who are accustomed to handle poetry. Joachim also made a deep study of the art of song. But the concerto form gave him his freedom on a larger scale. The first effect of his reaction against Liszt was to make him diffident about the more improvisatorial features of musical art-forms. Thus, both he and Brahms were eminently capable of designing an impressive or mysterious introduction. But the tendencies of progressive music in the 'fifties were all for works consisting of introductions to introductions to introductions, without any prospect of a clear answer to the question which Beethoven put to a famous improvisatore after twenty minutes of stimulated expectancy: "When will you begin?" And so Joachim and Brahms formed the habit of always beginning at once; and the few examples of an introduction in Brahms's works make us inclined to regret that he did not more often take the risk of rousing expectation.

Now it is a fundamental necessity of concerto form that it should have large spaces of discursive interlude for the solo instrument. Joachim's character made any frivolity in such interludes unthinkable; his enormous powers as a violinist gave him freedom to develop the full resources of his instrument, and he had an inexhaustible inventiveness in ornamentation, inspired by instincts akin to those of Bach and Beethoven. Accordingly his own classical conservatism set him free in the spacious interludes which are as necessary to the concerto as parks to large towns and lungs to the human frame. The Hungarian Concerto thus became a composition from which Brahms was proud to learn. The forms, in their general aspect, are four-square and youthfully weighty in their completeness. To ask for compression would be to fall into the commonest of donnish errors. It is obvious that these large forms lay an enormous burden on the function of ornamental detail that is to fill them out. But herein Joachim's mastery is neither youthful nor middle-aged; it is absolute. Nowhere outside Bach and the last works of Beethoven is there to be found any such ornamentation as that of Joachim's violin works. There are plenty of good schools and formulas in this matter; but with Joachim, as with Bach and Beethoven, the ornaments are only in small part formulas, and are mostly individual inventions as pregnant as any theme. Brahms himself never attempts such a style. Still less does it come within the imagination of the mere virtuoso player. Virtuoso ornamentation, even when it is as good as Liszt's, consists in knacks which, if more difficult than harp-glissandos, are hardly more intellectual. The ornaments of the Hungarian Concerto (quite apart from the Hungarian formulas which I purposely refrain from quoting in the musical examples) are like Bach's. Play them slowly and you will find them to be living melodies with real harmonic meanings.

One by-product of this style is that Joachim's violin-writing is almost always, even in his smaller works, extraordinarily difficult. He had a large hand, and extensions were easy to him which give great trouble to most players. He retained his left-hand technique in full efficiency to his last days, long after he had given up playing works that depended on staccato bowing. The Hungarian Concerto shows, especially in the finale, that in his physical prime his bow-arm was as wonderful as his left-hand. Above all, the concerto shows that he had the greatest of all technical gifts: the staying power without which Beethoven's Violin Concerto is inaccessible to players who think nothing of its individual passages. Beethoven writes no such difficulties as turn up in every passage in the Hungarian Concerto; but he demands the same kind of staying power. The difficulties of a big piece of music cannot be measured by the mere fact that its passages correspond to exercises of such and such a grade. Violinists, for example, usually defer the practice of harmonics in double-stops until they have mastered more necessary things. There are no double-stop harmonics in the Hungarian Concerto. But pieces that have room for such follies are easier to play, though they may be harder to practise at first. Most violinists will probably agree that the Hungarian Concerto is the most difficult work ever written for the violin. Its difficulties all have the double quality of being the work of a composer who could play them, and of being the most straightforward and economical expression of his thought.

The concerto opens with the following grave theme, typically Hungarian in its minor mode with raised fourth, and also in its later cadences.

Ex. 1

The orchestra works this up in a broad symphonic exposition which soon comes to a grand forte modulating deliberately to F major, where a second group begins with a theme rhythmically derived from ex. 1, but continuing in a vein of its own.

Ex. 2

An important new theme is given to the oboe, an instrument which it suits to perfection, though it afterwards comes with new meaning from the solo violin.

Ex. 3

Then with an impatient gesture—

the orchestra seems about to rouse itself to action; but with subtle dramatic purpose it soon comes to a series of dying cadences in F; and the solo violin makes its entry in a way not to be found in any other concerto. It begins quite quietly on its middle strings with dreamy meditation over the dying cadences, which have moved back to the home-dominant; but it soon gathers energy and in due course reaches a climax from which it descends to take up the first theme.

And now Joachim shows a freedom and truth of form that place him far above any epigonoi of the classics. The violin immediately follows ex. 1 by ex. 3 in tragic D-Minor harmony, and thence proceeds to a new theme which is to have the function of leading to the second group in F major.

Ex. 5

The solo exposition has thus entirely avoided the effect of a transcription of the opening tutti, and by this very freedom welds the whole movement into a more highly organized unity. Other unorthodoxies are to follow; but at present the transition leads to a quite regular reproduction of the whole second group (exx. 3 and 4) suitably expanded in terms of the solo violin,. After this the orchestra bursts in with the first forte of the opening tutti in F-Minor. This leads to a sustained development of ex. 2 passing through several keys with beautiful changes of orchestral tone. This is another unorthodox feature, which gives the orchestra more freedom than the normal scheme would allow. But here again the purpose is classical in its dramatic truth. The abrupt entry of the solo violin with a new counterpoint to ex. 2

Ex. 6

reveals itself as the explanation of the previous development and lays the foundation for the coda. The violin takes the rest of the development into its own control, making energetic use of ex. 5. In a few decisive steps it leads to the home-tonic and so to the recapitulation, of which solemn warning is given by the whole orchestra playing pianissimo below the climax of the violin passages.

In accordance with Mozart's principles the recapitulation follows rather the course of the opening tutti than that of the first solo. One of the most ingenious details is the passage of chromatic octaves with which the violin accompanies a quiet version of the first forte. Joachim himself compared this to a neighing horse. It is not the only striking feature in a recapitulation admirably free from anything like mechanical stiffness.

The coda is largely occcupied by a cadenza, beginning, like the usual extemporized cadenzas, with the violin alone, but joined at intervals by a flute and an oboe, each of which intervenes with ex. 6. Thus the cadenza sums up the development. Then the orchestra re-enters, the violin once more gives ex. 3 in the tragic D-Minor of its first solo; and then rounds off the whole structure with ex. 5.

After a meditative introduction the slow movement (entitled *Romanze*) begins with the following theme—

Ex. 7

The second part of this melody is worthy to rank, like Matthew Arnold's "touch-stones of poetry," among those things in great music which we may keep in mind as standards of beauty. I quote the whole strain:

Ex. 8

The typically Hungarian figure of its cadence becomes the main figure of a square-cut but agitated middle section in E minor. When this is completed, a short passage leads to the return of exx. 7 and 8 in the violoncellos accompanied by a most gorgeous ornamental counterpoint in the solo violin.

The cadence-figure of ex. 8 is used in fresh ways in the quiet coda, which also resumes the features of the introduction.

The finale begins by taking up the last notes of the *Romanze* in the full orchestra as a call to action. After some dramatic questionings the orchestra settles down to dance-rhythm over which the violin plays a theme in perpetual motion. (Note again the Hungarian minor scale with its sharp fourth.)

Ex. 9

This is worked out as a rondo on the largest possible scale. The transition passages are again admirably free and unexpected in their digressions and in the deftness of their returnings. Their influence on the finale of Brahms's D-Minor Concerto has already been mentioned. A detailed analysis of the whole movement would be well worth the trouble of writing or even of reading it; and experienced composers will not underrate the difficulty of inventing and developing a *perpetuum mobile* theme. Such stiffness as may be imputed to Joachim's phrase-rhythms disappears in the finale. The other main themes are: the first episode—

Ex. 10

the middle episode—

Ex. 11

and the entirely unexpected new presto theme of the triumphant coda.

Ex. 12

Presto

The drastic simplicity of such themes is deceptive: there is drama behind and around them.

Eduard Hanslick

Memories and Letters

Translated by Susan Gillespie

Eduard Hanslick (1825–1904), one of Brahms's closest Viennese friends, was born in Prague. His father was a scholar and librarian who taught music privately. His mother, the child of a successful Jewish banking family, inspired Hanslick's love of theater and literature. Hanslick studied law and worked for the Ministry of Culture for most of his life. But his real vocation was that of a writer on music. He lived in Vienna from 1852 on. From 1864 until the late 1890s, most of his work appeared in Vienna's most influential daily newspaper the Neue Freie Presse. *In 1856 he began teaching music history and aesthetics at the University. His two-volume history of Viennese concert life, which appeared in 1869 and 1870, remains a vital source. Hanslick also played a significant role as an official evaluator of musical activities, ranging from the quality of pianos to that of curricula. Hanslick perfected the quintessentially Viennese literary form, the "Feueilleton," a brief essay of opinion printed on the first page of the daily papers of Vienna, "under the line" which separated the news from the essay. Hanslick was identified in Viennese society with the same liberal bourgeois group as Brahms, a community made up of professionals, academics, and musicians, as well as many Jews and industrialists. He was disliked and mistrusted not only by Wagner, Bruckner, and their followers, but by nativists, anti-semites, and conservatives. Hanslick was, however, sympathetic to young composers and late in life took a benignly supportive stance toward the young Gustav Mahler.*

This excerpt is a complete translation of "Erinnerungen und Briefe," in Am Ende des Jahrhunderts [1895–1899]: Musikalische Kritiken und Schilderungen. *Die Moderne Oper, part VIII (2nd ed. Berlin, 1899), pp. 372–409.*

I

Friends and admirers of our dear master are constantly importuning me not to withhold a collection of his letters from the general public and from the loving interest of those who stood closer to him. Often the collection of Billroth letters is mentioned, whose incalculable significance, not only for his friends, has been demonstrated by the extraordinary success of a third edition.[1] The letters from Billroth to Brahms that are published in this selection could not but increase the demand for the answers of the latter. Unfortunately the two sides are unequal. United in deeply felt friendship and mutual admiration, the two men were fundamentally different in many things, and specifically in their correspondence. For Billroth's open, communicative spirit, letter-writing was a need; for Brahms it was a burden. When Billroth came home late at night after a productive or socially active day, he lit his lamp and wrote until midnight—confiding, often quite voluminous letters about the impressions that the concert or play he had just seen, the latest book or the newest acquaintance had made on him. In this way he seemed to enjoy his pleasure all over again, and as with his joys, so also with his trials, which he shared willingly with us.

Not so Brahms. Often, when I entered his apartment to find him at his desk, he would point with a heavy sigh or an ill-tempered curse to a stack of letters: "I am supposed to answer all that!" On occasion the accursed pile had grown to alarming proportions: business letters from publishers, concert directors, festival committees, interspersed with invitations from Viennese friends and acquaintances, tributes and autograph requests from out-of-towners. Brahms dealt with all of this as curtly as possible; he had attained virtuosity in the art of the extremely brief response. Where it was not a complete breach of etiquette, he used postcards, whose format considerately cut off any possibility of more extensive description. He wrote very fast and always used goose quills, in order not to be held up in his rush by a hard steel nib. The place and date are lacking on almost all of his letters; for a signature he made do with the abbreviation J. Br. His distaste for signing his full name grew stronger along with his worry that his letters might be snapped up and sold by autograph collectors.

Brahms had had an unfortunate experience. In a Berlin auction catalogue, among other autographs that were offered for sale, stood a "detailed letter from Johannes Brahms to his father." Horrified to see his most intimate family relationships and childish outpourings exposed to the curiosity of strangers, he wrote immediately to the bookseller in question; but a friend had gotten there before him, had already acquired the letter for Brahms and sent it to him. After that, Brahms was even more cautious and taciturn in his letters. He avoided confidences concerning his personal relationships, especially his youth, even in oral, and all the more in written communications. Judgments on modern musical trends or living composers—in a word, those things that would be of greatest interest to us—are only very rarely found in his letters, and then only in bare outlines. That with every passing year he was sought after more annoyingly by autograph hunters can be imagined. Brahms took care of this piece of business alla breve too: five lines for notes tossed off unevenly, a theme of two or at most three bars, and his signature. Period.

Once, however, there was a case of an autograph that went far beyond this easy model; a formal letter that was intended for publication. The music writer La Mara (Fräulein Marie Lipsius in Leipzig), to whom we are indebted for numerous interesting publications, asked Brahms for his permission to reprint in a volume of musicians' letters several missives of his that had found their way into her hands. The courteous request of this lady, with whom he was personally acquainted, seemed to upset him greatly, as the following letter to me of May 1885 shows:

Dearest friend! The enclosed two letters will make the situation clear to you. Impractical as always, I recently did not wait for your card, but gave Dr. Fellinger, who was visiting me, a letter addressed to you and the unsealed one addressed to Lipsius—with my instructions to mail the latter in case he did not have a chance to show it to you in Vienna. But Mrs. Fellinger copied the letter. Thus I can send it to you after the fact and ask you for a favor. Read it and tell me whether it is foolishness or contains same! I consider myself capable of all kinds of things in this regard—but I would be happy to hold my tongue! I can very well write another one in retrospect, or make changes in this one: so, I ask for your opinion!

Give Simrock my best regards, and [tell him] I am writing to him either yesterday or tomorrow! But the devil take it, if one is plagued like this with letters from and to Miss Lipsius, then the already scant desire to write letters is entirely for the birds.

So, you, too, forgive the peevish letter—but this business annoys me. My heartfelt greetings; live as well, contentedly, and happily as you deserve.

Cordially, your J. Brahms.

For further explication I permit myself to append Brahms's letter to Fräulein Lipsius, from the *Musikerbriefe* which she later published:[2]

2

Vienna, May 27, 1885

Dear Fräulein!

Indeed I have the temerity to ask you to leave the letters in question unpublished. I know and admit that I never write otherwise than reluctantly, hurriedly, and carelessly, but I am ashamed when an example like yours comes to my attention. It takes a kind of courage to write to an unknown, educated, well-intentioned man as carelessly as I did in this case. But even admitting that such letters get printed, to give one's express approval to that—that would be something else than courage! If you will permit me to state expressly here that no one can do me less of a favor than to print letters of mine—nevertheless I will be glad to make an exception for this one. You can include it in your book all the more easily since your readers will learn from it that not you, but I have been careful not to draw from the intended inclusion of my letters any conclusion as to the content and value of the remainder of your book.

There are, as I know not only from Schiller and Goethe but also from the most enjoyable personal experience, plenty of people who write letters gladly and well. But then there are also people like me, and their letters, if the writer otherwise deserves it, should be read and interpreted with indulgence and great care. For example, it pleases me to save a letter from Beethoven as a memento; but I can only be horrified when I imagine all the things such a letter may be taken to mean and explain!

I feel similarly about the posthumous works of a musician. How eagerly I have always tracked down such traces, studied and copied them many times. For example, how dear to me, in the cases of Haydn and Franz Schubert, were these countless, superfluous proofs of their diligence and genius. I have always wished that such valuable and instructive treasures would be copied for larger libraries, so that they would be available for the person who is seriously interested in them. I do not wish to elaborate on the very different sentiments with which I see these beloved treasures in print — or myself work to ensure that this is done, at least, in an orderly fashion! It is unbelievable how in this case and that things get misunderstood and misinterpreted, and whether such publication is necessary, good, or superfluous and even harmful — I don't know!

Taking into account the risk that you will find the beginning of this epistle to be vain hypocrisy, I remain your respectful, devoted

J. Brahms.

How characteristic, how substantive this letter is in all its brevity. It proves that Brahms lacked only the desire, not the talent for writing. Once he saw himself compelled, in place of his precious postcard, to get out a clean sheet of stationery and exercise some care in style and expression, he could write masterfully — clearly, concisely, not at a loss for any sharply descriptive term. Since for him thoughts were there in order to be kept silent or to be expressed in musical tones, he mistrusted his ability to express them in firm literary form. And yet he was compelled to express his written thanks, now for a high honor, now for the election to an academy — for Brahms nothing could be more unpleasant! In such cases it was his custom to come grumbling to me with his draft. Not only did I not want to alter a word, but I was forced to admire many a sentence for its precise expression and sculpted form. Brahms always instinctively found the right medium between excessively humble modesty and proud self-confidence. Once he wanted to sweeten the onerous task by at least making a joke. He walked in with an entirely unaccustomed, mysteriously pleased expression and whispered that he had written something quite new and wanted to show it to me — not a soul had seen it yet. After he had kept me dangling for some time in the most delighted anticipation, he cautiously pulled out his draft of an acknowledgment letter (if I am not mistaken, for the Order of Maximilian) and gloated over my disappointment.

It is regrettable that Brahms was only very rarely and reluctantly induced to respond by letter to musical questions. His profound musicological and technical knowledge, combined with such clear, sharp judgment, could have provided a treasure trove of information, whether he was speaking about his own projects and compositions or those of others. Brahms was capable, in private conversation, of commenting on musical matters with such fluidity and liveliness, especially if they were of current interest — matters of the Musikverein, programs of our larger concerts, etc. With pen in hand he became monosyllabic. As for speaking about his own compositions or plans, his own reticence held him back all his life. Just as sensitive was the response of his modesty to praise from others. His unwillingness to pass on flattering letters that had been sent to him was very difficult to overcome. The request by the widow of Hans von Bülow that Brahms entrust to her, for purposes of publication, several letters of her husband's caused Brahms great uneasiness, for Bülow's letters overflowed with enthusiasm and devotion. Nevertheless, Brahms could not give Mrs. Marie von Bülow a negative answer. So he sought out from among his large correspondence with Bülow five or six insignificant notes, in which nothing was discussed but concert programs, apartment furnishings, and other practical matters, and brought them to me. I declared that it was an injustice to Bülow to attempt to represent this brilliant virtuoso of letter-writing, as well, in a published collection, by means of such trivial and uninteresting scraps. Brahms thanked me sincerely for my plainspoken veto and decided, with a heavy heart, to deliver more extensive and substantive letters of Bülow's to his widow.

On the occasion of his adaptation of German folksongs, Brahms sent a number of letters with a significant musical content to Professor Spitta in Berlin. Another extensive and content-rich letter was occasioned by youthful compositions of Beethoven's, with which he had become acquainted through me—the Cantata on the Death of Emperor Joseph II and the Cantata on the Accession of Emperor Leopold II.[3] Both works had never been printed and were thought to be lost. A   3
musically educated businessman, Herr Friedman, had purchased the two scores, copied in a clear hand, from a second-hand dealer in Leipzig and sent them to me to examine. I was just about to leave for Karlsbad and sent the cantatas, after leafing through them hurriedly, to Brahms, who wrote me the following letter about them in May 1884:

Dear friend! You departed and left me a treasure, without having looked at it yourself. I must write you a few words of thanks on the subject so that you will have an idea what the treasure signifies. For it is quite beyond doubt that with this the two cantatas have been found which Beethoven wrote in Bonn on the death of Joseph II and the accession to the throne of Leopold II. In other words, two important works for chorus and orchestra from a time to which until now we could not ascribe any compositions of significance. If it were not for the historical dates (1790), we would certainly guess at a later period—but only because we would know nothing of this earlier time! But even if there were no name on the title, one could guess no other author—it is all Beethoven through and through! There is the beautiful and noble pathos, the grandeur of the feelings and fantasy, the power, yes even violence of expression. And then there is the voice-leading, declamation, and in these last two areas all the peculiarities that we can observe and ponder in his later works.

First, I am naturally interested in the Cantata on Joseph II's Death. On this subject there can be no "occasional music"! If we were to celebrate today that unforgotten man, who is still not replaced, we would do so as warmly as Beethoven and everyone else did at that time. And for Beethoven it is not occasional music either, when one considers that the artist never stops developing artistically, nor struggling, and that one is probably more likely to

observe this in a younger artist than in a master. The first lament is already entirely Himself. You would not doubt it at any note or at any word. A recitative follows, extremely lively: "Ein Ungeheuer, sein Name Fanatismus, stieg aus den Tiefen der Hölle ..." [A monster, his name fanaticism, climbed out of the depths of hell ...]. (In an aria he is trodden to death by Joseph.) I cannot help myself: at this point it is a particular pleasure for me to think back to that time and—as the strong words indicate—to the way the whole world realized what it had lost in Joseph. But the young Beethoven also knew what great things he had to say, and said them loud, as is appropriate, in a powerful prelude. And now, to the words "Da stiegen die Menschen ans Licht" [Then mankind ascended toward the light], comes the magnificent F-major movement from the finale of Fidelio.[4] There, as here, the touching,   4
beautiful melody is given to the oboe. (Admittedly it doesn't agree with the vocal part, or only with great difficulty.) We have many examples of the way our master used his ideas a second time in a different place. Here I find it especially pleasing. How deeply Beethoven must have felt the melody in the cantata (in other words the meaning of the words)—as deeply and beautifully as he did later when he sang the love of a woman—and of liberation—to its end. After more recitative in arias, a repeat of the first chorus closes the work; but I don't want to describe it further; nor, in any case, the second cantata. For here the music itself is more interesting than any particulars concerning Beethoven.

But now, dear friend, in my thoughts I already hear you asking when the cantatas will be performed, and when they will be printed?[5] And here my joy is at an end. Printing has   5
become so much the fashion, especially the printing of things that have no claim to it. You know my longstanding fond wish that the so-called complete works of our masters—even in the case of their secondary, but certainly in the case of their most important works—should not be printed all too completely, but—and here really comprehensively, should rather be incorporated in good copies into the larger libraries. You know how eagerly I have sought, at all times, to get to know their unpublished works. However, to possess everything of many a beloved master in print is more than I wish for. I cannot find it right and proper for amateurs and young artists to be seduced into filling their rooms and their brains with all the "complete works" and thus confusing their judgment.

The honor of a complete edition has not yet fallen to our Haydn.[6] And a really complete   6
edition of his works would be as impossible as it would be impractical; but perhaps—and how desirable, in comparison—a selection copied from among them, and this in multiple copies, in our public libraries. How little, in comparison, is done regarding new editions of various works whose study and transmission would be desirable. So, for example, older vocal music of all sorts. You will object that they are not needed, either—but they should be and they will be more and more, without a doubt. Here sacrifices would be quite in order and would certainly be worthwhile in every respect.

But these are vast themes, I won't fantasize more variations on them for you; they develop all too exclusively from a minor key, and I know very well that the same are quite possible and necessary in major.

But come soon and share the very special feeling and pleasure of being the only person in the world besides myself to know these deeds of a hero.

Cordially your   Johannes Brahms.

II

Brahms, whose works were composed in large part (and probably the most beautiful part) in Austria, by no means limited himself to his own musical creation. He also developed a varied practical activity that richly benefited the arts in Austria. An almost negligibly tiny part in all this was played by instruction. This is the activity, even if it is only practiced to a modest extent, that disturbs the musician most sensitively in the sphere of his own musical thought, and therefore it seems to be qualitatively the most unwelcome. As far as I know, the well-regarded concert singer and voice teacher Frau Neuda-Bernstein is the only talent in Vienna who can boast of having enjoyed piano lessons with Brahms.[7] In his capacity as a member of   7 the board of directors of the Gesellschaft der Musikfreunde, which enjoyed an inestimable advantage as a result of having such a great authority in its midst, Brahms worked zealously for the promotion of musical education in its broadest extent. Brahms was able to have a strong influence on the programs of the concerts of the society, and also on the naming of professors at the conservatory, as well as artistic directors. He occupied a position as conductor in Vienna on two occasions, each time only for a short period: with the Singakademie (1863) and the concerts of the Gesellschaft (1872–74).

Another musical office that Brahms occupied, not in the public eye, but influentially and with quiet seriousness, was his membership of more than twenty years on the Commission for the Conferring of Artists' Scholarships [Kommission für Erteilung von Künstler-Stipendien]. In 1863, the Ministry of Education had given life to this new institution whose activity consisted in the awarding of annual scholarships to deserving and talented artists who have already emerged as creators of independent works. As a result of this measure, a separate, permanent budget was created for the first time, dedicated by the state to the education and support of individual artists. Three members of the commission were named in each of the three sections (poetry, visual arts, music), and together they evaluated and judged the requests that had been submitted. The section on music was entrusted to me, and thirty-four years later it still rests in my hands. At first Esser and Herbeck were my colleagues; later Brahms took Esser's place, and Goldmark Herbeck's.[8] Unfor-   8 tunately Goldmark, on account of his extended stay in Gmunden, was only rarely in a position to participate in the evaluation of the compositions that had been submitted. Therefore the business at hand was almost always dispatched only by me and Brahms. In general, I would go over the submissions, which were usually very numerous, alone, discard whatever was not in accordance with the guidelines or was unquestionably bad, and then consult with Brahms about the rest. If there were only a few submissions that invited more serious consideration, I would make myself comfortable on the sofa with a cigar and read the pieces that had been sent in. In this I had frequent occasion to admire Brahms's rapid comprehension and the accuracy of his judgments. When there was a larger quantity of compositions that demanded more exact evaluation and mutual consideration, then I would send them with my recommendation to Brahms, from whom I would receive the whole, often very weighty package back complete with his written comments. These were generally kept very short—for his suggestions almost always corresponded to mine—but usually peppered with satirical remarks about this or that talentless supplicant.

Thus Brahms was untiring in his efforts to serve his adoptive fatherland Austria with word and deed in affairs of music pedagogy. In the summer of 1889, when Brahms received the Austrian Order of Leopold at the request of the Minister of Education Dr. von Gautsch, there was a general feeling of happiness and gratification. When I wrote to congratulate Brahms (with a certain amount of feigned surprise) on receiving this distinction, I received the following answer from him:

Ischl, 1889

Dear friend! A thousand thanks for news of you, which I had been looking forward to quite eagerly. I hope your plans remain as they are, or become even more favorable once you get to Ischl.

What surprised and astonished me was your astonishment and surprise about my medal and the fact that the people "in high places had such a clever idea." The latter thought had never crossed my mind at all, when I wondered to whom I might actually owe the medal. There are, after all, very complicated machines at work in the state; this time I believed you, above all, to be in complicity and one of the instigators. Otherwise I am looking about myself in a futile effort to figure out who might have suggested and promoted it. In general, there is more to it than mere artistic attainment, and as far as all this "more" is concerned—whatever name it may go by—I have precious little to show for myself.

This time, for the first time, I was at least well-behaved afterwards, as I answered the many telegrams, letters, and cards! I had such a friendly impression that the Austrians as such were happy about it that I necessarily had to thank them politely. I would like to ask you in all earnestness to tell me how I should comport myself toward those "high places." May I at least be permitted to wait until after the official notification? Should I write to the Ministry of Education, or to His Majesty directly? Or should I request an audience?

You will find me here until—I must finally leave for the music festival in Hamburg! I must, for my Honorary Citizen adventure was entirely too lovely and agreeable, with

everything that came along with it.[9] *However, I am alarmed to see my telegram to the mayor*   9
in print! It sounds altogether foolish, "the greatest beauty, which can only come from human
beings"—as if apart from that I had been thinking of eternal salvation! But our dear Lord did
not occur to me at all in that connection, I was only thinking in passing about the so-called
gods and the fact that when a pretty melody occurs to me it is far preferable in my mind than
an Order of Leopold, and if they should grant me a successful symphony, it is dearer to me
than all honorary citizenships. With cordial greetings; come soon!

III

Before he became a regular summer guest at Ischl, Brahms's custom had been to
spend his summer vacation alternately in Baden-Baden, Wiesbaden, Thun (in
Switzerland), and a few times in Pörtschach and Mürzzuschlag. From all these
places I received greetings from him; letters or notes, which without claim to any
significant content still contained one or the other interesting piece of personal
information, striking expression, or lovable trait. I have the sense, and submit
myself willingly to it, that after any great loss our hearts hold fast to even the most
modest tokens of memory. In the case of the following letters from the 60s and 70s,
I was thinking first of Brahms's special friends and admirers. But where didn't he
have those!

The first letter refers to Brahms's selection as director of the Vienna Singakademie
in the year 1863. The invitation reached him in Hamburg and found him not
entirely decided to accept it. "It is," he wrote to the head of the association, "a
particular kind of decision that entails giving up one's freedom for the first time.
However, whatever comes from Vienna sounds twice as beautiful to a musician,
and whatever calls him there, tempts twice as strongly."

To me he wrote in the summer of 1863 on that subject:

My dear friend! You will be surprised that the most delighted and grateful reply does not
arrive more rapidly than your own and other friendly letters reach me. But I feel like someone
who is praised undeservedly and would prefer to hide for awhile. I, who after receiving the
telegraphed dispatch (from F., who always has to have the upbeat!) firmly desired to be
satisfied to have received such an honorific offer and not to tempt the gods further. But now I
shall accept it all the more certainly, and come. And since for my part there is no remaining
question except whether I have the courage to say "yes," why, it shall come to pass. If I had
declined, my reasons would only have seemed strange to the Academy and to you Viennese in
general. Here I must also send you my most sincere thanks for your book On the Beautiful
in Music,[10] *to which I owe many hours of enjoyment, of clarification, indeed literally of*   10
relief. Every page invites one to build further on what has been said, and since in doing so, as
you have said, the motives are the main thing, one always owes you double the pleasure. But
for the person who understands his art in this manner, there are things to be done everywhere

in our art and science, and I will wish we might soon be blessed with such excellent instruction on other subjects. For today, with cordial greetings and thanks, your

Joh. Br.

* * *

The following letter from August 1866 refers to the Waltzes for Four Hands, op. 39, which were dedicated to me.

Just now, writing the title of the four-hand waltzes, which are to appear shortly, your name occurred to me quite of its own volition. I don't know, I was thinking of Vienna, of the pretty girls with whom you play four-hands, of you yourself, the lover of all that, the good friend and what not. In short, I feel the necessity of dedicating it to you. If it is agreeable to you that it should remain thus, then I thank you most sincerely; but if for some reason you do not wish it, then express yourself on the subject and the printer will receive the counter-command. It consists of two volumes of innocent little waltzes in Schubertian form. If you don't want them and would rather see your name on a proper piece with four movements, "your wish is my command." In the next few days I am leaving for Switzerland. Shall I complain to you about the fact that I was not in Vienna last winter? My arrival next year can express it better. In considerable haste and old friendship your

Joh. Br.

* * *

Hermann Goetz, the composer of the *Taming of the Shrew,* had left behind at his death a great opera, *Francesca di [sic] Rimini,* which was performed for the first time on 30 September 1887, in Mannheim, as completed by Ernst Franck. Concerning the quite widespread belief that Brahms had a hand in this completion, the latter wrote me from Baden-Baden in October 1877:

Dearest friend! In the N. Fr. Presse [Neue Freie Presse] *it says that I completed the* Francesca di Rimini. *This is not true; Franck orchestrated the overture and the third act alone, following the sketches; I merely looked his work over and was enormously pleased at its lovely seriousness and diligence, which I would not have thought him capable of. On the occasion of the* Taming of the Shrew, *by the way, he demonstrated the same loving devotion, then as now with the best of results. He can really not be praised enough for what he has done for Goetz (his idol),[11] and if you had known that excellent man and most estimable artist, you would have had the most intense joy over little Franck, to whom alone Goetz owes a peaceful death and his Francesca owes her life.*

11

But the notice to which you refer is found in many papers; I, however, do not like to write. Wouldn't you like to devote a couple of words to this? I can only excuse the fact that I let it go for so long because if the opposite were the case I would most assuredly remain silent.... Actually I had written so small because I wanted to chat with you quite unhurriedly, but since then the pen has lain idle for hours. I have been spoiled for letter-writing. I hope to enjoy a few fine fall days here in Liechtenthal (near Baden-Baden). But it won't last long and then the Karlsgasse and the others will reclaim me. Dessoff comes by often and is very pleased—even when he sees new notes of mine. But now transmit my best greetings to your own and other households! Until our next happy reunion!

*   *   *

A letter from Pörtschach from September 1878 refers to the Hamburg Music Festival with which the anniversary of the Philharmonische Gesellschaft in that city was to be celebrated.[12] I had received an invitation to it, along with the urgent request to give the committee word as to whether Brahms, from whom no answer had been received, could definitely be expected in Hamburg. Brahms responded to my inquiry as follows:

12

Pörtschach am See, September 1878

You have preached the doctrine of deportment to me in public once before; I do not wish that it should happen again through no fault of my own, and therefore I am telling you that it is the fault of the Hamburgers if I do not appear at their festival. I have no occasion to display good breeding and gratitude; on the contrary, a certain amount of incivility would be appropriate, if I had the time and inclination to ruin my mood with it. But now I won't spoil yours either by detailed descriptions and will therefore say only that despite an inquiry there has been no mention of any honorarium or other remuneration. This is a highly questionable valuation of me, poor composer, and I lose every right, for example, to sit next to your wife at the feast table! So I beg this time for consideration toward my already damaged reputation as a well-bred fellow. In the matter of the symphony I ask for no special consideration, but I fear that if the conducting is not entrusted to Joachim, as I wish, there will be a miserable performance. Now, the dinners in Hamburg are good, the symphony has a propitious length—you can dream yourself back to Vienna while all this is going on! I am thinking of going to Vienna quite soon, but I have again been excellently pleased in Pörtschach. With cordial greetings for you and your wife.

Your J. Br.

*   *   *

In spite of this very dubious reply, Brahms came to the festival after all, and it went off brilliantly and enjoyably. Clara Schumann, at that time already sixty years old, played Mozart's Concerto in D Minor with perfect mastery and youthful fire. The following evening [28 September] brought Brahms's Second Symphony, which he directed himself after a welcome that included an orchestral flourish and a laurel wreath. Joachim played the first violin. After the symphony, the ladies from the chorus and the first few rows of seats in the audience threw Brahms their bouquets. He stood there, as it says in his lullaby, "covered with roses, trimmed with carnations." During the outing to Blankenese many interesting and famous artists found themselves on the deck of the steamer in animated conversation: Brahms, Ferdinand Hiller, Niels Gade, Friedrich von Flotow, Theodor Kirchner, J. [*recte* Karl] Reinthaler, and others.

* * *

In May of 1880 I had received the newest volume of songs (op. 84) in Karlsbad and written to him, quite captivated by the *Vergebliches Ständchen* (no. 4). He responded from Ischl:

I am full of pleasure as I thank you for your letter, for it was really a very special one for me, and I am in an extremely good humor as a result of the good-humored correspondence! In my position, one can't write a great N.B. after something just because one thinks one is in a position to do so, but it is the most pleasant form of flattery when someone else does.

And this time you have hit my bullseye! For this one song I would give up all the others and the W-album in the bargain.[13] But from you the confirmation is of immensely serious value to me! I have known for a long time that your excellent sniffer doesn't miss any really excellent morsel (this is more annoying when we are eating oysters).   13

With dedications I am in a bad spot. I owe so many, more or less, that I hesitate to begin paying them back. I must think up a special method of proceeding, perhaps by publishing a thematic catalogue in which a fancy name appears next to every piece?! Talk that over with Simrock some time. —

It would be very nice if you would come to Ischl; it is really splendid here and taking walks extremely pleasurable.

Whether I am actually going to Bayreuth? Bülow, who is going there in August with his bride, is also trying to seduce me or rather asks me whether I would like to join them.[14] If you should happen to be about to throw away a Bayreuth brochure in a fit of annoyance, then put a postal wrapper around it instead and send it here; for us such things are exotic and interesting.   14

Please give my best regards to Simrock, Dvořák, and even better ones to your singer. And you yourself are warmly thanked, again, for your friendly words.

* * *

In Karlsbad I had thanked Brahms cordially for the third and fourth volumes of his Hungarian Dances for four hands, which he has played there so often with my wife. In these two volumes, Brahms really works little miracles of harmonization and rhythm, which raise the art of the "arranger" far above that of the anonymous "singer" of these simple folk melodies. One should give the same melodic raw material to another composer, and see what he or she would make of it! By the way, two of these pieces are entirely Brahms's own invention, without his finding that important enough to boast about.[15] Brahms wrote back to me in Ischl: 15

I am so pleased about your pleased and nice words that I must let you know immediately. You know, the things give me pleasure myself, for once. How happy I am if others feel the same way and are kind enough not to make a secret of it! With best greetings to your second half and your second pair of hands cordially your J. Brahms.

IV

Brahms's general education was much more comprehensive and deep than one might think on superficial acquaintance with him. The things that had been denied him through the hardships and deprivations of his youth he later made up with persistent energy. An admirably quick gift of comprehension and an equally extraordinary, never-failing memory supported him in his studies. Often one would only discover years later, after some cue gave him the necessary impetus, how well versed he was in literary matters. It never occurred to him to flaunt his wide reading; he preferred to hide it. The absolute opposite of Liszt, who constantly tosses around Dante, Shakespeare, Goethe, Michelangelo, and Albrecht Dürer in his musical essays, along with Plato, Spinoza, Kant, and Hegel, of whom he himself has scarcely read a single chapter. Perfectly obnoxious, in Brahms's eyes, were those newest critics who quote Schopenhauer and Nietzsche the minute they take up a new opera or symphony.

How intimately Brahms knew our classical literature, how deeply he had absorbed the masterworks. Some of his literary sympathies were not entirely comprehensible to me, for example the fact that he could read Jean Paul over and over again, right into his old age. The same was true of the comic novels of Swift and Fielding, the latter in German translation. He had no talent for foreign languages and never learned enough French for even the most minimal household use. He approached the latest literature with a very hesitant selectivity. The trouble with the new books is undoubtedly the fact that they prevent us from re-reading the old ones. The realistic products of our modernists incited Brahms's dislike; but he read the novellas of Gottfried Keller and the poems of his friend J. V. Widmann in Bern with never-failing pleasure.

Brahms even followed politics—that otherwise avoided and despised Cinderella subject for artists—attentively. In one of his letters I even find passionate involvement with a particularly Austrian incident. In June 1883 he writes to me from Wiesbaden:

Dearest friend! I must shout out my hurrah to someone, my happy, firm hurrah to the professors in respect of your letter to Rector Maasen.[16] *One must be as much an Austrian as*   16
I am, love the Austrians as much as I do, to feel sad every day I read the newspaper, and then suddenly, as now, to feel such a deep pleasure. Unfortunately, I regularly read only the Fremden-Blatt, *which a princess-friend of mine receives here and sends to me. I am still grateful to Lamezan for the box on the ear he gave the paper this winter. If I could only get the confiscated issues, I would subscribe to the* Neue Freie Presse!
And friend Billroth still doesn't want to become a Wagnerian? What is he waiting so long for; sooner or later he will have to do it.

Brahms had become a good Austrian and at the same time remained a faithful Reichs-German. He read the historical works of Sybel and Treitschke, and finally Oncken's book about Kaiser Wilhelm, with the warmest sympathy and interest.[17]   17
He had a passionate admiration for Bismarck, was pleased to receive presents of each of his portraits, loved his speeches, and was familiar with everything that had been written about the Iron Chancellor. Three weeks before his demise, when the treacherous illness had robbed him of all pleasure in living, he complained to his friend Herr Arthur Faber that he could no longer retain what he had read. "I only want to read about Bismarck; send me the book by Busch, *Bismarck and His Men.*"[18]   18
Rodenberg's *Deutsche Rundschau* counted him among its most appreciative readers.

Among modern painters there were two in particular whom Brahms held in high esteem: the old master Adolph Menzel and Max Klinger, who had achieved fame in our days. The affection was returned in both cases. Menzel, who despite his advanced age always remained fresh and agile, visited Brahms repeatedly in Vienna, and celebrated him with exceptional attention in Berlin. Klinger was inspired by Brahms's music to create many of his most notable works. After receiving Klinger's most recent illustrated book *Fantasies,*[19] Brahms immediately wrote to me: 19

Dear friend! Just to look at the newest Brahms-Fantasy is more pleasure than to listen to the previous ten![20] *But since I cannot very well bring them to you, I would like to ask you to pay*   20
a call on me—and to bring some time, for it takes at least as long as the above-cited ten or other earlier ones.

As much as the brilliant boldness of Klinger's illustrations impressed me, I was not able to share Brahms's rapture in every case; least of all at the cover illustrations of the songs that were published by Simrock.[21] Quite incompetent to give an expert   21 opinion, I was nevertheless unable to conceal my feeling that here the one-sidedly realistic and violently characterizing manner pushed beauty too much into the background, even damaged it without compelling necessity. I could not comprehend why, for example, Homer had to be portrayed as a repellently ugly old man with tufts of white hair all over his stark naked, miserable body—or why the charming melody of one of Brahms's songs is reflected in Klinger's work not as the figure of a lovely girl, but rather as a coarse and ordinary one. "You are not wrong," Brahms replied," but all that does not bother me—it is a work of genius." I had to think of Eitelberger,[22] who in a mood of wild opposition once cried, "That damned thing beauty—it is responsible for all the problems of painting!"

Brahms expressed his gratitude and admiration for Max Klinger by dedicating to him the *Vier ernste Gesänge,* op. 121. From Brahms, who was always remarkably sparing with his dedications, and in recent years almost entirely avoided them, this dedication meant more than a little. It became all the more significant since the *Vier ernste Gesänge* remained his very last work.[23] Yes, these not merely serious, but inconsolable strains of death and decay were a prelude to Brahms's departure from this life, although he did not suspect it. Since then Herr Sistermans has performed them as a kind of requiem for the master himself in almost all German cities, one after the other, which added a memorial meeting for Brahms to their concerts or music festivals. Certainly these *Vier ernste Gesänge* had always been perceived and interpreted as a certain premonition of his own death, although Brahms was still in good health when he wrote them. I thought in my own mind that they had an immediate connection to the death of Clara Schumann, which left him deeply shaken. But today I must declare this supposition to be erroneous. Brahms's intimate friend Herr Alwin V. Beckerath, one of the most well-informed supporters of music in the Rhineland, writes to me from Crefeld on this subject:

Brahms came (in May 1896) directly from Bonn, from Frau Schumann's funeral, to the country home of my brother-in-law Weyermann in Honef, where we were celebrating a small private chamber music festival together with Barth from Hamburg and a few musicians from Meiningen. On the first day Brahms was very agitated, but the beautiful, still country and the comfort of the household soon began to do him good, and instead of one day, as he had originally planned, he stayed five. On the second day he told Barth that he had something new, and would like to show it to us some time in a quiet moment. We accompanied him with pounding hearts to a remote room, where there stood an upright piano, and there he performed the Vier ernste Gesänge *for us, from the manuscript. "I wrote these for myself for my birthday," he said. From this you see that these compositions do not stand in any causal relationship to Clara Schumann's death. Besides the* Vier Gesänge, *he also brought new organ pieces* [op. 122]. *We were all deeply moved and a sorrowful premonition filled my heart—unfortunately it proved to be right.*

Toward the end of his life Brahms had to overcome two painful losses in quick succession: in February 1894 Billroth died, in May 1896, Clara Schumann. It was in perfect accord with his strong, solid, and taciturn nature that he wanted to speak and hear as little as possible about it. As soon as he learned of Billroth's death, he came to me full of sympathy, but admitted that he felt something like a "feeling of liberation" on account of the fact that he no longer had to witness the sad withering-away of our friend, that giant of intellect and physical strength. He expresses this later, too (from Ischl), in a few lines to me that refer to my *Billroth Recollections*, which were published in the *Neue Freie Presse:*

Let me thank you very cordially for the sincere joy which your Billroth essays have given me. This is a sacrificial offering of rare beauty and a sign of friendship of the sort that can only be given by a good man. Even people who were not so close to him will read your words with delight; doubly so everyone to whom Billroth was dear.

As for me, let me confess why they did me particular good: they have freed me from the memory of the sick Billroth; not until now have I been freed from the painful feeling and memory of the last years and think and love the man as I knew him earlier and as you have sketched him so lovingly . . .[24]

24

Billroth and Brahms were joined in the most intimate personal friendship; Billroth, in addition, felt an enthusiastic admiration for Brahms's compositions. Just as he never tired of playing these through with me in four-hand versions, so also he never failed, after the premiere performance of any new Brahms piece, to write to me about the impression he had received. I had spoken to Brahms once about these so detailed, beautiful musical letters of Billroth's, and Brahms, otherwise so uncurious and even less eager for praise, expressed the wish to see something of these unpublished critiques written in the spirit of friendship. I quickly gathered up three or four of Billroth's letters and sent them to Brahms. Just a moment too late, I was dismayed to remember vaguely that in one of these letters there was a cutting remark about Brahms. Billroth, namely, comparing Brahms with Beethoven, made the observation that our friend, along with the great advantages of his model, also shared some of the latter's personal weaknesses; that like Beethoven he was often inconsiderate and painfully harsh toward his friends, and that he could no more rid himself completely of the effects of his neglected upbringing than Beethoven could. I was not only perfectly miserable that I had acted so carelessly toward my two best friends, but had to fear, in the balance, that Brahms, in one of his sarcastic moods, might tease and embarrass Billroth about his remark. Brahms rescued me promptly from my distressing state. His answer to my letter of apology is as remarkable and straightforward as it is revealing about his character:

*Dear friend! You need not worry yourself in the slightest. I barely read the letter from
Billroth, stuck it back in its envelope, and only shook my head quietly. I shouldn't mention
anything to him about it—oh, dear friend, unfortunately that is quite automatically how these
things go with me! The fact that even old acquaintances and friends think one to be
something quite different than what one is (or, in their eyes, pretends to be) is an old
experience of mine. I know that earlier I would have kept silent in such a case, dismayed and
taken aback—nowadays I am long since calm and take it as a matter of course. To you, good
and kind-hearted man, that will seem hard or bitter—but I hope that I have not strayed too
far from Goethe's dictum: "Selig, wer sich vor der Welt/Ohne Haß verschließt"* [Blissful is
the man who can shut himself off from the world without hatred].[25]   25

Very cordially your

J. Brahms

The two last letters of Brahms that I possess have a long history. They concern
several letters of Robert Schumann (from Endenich sanatorium, near Bonn) to his
wife and to Brahms. The latter, who knew of my enthusiastic veneration for
Schumann, the musician and the man, had sent me the letters to make copies of
them more than twenty years earlier. I would have liked very much to see them
printed, these touching communications, which show us the ailing Schumann in a
kind of mild and transfiguring light. He therefore asked Clara for her permission.
She gave it, by letter, after some hesitation. But later, with the anxiousness that was
peculiar to her, took it back again. Since neither Brahms nor I had the slightest wish
to oppose the sentiments of the venerated woman, we did not speak further about
this matter. Not until after Clara's death did our conversation turn to it again; in a
letter to Brahms I expressed the wish that these last utterances of Schumann's might
not be be lost to his faithful congregation. Brahms initially responded to my
presentation with the following note (July 1896 from Ischl):

*With my whole heart in agreement with you, I am sending this on ahead only because it will
probably become a longish letter that reiterates my yes, and I am also occupied with the
thought of writing to Marie Schumann.—So: until then!*
Very cordially your J.B.

And in fact the "longish letter" (it reached me at the end of July in Heringsdorf) did
not keep me waiting for long. It reads:

*Dearest friend! Everything that you write is accurate and true and of concern to both of us. So
I shall only say briefly that a portrait of Robert Schumann in Endenich from your pen was
always my fervent wish. Like you, I had Clara's consent. Then came N.N.'s involvement and
her change of heart. It affected me more severely than it did you—but for your sake, which I
tried, like other things of this sort, to get over in silence.*

Confidential dealings with women are difficult—the more difficult, the more serious and confidential the matters at hand. In this case one must take into account as a mitigating factor the fact that Frau Schumann did not see her husband at that time and it is understandable that she did not like to hear mention made of the sick man. Now Maria is in possession of the entire written estate and may dispose of it. Again I ask you to consider how difficult her situation or that of the three sisters is—toward such a possession!

I do not believe they will do anything without asking me for advice; but whether they will do anything on my advice, I do not know. In any case I would like to present our case to Maria and ask her to entrust us with the remaining material (relating to Endenich), or initially to give her friendly assent for you to use whatever is now in your hands.

Now it is my urgent wish that you should not hurry with the publication *of your work. For it is possible that we may receive everything relating to this question, and then: I am the only one who came together often with Schumann during that time, and you are the only one to whom, rather than to my own pen, I should like to entrust my memories. Nothing remarkable will come of them, but still—shouldn't we spend a few quiet hours on it?*

In earnest friendship your

> *J. Brahms*

One can see that the matter weighed on his mind. He reports to me on the same matter in early September 1896 from Karlsbad with the following lines:

I would have sent the enclosed letter from Marie Schumann to you long ago, if I had been certain of your address. I had sent your letter to Marie at that time and asked her to entrust us with additional material having to do with Endenich. I referred in a precautionary way to the passage about "us children" by saying: they would probably overlook a certain sensitivity in this matter on your and my part. Women, etc.

Perhaps we may yet find other suitable material in Vienna—if not, we have done our best.

In the letter that Brahms mentions at the outset, Fräulein Marie Schumann answers him in the affirmative (Frankfurt, 17 August): "Do what you feel is right, in my mother's memory, and that will suffice for me." However, she responds to the wish to receive yet other letters of Schumann's with the words: "I must first have read the material through in tranquility myself and gained an overview before I give anything out of my hands. But for that *several years* will be required."

So it then remained, with only those few letters published which Brahms had communicated to me so many years ago and to which Joachim made a very valuable addition.

*   *   *

One had to have known Brahms for a long time to get through to the golden underlayer[26] of his taciturn being. He was as indefatigable in generous deeds as he was inexhaustible in the art of keeping them a secret. How many young musicians he voluntarily helped with a loan, "payable at some undetermined future time," that he never intended to remember of his own accord! He spared no pains to give moral support, encouragement, or recommendation to aspiring talents. Very different from certain world-famous artists, who are more likely to help out with money than with their patronage, but preferably with neither. Brahms took pleasure at every deserved success of others. It is known how energetically he expedited the general recognition of Dvořák. As honorary president of the Wiener Tonkünstler-verein [Viennese Society of Composers], whose evening receptions he attended regularly and with pleasure, he was a zealous promoter of competitions, especially chamber music competitions, to bring young talents to the fore. When it came to the examination of the anonymous manuscripts that had been submitted, he showed astonishing acuity in guessing, from the overall impression and technical details, who the author was, or at least his school or teacher. Last year Brahms was very interested in an anonymous quartet whose author he was quite unable to identify. Impatiently he waited for the opening of the sealed notice. On it was written the heretofore entirely unknown name: Walter Rabl. He was awarded the prize at Brahms's recommendation; the piece was performed publicly and recommended to Simrock, who immediately published it.[27]

26

27

* * *

Not always courteous in his manners, Brahms nevertheless possessed a pleasing courteousness of the heart. How much he enjoyed it when he could give pleasure to others, especially if it could be surprise! Thus one Sunday morning I found him busily packing several bottles of champagne into a basket. "They are for . . . , whose new orchestra piece is being performed today. When he sits down with his family to dine after the concert, he shall have a pleasant surprise!"

Shortly before his last illness, the wife of an excellent composer who lived in Bohemia visited him. Brahms encouraged her, telling her how advantageous it would be for her husband's career to move to Vienna. "Yes," the woman said, "if only life in Vienna were not so expensive for a large family!"—"If that's all it depends on," replied Brahms, "then take as much of my wealth as you need, without further ado; I myself need very little." The good woman broke out in such intense tears of emotion that she could not respond.

* * *

In Brahms there lived a powerfully developed sense of justice that to strict jurists might perhaps have seemed all too sensitive. A characteristic story, at whose beginning I was present, but whose conclusion I did not learn about until Brahms's very last days, may serve to confirm this. Once at Brahms's apartment I met a pale, interesting-looking woman of about forty, the divorced wife of a retired officer (if I am not mistaken, he lived in Bavaria). This woman, whose nervous loneliness was kindled to flickering life only in the presence of ardent music-playing, was an enthusiastic admirer of Brahms's music and no less of the composer himself. The latter visited her occasionally in her nearby apartment Auf der Wieden, moved more by humane compassion than by personal sympathy.

One day, it may have been twenty-five years ago, Brahms told me that Frau Amalie M. had died and left him some music, attractively bound volumes of Brahms's piano compositions from his first period. Every title page showed, in a delicate hand, the name of the deceased. Brahms offered me these volumes, which I accepted gratefully and still possess. Then he never again spoke of this female admirer. Not until three weeks before his death did the critically-ill Brahms tell his friend Simrock that at that time he had been named by Frau Amalie as the sole heir to her quite considerable fortune. He had felt this disposition to be a severe injustice toward her former husband, had hurried without delay to the notary and renounced the estate in favor of the husband. The latter was informed at once, came to Vienna, visited Brahms and, with thanks, took possession of the estate that had been ceded to him.

Anyone who has become lovingly accustomed to living with Brahms now feels as if our music has lost its backbone. But these insignificant pages are devoted not to his great significance as a musician. They are only intended to contribute to the understanding of the character of the noble, rare man in whom his circle of close friends has lost no less than the musical world has lost in the artist.

Notes

1   *Briefe von Theodor Billroth,* ed. Georg Fischer (1st ed. Hannover and Leipzig, 1895; 3rd ed. 1896). [Ed.]

2   *Musikerbriefe aus fünf Jahrhunderten,* ed. La Mara [Ida Maria Lipsius] (Leipzig, 1886), II, 348-50. [Ed.]

3   WoO 87 and WoO 88. [Ed.]

4   The *sostenuto assai,* where Leonora unlocks Florestan's chains and exclaims, "O Gott, o Gott, welch ein Augenblick!" [Ed.]

5   On Brahms's initiative, the Cantata on the Death of Joseph II had its premiere performance by the Gesellschaft der Musikfreunde in November 1884. [Hanslick's note]

6   A complete Haydn edition was begun by Breitkopf & Härtel in 1907 under the editorship of Brahms's friend Eusebius Mandyczewski, but only reached ten volumes. A new edition from the Haydn-Institut in Cologne began publication in 1958. [Ed.]

7   Probably the same Rosa Bernstein mentioned in Max Kalbeck, *Johannes Brahms* (Berlin, 1904-14), II, 135. [Ed.]

8   Heinrich Esser (1818-72) was one of the main conductors at the Imperial Opera. In 1860-61 he was artistic director. Esser also conducted at the opening of the new opera house in 1869, leading, among other things, an overture he had written for the occasion. Johann Herbeck (1831-77) took over the directorship of the Opera between 1870 and 1875 and was concert director of the Gesellschaft der Musikfreunde. Karl Goldmark (1830-1915) was a prominent composer who settled in Vienna after 1860 and is best known for his "Rustic Wedding" Symphony and several operas. [Ed.]

9   In the spring of 1889 Brahms had been awarded the Honorary Freedom of Hamburg; the formal ceremony took place on 14 September. Five days earlier Brahms's *Fest- und Gedenksprüche,* op. 109, had their premiere by the Cecilia Society: that must be the "festival" to which Brahms refers in this letter. [Ed.]

10   Hanslick's influential work *On the Beautiful in Music* [*Vom Musikalisch-Schönen*] was published in 1854. [Ed.]

11   Hanslick uses a play on words—the German "Götze," idol, is almost identical with Goetz's name. [Trans.]

12   The festival took place on 25-28 September. [Ed.]

13   Perhaps a reference to the Waltzes, op. 39. [Ed.]

14   Brahms never visited Bayreuth. [Hanslick's note]

15   Based on remarks by Joachim, Brahms's biographer Kalbeck identifies three dances, nos. 11, 14, and 16, as "ureigenster [most authentic] Brahms." See Kalbeck, *Brahms* I, 66. [Ed.]

16   In the year 1883, in a debate in the Lower Austrian Parliament, in which, as Rector, he represented the University, Professor Maasen had come out in favor of a Czech-language elementary school. [Hanslick's note]

17   Brahms had in his own library works of Heinrich von Sybel and Heinrich von Treitschke. See Kurt Hofmann, *Die Bibliothek von Johannes Brahms* (Hamburg, 1974). The Oncken book is Wilhelm Oncken, *Das Zeitalter des Kaisers Wilhelm* (Berlin 1888-92). [Ed.]

18   Moritz Busch, *Bismarck und seine Leute während des Kriegs mit Frankreich* (Leipzig, 1878). [Ed.]

19   Max Klinger, *Brahms-Phantasie* (Leipzig, 1894). [Ed.]

20   Brahms, op. 116, *Fantasies for Pianoforte.* To these seven fantasies Brahms clearly also reckons the three *Intermezzos,* op. 117. [Hanslick's note]

21   The song collections opp. 96 and 97, whose title pages are reproduced in Kurt Hofmann, *Die Erstdrucke der Werke von Johannes Brahms* (Tutzing, 1975), pp. 204, 206. [Ed.]

22   Rudolf Eitelberger (1817-85) was the most significant and influential art historian of his day in Vienna. A medievalist, he was the founder of the Viennese school of art history. He was also instrumental in reorganizing the Academy of Fine Arts and the museums of the city. [Ed.]

23   The Eleven Chorale Preludes for Organ, composed in June 1896, were published posthumously in April 1902 as op. 122. [Ed.]

24   Every time I attend a performance of *Wallenstein's Lager,* I take pleasure in the lines: "Ein Hauptmann, den ein Anderer erstach, Ließ mir ein paar falsche Würfel nach" [A captain, who had stabbed another, left me a pair of loaded dice]. These two lines, a small eloquent memorial to the collaboration of two great poets, are by Goethe. He had inserted them into Schiller's manuscript to motivate the peasant's acquisition of the false dice. A similarly improving addition, insignificant but interesting, may be found in Schumann's opera *Genoveva*; but with the difference that here it was not the older, more experienced poet who was helping the younger, as in *Wallenstein's Lager,* but the much younger one helping the elder, the student helping the master. Fourteen bars in *Genoveva* are by Brahms. We only learn this now, forty years after Schumann's death, and only—how strange!—from the latest (fourth) edition of Billroth's letters. In response to a remark of Billroth's that he did not believe Brahms would compose an opera, the editor of Billroth's letters (4th edition, 1897), Dr. Georg Fischer, makes the following note: "Brahms did not compose an opera. But it has been unknown until now that he participated in an opera, even if it was only with fourteen bars, by writing the conclusion of Siegfried's song in the third act of Schumann's *Genoveva.*" This occured in the year 1874 as the opera was about to be rehearsed at the Royal Theatre in Hannover. Frau Clara Schumann sent the singer Max Stägemann, who had been cast in the role of the Palatine Count, the Brahms addition, with the explanation that she was not only completely in agreement with it but thought this conclusion to be very desirable from the point of view of its effect. The addition is not found in the score as Schumann had edited it after the premiere in Leipzig (1850), as it was copied later for Munich, Vienna, and Wiesbaden, or in the printed piano reduction prepared by Clara Schumann [1851]. For Hannover, the fourteen bars were stitched into the score as an addendum. When I compare this addition (which I have before me in the form of a copy) with Schumann's original, in which it is lacking, I can't help admiring the correctness of Brahms's perception. He felt that in Schumann's version the song has no satisfying conclusion, but that instead there is a questioning half-cadence on the dominant chord; further, that this half-cadence ("Mich trennt keine Macht mehr von dir!" [No longer will any power separate me from you!]) is followed much too quickly and abruptly by Siegfried's words "Wer sprengt so eilig ins Thor herein?" [Who gallops so hurriedly through the gate?]. Thus it was as much in the interest of the drama as of the music alone that Brahms separated the two so heterogeneous halves of this scene by means of the insertion of his fourteen helping bars. Today this has little practical relevance; *Genoveva,* musically so noble and deeply felt, but dramatically hesitant and anemic, finds all doors closed to it—with or without the Brahmsian insert. But for the history of the opera and for the admirers of Brahms and Schumann it is a particularly appealing item. [Hanslick's note]

25   The quote is from Goethe's poem "An den Mond," written between 1776 and 1778. [Trans.]

26   The reference is to the practice of painting over a gold sizing. [Trans.]

27   This was the Piano Quartet (with clarinet), op. 1, published with a dedication to Brahms. Brahms had mentioned the Rabl work in a letter to Simrock of 3 December 1898. See *Johannes Brahms Briefwechsel* (Berlin, 1908–22), XII, 208. [Ed.]

Gustav Jenner

Johannes Brahms as Man, Teacher, and Artist

Translated by Susan Gillespie

Gustav Jenner (1865-1920) became Brahms's only real pupil in composition. He studied privately with Brahms during the winter and spring of 1888, then remained in Vienna until 1895 studying counterpoint with Eusebius Mandyczewski. In that year Jenner was appointed academic musical director at the University of Marburg, where he worked until his death. Jenner's memoir of Brahms is one of the most valuable sources for the latter's ideas on compositional technique, about which he spoke rarely.

The excerpts are taken from Johannes Brahms als Mensch, Lehrer und Künstler *(Marburg, 1905), pp. 1-9, 11-13, 16-31, 35-46.*

It was in Leipzig in late December of the year 1887 that I first met Brahms. He had travelled there to oversee the performance of two of his newest works, the Double Concerto and the Piano Trio in C Minor,[1] and he knew that I was coming from Kiel to visit him, to ask him to give his opinion of my musical abilities based on a selection of my compositions. This is how it had come about.

On the advice of one of my teachers I had sent several of my songs to Simrock[2] in Berlin to inquire whether he might be inclined to publish them. But Simrock wrote back that he was just on the point of leaving for his summer vacation and therefore would not be able to give me an answer until nearly fall. Then one day I got a call from Klaus Groth,[3] who was very fond of me and a loyal advisor in every respect. I can still see him standing at the gate of his garden waving his arms as I came into sight: "Come quickly," he called, "I have good news for you!" And, beaming with pleasure, he handed me a letter from which I learned that on his summer vacation in Thun, Simrock had paid a visit to Brahms and shown him my song manuscripts. It seemed that these had piqued his interest, but he had advised Simrock not to print them. Now he wished to learn more about me and to meet me whenever the opportunity should arise.

With this, far more was accomplished than the publication of the songs, which didn't matter much to me in the first place. My long-cherished secret wish to become personally acquainted with Brahms was about to come true, and in what a splendid fashion! It may be safely assumed that I would gladly have departed at once; however, since my means did not permit such a long journey on short notice, I had to console myself for the time being with the prospect of the favorable opportunity Brahms had mentioned. This finally arrived, as mentioned above, at the end of the year. Groth wrote to Brahms to ask whether he would like to see me in Leipzig and received the reply that I would be welcome.

In Hamburg, as had been arranged, my friend Julius Spengel[4] joined me, and then we went on to Berlin to see Joachim. There, for the first time, I experienced one of the Joachim Quartet evenings. Immediately after the concert we set off with the quartet for Leipzig and arrived late at night at the Hotel Hauffe. I will never forget the feeling that came over me as I saw on the guest list the name "Johannes Brahms, Vienna." He had already gone to bed. Through an odd coincidence I was given a room directly adjacent to his, and, as I entered, the sound of hearty snoring announced the presence of the great man. I undressed quietly and lay down with a strange feeling of mingled awe, pride, and anxiety.

When I descended the following morning, Brahms had already breakfasted. He was smoking with evident relish and reading the newspaper. I was almost taken aback when I saw him: for I had pictured him—I don't know why; perhaps I was thinking of our German types—as being tall, and so at first I could hardly grasp the fact that this short plump gentleman was Brahms. But the sight of his head banished all doubts.

Brahms received me with a pleasant and direct friendliness, indicated that he understood why I had come, and was able, with just a few brief questions, which he posed quite casually, to help me over the first awkwardness and shyness, so that in no time I was convinced of the kindness of his nature and placed my unqualified trust in him. He also made sure that I could thoroughly enjoy the wealth of beautiful new experiences that there were for me to enjoy during those unforgettable days. Once during a walk he put his arm in mine familiarly, remarking that he didn't see well, which was quite true, and said: "If you have brought along something nice to show me, then you may just leave it in my room." On New Year's Eve a large number of us were gathered around Brahms, and as the bells announced the New Year, someone stood up and spoke the simple lines: "We waited for the New Year, now it comes; and with it a good spirit, Johannes Brahms." I felt that these words had a special meaning for me; I knew that for me it really was the beginning of a New Year, a new time, a new epoch in my life, even though I could not yet imagine, at that time, to what an extent this would be true.

After the chamber music concert, in which Brahms himself had played the piano part of the C-Minor Trio, the reception at the inn with the Leipzig musicians and patrons lasted inordinately long. The holidays had come and gone. Joachim, Hausmann, and Spengel had already departed, and I, too, would soon have to think about leaving. But Brahms had not yet said anything about my work, and that was the reason I had come. True, he had said quite often, in the presence of others, that I had talent, as a kind of social legitimation, but I was still hoping for an hour of private conversation.

It was after three in the morning when we arrived at the Hotel Hauffe that night. How overjoyed, and at the same time amazed I was, when, at that hour, as he was saying goodnight, he announced that he would be waiting for me at 7 in the morning in his room, to talk with me about my compositions. I arrived punctually at the appointed time and found him fresh and rosy, the soul of geniality, at his breakfast. The busy days, which in addition to the concerts had placed unusual social demands on him, seemed not to have affected him in the slightest. From a very large case he extracted two equally large cigars and lighted one of them. Every puff betrayed the enjoyment of the connoisseur. In the presence of such strength I didn't want to betray any weakness, and so I bravely lighted up the proffered cigar, although I was not comfortable smoking so early after having been up all night— and then the genuine article! I also could not prevent my cigar from going out now and again; Brahms, undeterred, helped me to relight it. At the same time he was examining my work.

I had brought with me a trio for piano, violin, and cello, a choral piece with orchestral accompaniment, women's choruses *a capella,* as well as some songs, and I found that he was minutely prepared, down to the tiniest detail; just as later, without exception, he never went over pieces with me that he had not thoroughly scrutinized ahead of time. After some preliminary remarks to the effect that he had received a generally positive impression of my compositions, he first handed back the choral work with orchestral accompaniment, which had turned out rather long, with the words: "Too bad about the pretty little poem." It was Klaus Groth's "Wenn ein müder Leib begraben." The women's choruses suffered the same fate; I got them back with the equally uncomforting assurance: "This kind of thing is very hard to do."

But then he went over the trio and the songs with me all the more exhaustively.

At the first movement of the trio there was much turning of pages back and forth. With devastating precision Brahms demonstrated to me the lack of logic in the structure; it was as if in his hands the whole thing dissolved into its component parts. With growing horror I saw how loosely and weakly they were joined together. I realized that the bond that was supposed to hold them together was less an internal than an external one; it was nothing more than the device of the sonata form. The essence of form began to reveal itself to me, and I suddenly realized that it is not enough to have a good idea here and there; that one has not written a sonata when one has merely combined several such ideas through the outward form of the sonata, but that, on the contrary, the sonata form must emerge of necessity from the idea. I was already making the discovery that precisely those passages from which I had promised myself the most did not seem to interest Brahms at all. At such enthusiastic passages, where my heart beat faster and my eyes focussed expectantly and anxiously on his, he calmly and coolly criticized "sleepy, lazy" basses, pointed out weak harmonies, suggested replacing a few notes with others that were more logical and, at the same time, allowed the idea which had gotten stuck in my harmonies, had lost its ability to develop, so to speak, to emerge clearly and powerfully.

It was a painful disappointment for me to realize that often, when I thought I had done the best work, this was just when my imagination had faltered. The whole, moreover, was lacking that broad and deep undercurrent of feeling that produces the unity of effect in a work of art, by finding the same lively expression throughout the work and giving all the separate parts, however disparate and far removed from each other they may be, its distinctive stamp. Sentences such as "That could just as well have been something else" gave me, even then, much food for thought. After only a few moments I had come to the depressing conclusion that my entire composing career betrayed the tendency to succumb weakly to whatever inspiration happened to strike me, that it indulged in childish pleasure over "beautiful" details, that it was nothing but purposeless groping: in other words, dilettantism. Brahms showed me how my eye had fastened with truly touching tenderness on unessential things, while overlooking the essential ones that made all the difference. Naturally these weaknesses showed up most glaringly in the slow movement; but it is understandable when I must confess that precisely this movement, with its youthful enthusiasm, was my favorite. And thus, to my bitter disappointment, the entire glory of this beloved adagio melted away before my watching eyes into empty nothingness. For my suffering, which Brahms probably sensed, he offered only the dubious consolation that "such a long adagio is the most difficult of all."

In the scherzo I had attempted to be "original." Following a public performance, my friends in Kiel and, if I remember correctly, even the newspapers had loudly praised the originality of this section. Unfortunately it did not hold up either; its originality was slowly but surely transformed into pure nonsense. We came to the end of this movement remarkably quickly, and Brahms said well-meaningly: "Of course, you *will* promise me not to write anything like this again."

The finale was a rondo. Here I did relatively well. I was amazed when Brahms stopped at a phrase that did not seem to me to deserve any particular attention, with the words: "You see, that is a good sign." I remembered clearly that when I had worked on this passage it had flowed from my hand without particular effort; but since no further explanation was forthcoming, it remained completely unclear to me what agreeable characteristics this passage actually contained. Only one fact seemed to be beyond doubt, that there must be things in musical creation of which I knew absolutely nothing. And so Brahms turned my attention from dreamy sentiments down toward the depths, where I could only guess that in addition to feeling there must be another factor at work which in my case, for lack of ability and knowledge, was operating only very imperfectly: understanding. I saw not only that I had to learn, but also, at the same time, where I had to learn. At present I was lacking a solid foundation of knowledge. I began to comprehend why Brahms, when I had answered his question as to what I was doing by telling him that I was learning instrumentation, had laughed out loud and asked disparagingly whether I didn't know that that "had to be learned, even when one's five senses were in good working order." The feeling that I was on the wrong path grew more and more distinct. . . .

With the songs I got off a bit more easily. It is true that here, too, to my great discomfiture, several were immediately laid aside without even being considered: these were the great, powerfully expressive ones, for which I had such high expectations. But then on the other hand some of the small ones were looked at closely. Now a few words of recognition were spoken, for example: "That is something you don't forget, once you have seen it," or: "That could have turned into a good song."

After all that I felt like someone who, after a long journey on the wrong road, believes that he is nearing his destination, only to become suddenly aware of his error and see the goal recede behind the faraway horizon, unreachable for his failing powers. The friendly and confiding manner with which Brahms had received me in the previous days had given me a certain security and self-confidence that now, to tell the truth, began to wobble perilously. But in spite of the unmercifully hard criticism that my compositions had experienced at his hands, not an ironic, much less a mean word was ever spoken, and everything seemed to be softened by a good will that won my confidence: he showed me without leniency or any possibility of objection that I didn't know how to do anything. But the high vantage point from which he made his judgments, which I could only intuit but not comprehend, actually gave me courage. For before my eyes a new world was dawning. I saw the correct road to the land of true art clear and palpable in front of me, even if that realm itself was still lost in fog.

I had come to Brahms for the purpose of asking his advice; this had also been Klaus Groth's understanding. Neither he nor I would ever have conceived the bold idea of asking Brahms to take me on as his student; for we both knew perfectly well that Brahms lived as a private gentleman in Vienna and did not teach. I was merely to get from him confirmation of the fact that I was not without talent, along with a few pointers for the immediate future. I did, of course, notice that in his comments on my work Brahms repeatedly used the phrase, "Yes, I might be able to be of use to you"; whereby he expelled the first syllable quickly and energetically in a manner peculiar to him. But I didn't rightly know what to make of these words; at least in my timid state I didn't dare to interpret them to mean that he might be prepared to instruct me, and so I asked him modestly for his advice. After a strict examination of what I had done up until that time, Brahms said: "You see, you haven't yet learned anything proper about music; for everything you are telling me about theory of harmony, attempts at composition, instrumentation, and the like, is in my opinion worthless." Then he asked me how old I was, and when he heard that I had just completed my twenty-second year, he made no secret of his qualms that it might already be too late, and then he continued: "First find a teacher who will instruct you in strict counterpoint; the best ones are among the cantors in the villages; he doesn't need to be so famous as Mr. X (here he gave a well-known name). It is absolutely essential that one see the world through this glass for a good long time. You will have plenty to do there for several years. But write to me."

On the same day I travelled back to Hamburg, where I remained for some time....

I wrote a letter to Brahms in which I poured my heart out confidingly and finally asked him to make an exception and take me on as his student. Then I went to Klaus Groth to tell him about it. We did not remain in uncertainty for long: Brahms answered immediately from Vienna with the following words:

Honored and dear sir:

I must overcome a certain shyness—but finally I have no other advice for you than to come here and study with Mr. Eusebius Mandyczewski.[5] Mr. M. is a young, very able man who will certainly be agreeable to you in every way. Whatever you might wish to have from me is at your service in full measure. I would hope that you might be able to come to a decision quickly so that you could make use of the rest of the winter! The summer will probably mean a long pause. 5

In great haste and with warm greetings for you and Klaus Groth,

> *Your devoted*
>
> > *Joh. Brahms*

The decisive turning point in my life had arrived. Thanks to the sacrifices of high-minded friends in Kiel, whose names have been withheld from me to this day, I was able soon afterwards to depart for Vienna, where on 13 February 1888, in the morning, coming straight from the station, I walked into Brahms's room.

Again it was early in the morning, again he offered me one of the big cigars from the familiar bulky case, and again I was unable to prevent it from going out repeatedly as I talked. But already at the second match Brahms said: "You don't seem to deserve a good cigar," and never again until the day he died did I receive one of the "genuine ones," but was always, unlike others, made to settle for an Austrian imitation.[6] At the same time I was soon to experience what he meant by his words in the letter "Whatever you might wish to have from me is at your service in full measure." First he introduced me, at the archive of the Gesellschaft der Musikfreunde, to Mr. Mandyczewski, who was to be my counterpoint teacher; then for the first time I ate lunch with him at the Red Hedgehog [*Zum roten Igel*],[7] and after lunch he took me to look for an apartment, whereby he exhibited a weakness for the older buildings. On these strolls through the city he immediately drew my attention to what holy ground we were treading on. In front of one house he would say, "This is the 'Eye of God,'"[8] and in front of another "Hats off, this is where *Figaro* was written." We were in the Rauhensteingasse, too. 8

Finally in the so-called "Freihaus auf der Weiden," near his own apartment, we found a room that suited my needs. "The young man is fond of music," Brahms said

to the landlady, "Will he hear a little piano playing, singing or such, here from time
to time?" She was afraid she couldn't oblige. "Well, then it is not so important."
Then he gave me one of his coffee-makers, plate, spoon, knife, and fork, so that I
was comfortably installed right on the first day. His library was open for my use,
and his purse likewise. I could have as much money from him as I needed, but I
never found it necessary to take any and never did borrow anything. In the evening
he took me with him to the Vienna Tonkünstler-Verein (the composers' association),
of which he was the Honorary President, and advised me to become acquainted
with a Dr. Rottenberg,[9] who was about my age and whose friendship has become   9
infinitely dear to me.

It was agreed that my counterpoint work with Mandyczewski should begin at
once. With him I limited my work to strict counterpoint, bringing my free compositions to Brahms, not necessarily at any agreed-upon time; rather, whenever I had
finished a piece, I gave it to him, and a few days later it would be discussed in the
morning between 10 and 12. In regard to the counterpoint studies, he merely
inquired now and again how far I had gotten, for example when he visited me in
my room and happened to find me working on such a project.

In the beginning I would pick him up every day at half past twelve to go with
him to lunch at the Red Hedgehog. Then, as was his custom, he would take his
coffee either there, or, if the weather was fine, in the Stadtpark,[10] and afterwards he   10
would take a longish walk, often in the Prater.[11] As a rule I could not afford this   11
luxury, namely the time. But in the evenings, generally after a concert or after the
opera, we would meet again in the Hedgehog as agreed, usually with Rottenberg,
often, too, in a small group with the Kalbecks, Doors, Brülls,[12] and other Viennese   12
musicians. Sometimes he would also bring strangers to whom he would graciously
demonstrate the superior qualities of the Hedgehog. When there were a lot of
people present he had a tendency to be reticent, or else he would bubble over with
good-humored jokes and high-spirited witticisms that spared no one. With deep
nostalgia, however, I think back to those splendid evenings on which Rottenberg
and I sat alone with him in the low-ceilinged back room, where his portrait now
hangs, and the taciturn Brahms warmed up and allowed us a glimpse of his deep
and strong human soul. But he never, on such evenings, spoke of his work, and
extremely seldom of himself and his life. It is true that during our lessons I often had
the good fortune to hear him speak of himself; it was nearly always in a state of
excitement. The occasions when he spoke calmly about himself were more infre-
quent; this occurred on long walks, for example when he had made a few children
happy with candy in the Prater, or when I walked home with him in the evening.
Then I could make bold to ask him about this or that aspect of his life or his works
without being immediately rebuffed. Unfortunately, in the second winter I already
had to deny myself the pleasure of eating lunch together with Brahms every day,
since the Hedgehog grew too expensive for me. Brahms, it is true, always maintained

that the Hedgehog was the cheapest restaurant in Vienna, and in fact he understood how to manage in such a way that he always paid less than I did and yet ate better. He was quite extraordinarily frugal in his daily life: 70-80 Kreuzer[13] were the most   13 that he required for his midday meal, including a small glass of Pilsner beer or a quarter-liter of red wine. In the evening he scarcely drank any more than that. It is only because the opposite has been asserted so often that I feel it is my duty to describe this in such detail, in accordance with the truth.

The first two weeks in Vienna were rounded out with a task that I had taken on in order to raise money. Under the circumstances to which I have alluded, which alone had made it possible for me to stay in Vienna, I felt that I should apply for a scholarship that was offered at that time, and I told Brahms about it. He tried to talk me out of it: "I have never wanted to apply for anything like that." But finally he accepted my rationale and asked me to show him the pieces I had done for the application. I remember giving them to him with some hesitation and asking him whether I should send them in at all. But Brahms said: "Anyone who knows the slightest thing about it can recognize talent, and no one is going to expect you to turn out masterpieces." So I gamely sent them off.

In March my real studies with Brahms began. The first lesson is one I will never forget: it was bitter. On the same day on which he had encouraged me so nicely to send off my creations, he asked me whether I wouldn't bring him back the songs I had shown him in Leipzig, so that he could talk about them with me in more detail. During our lessons he always sat at the piano, my work lay on the music stand and I sat next to him. But no note was ever played on the piano, the only exception being when he wanted to give a concrete example of wrong notes or other bad parts of a composition by demonstrating their ugly effects. With a sole exception, namely once in Ischl when Rottenberg and I were called on to demonstrate some of my variations for four hands, I was never permitted to play anything of mine on the piano for him.

Since Brahms had judged the songs relatively leniently in Leipzig, I hoped to hear good things. But now he suddenly changed his tune. He took up one song after the other, showed me mercilessly, expressing himself forcefully, but always appealing only to my faculty of understanding, how poor these songs were. He criticized my poor pampered dears so roundly that there wasn't a good beat left in them and the tears leapt to my eyes. And yet that was only the introduction; I was about to feel his pedagogical rod even more sharply. He stood up and fetched a few loose yellowed sheets. It was the manuscript of those songs by Robert Schumann which Brahms would later publish himself in the supplemental volume of Schumann's works.[14] Then he sat down again at the piano, played and sang them for me,   14 especially that touching song *An Anna* whose melody Schumann used in the F-sharp-Minor Sonata, op. 11, with such enthusiastic sentiment that he could not forbear to weep tears of emotion, which came easily to him. "Yes," he said, standing up, "Schumann wrote that when he was eighteen; talent is what you need, nothing else will get you anywhere." Then, as if the cup of humiliation were not full, he handed me back the badly rumpled and wilted bouquet of my songs and dismissed me with the ironic words: "So, young man, continue to amuse yourself in this way," an expression to which Brahms was very partial and which I was to have to swallow many times more.

I stood as if thunderstruck. The situation could not have been made more bitterly or heartwrenchingly clear to me. Only recently he had called my work talented and done everything to bolster my self-confidence. Why then had he called me to Vienna to see him—not, finally, to tell me that I was without talent? In the days that followed it was necessary for me to keep this constantly before my eyes, in order not to despair completely. For I might as well say right away that Brahms never again spoke an encouraging word, much less a word of praise, about my work. In addition to this, his entire manner toward me changed from that day forward. True, when we were alone, he remained the same familiar, dear, paternal friend, but in any larger group I soon learned to remain completely silent, since I could be certain that he would respond to even the most harmless remark by cutting me off with an infinitely condescending: "Well, you are still quite young," or: "That is not so critical," or some similarly blunt remark. I will not deny that I fell prey to periods of complete despondency, even despair, to which I feared I would succumb. Of not inconsiderable influence, moreover, was the fact that my studies in counterpoint with Mr. Mandyczewski were only advancing with difficulty. The fruit of long hours of the most arduous labor was often only a few bars, and for a very long time I could not feel their positive effect on my work, so that however bravely I might resist, I could not but begin to doubt my abilities. My tranquility of mind threatened to desert me at work and to be replaced by a nervous haste by means of which I wanted to force more significant results more quickly.

Things went on like this for a considerable period, before I really learned how to work. Not until a whole year later did Brahms remark on some occasion: "You will never hear a word of praise from me; if you can't stand that, then whatever is inside you only deserves to go to waste." This sentence was my salvation. Why Brahms applied this strict and austere method of pedagogy toward me, whether perhaps he found something frivolous, immodest, or even arrogant in my demeanor, I do not know. But it is certain that he acted according to his dictum, repeated countless times: "One mustn't spoil the young." Perhaps, too, he was thinking of his own youth, of how many difficult battles he had fought through to their fortunate conclusion. "It is not easy to find someone who has had as hard a time of it as I have," he said to me once as I sat alone in the Hedgehog with him on his birthday; and then he recounted sad events which were, in part, already known to me from Klaus Groth's stories. "If my father were still alive," Brahms said, "and I were sitting in the orchestra in the first chair of the second violins, then at least I could say to him that I had accomplished something." He could speak with justifiable pride, for everything he was, he had become through his own efforts.

But sometimes he played a softer tune. Thus, later, he might have expressed his satisfaction by showing me, after my lesson, the most beautiful treasures from his collection, or playing for me works I did not know by Ph. E. Bach, Scarlatti, and others. Or he would read me foolish letters that had just arrived, like the one from a stranger in Kapstadt who wanted another piano, since he was very satisfied with the one that had just been delivered—this turned out to be the clumsy ruse of an autograph hound, a breed to whom Brahms was not exactly obliging. Or he would show me gifts from equally unknown admirers and tell me to keep them. Sometimes, on a beautiful spring morning, he would be prepared to give away everything that was lying around his apartment. His books he was very particular about. But, on one occasion, as he was returning a cycle of Rückert's[15] songs I had composed, he made me a gift of Rückert's poems, which he loved very much. The book contained a dedication and his signature. He scratched out the former with a knife, but let Rückert's name stand and only said: "Now, with just a little bit more depth." I also soon noticed that when certain passages were passed over without comment or individual pieces were not commented on at all, these were the ones in which there was the least to criticize. True, I learned nothing about their value, and it was therefore not at all out of the question that they might be of precious little significance. It was only in a roundabout way that I occasionally heard, for example from Rottenberg, whether the content of my work had been of interest to him. In his dealings with me, he was occupied solely with the measure of perfection.

Brahms lived in the Karlsgasse No. 4 on the upper floor, No. 8, in three rooms. One entered through his bedroom—a common inconvenience in Vienna. I have often lived in circumstances in which I had to pass through the bedroom of my landlord in order to get to my own: "If it doesn't bother the gentleman, then is doesn't bother us," was the usual comment. Over his bed there hung an engraving of J. S. Bach. Through a glass door one then passed into the simply furnished living room, in which stood the grand piano and the desk; above the latter hung the well-known medallion portrait of Robert and Clara Schumann, with a lovely dedication to Brahms in Schumann's own hand. Toward one side was the library, in which a lectern could also be found. The windows of the living room and the library, which faced toward the front of the building, were always closed, while the windows of the bedroom, which looked out on the courtyard of the Technical University,[16] were open day and night. During lessons Brahms was always dressed in slippers, trousers, and a wool shirt. Since he was nearsighted, he wore a pair of glasses, which he exchanged for a pince-nez when he went out.

Since it was common knowledge that Brahms could almost certainly be found at home in the morning, we were often interrupted by visitors. As soon as, from our seat at the grand piano, we caught sight of such a visitor through the curtain of the glass door, Brahms would flee with great bounds into the library, where I gave a signal by means of prearranged signs as to whether he should put on a jacket or not. He always did when a lady came by. It would be untrue if I were to maintain that Brahms was always polite to his visitors. On the contrary, I was often witness to embarrassing scenes, particularly in the case of visits by unknown artists in whom he had no interest. If he felt that someone was coming out of curiosity, or that someone wanted something from him that he was not inclined to give them, or that they perhaps even wanted something unreasonable, then he knew how to dispatch the visitor in an amazingly short time. It is not entirely without cause that Brahms developed a reputation as a boor, although few individuals could be as charming as he. Not long ago a famous artist told me that he only went to visit Brahms when he could be sure he would not be at home.

As far as my actual instruction was concerned, Brahms didn't give me any definite assignments. In general I could work on whatever I wanted. But in the beginning he recommended that I write songs with short stanzas and practice the form of the variation. "Writing variations is the smartest thing you can do for the time being." Later he asked for sonata movements and sonatas.

If I now attempt to share, from these lessons, some things that I believe are of general interest and may perhaps be of use here and there, it is not that I am deluding myself about the great difficulties I will face in this endeavor. The danger of saying things that are misleading or even false is in fact very great, since I am continually forced to generalize from a specific example. In this short study, it would not have been possible to apply the method of quoting each example, along with Brahms's corrections and observations. But anyone with any insight knows that generalizations drawn from individual statements, even when these are undoubtedly correct, are always risky in matters of art and often turn things that are correct in themselves into utter falsehoods. For this reason I would like to state that I have been very careful, both in my selections and in my presentation, and that every sentence is based on my personal experiences in the lessons. I would rather say too little than too much. Furthermore, I would like to state explicitly that I have always made Brahms's own words clearly identifiable through the use of quotation marks. Otherwise it is not he who is speaking; rather I am describing my own convictions, as they have been formed, admittedly, on the basis of my Brahmsian instruction. However, I am not so presumptuous as to suggest that it would be appropriate for me to identify myself or my opinions with his, based on this instruction.

Brahms's way of speaking had something abrupt, fragmentary about it. He was not one to discourse expansively on a subject. In contrast to so-called eloquent people who, when they speak, evince pleasure at their own words, he gave the impression that he spoke only reluctantly and only as much as was absolutely necessary. His sentences were uttered precisely and pointedly, and here he always hit the nail on the head; but he concealed far more, in fact often the main thing, without which his words could not be properly understood. This became all the more pronounced if he was in a situation in which he was forced to speak about himself. Everyone who was close to Brahms knows how abruptly and almost dismissively he could speak of his own works; on this subject, in particular, it was harder than ever to understand him correctly. He was quite conscious of the value of his works, but his nature, with its manly modesty, made it endlessly difficult for him to talk about himself. Often he tried to extricate himself with a joke, but naturally it is impossible that this should always have been recognized, so an awkward atmosphere could easily develop. Usually, when he spoke seriously about himself, he was in a state of embarrassment, which was often mingled with anger, if someone pressed him who he did not think had the right to do so. If, as was the rule, he did not feel confident from the outset that he would be understood, then he was capable, unless restrained by a sense of general regard for the person with whom he was speaking, of pulling the wool over that person's eyes in the most outrageous fashion, and with perfect equanimity. The saying "Since truth is a pearl, cast it not before swine," as Theodor Storm[17] has it, was sacred to him; and there were in effect very few individuals who were not sometimes reckoned among the swine. But he took it well, as I often had occasion to remark in my own case, if one protested and struggled valiantly to escape from this rather unpleasant circumstance. And if one succeeded in winning his confidence in this way, then he was also capable of finding that person worthy of the truth.

I have always retained the impression that of all song forms, Brahms valued strophic songs the most. This sentence can easily lead to misunderstandings, as Brahms indeed never expressed anything so definitive about it to me, but he did once say something similar to me about his own songs. Once, during a walk, Brahms began a conversation with the words, "There must be among my songs one that is called *Feldeinsamkeit*." I remarked as disinterestedly as possible that I was familiar with it. Now he told me how upset he had been that Klaus Groth had also expressed objections to the famous "Gestorben bin" and had even gone so far as to suggest changes in the text by Allmers.[18] He defended Allmers's text in the warmest of terms and added: "There is nobody about whom one can be certain that the Philistine won't come out in him someday." From the text we moved on to the subject of the music, and then, thinking of the wonderful effect of that particular piece and the genius expressed in its strophic form, I steered the conversation to the subject of the mysterious effects that are inherent in that form. Brahms picked up this theme, and in the course of our conversation uttered the following phrase: "My little songs are more appealing to me than my big ones," which, as an illustration of what has been said, could only mean that a successful strophic song was what he preferred. During my lessons, too, I always had this impression.

When he discussed a song with me, the first thing to be examined was whether the musical form fully corresponded to the text. Mistakes along these lines he criticized especially sharply, as a lack of artistic sense or the consequence of inadequate comprehension of the text. In general, he demanded that if the text allowed a treatment in strophes, this was what should be utilized. In order to become clear as to which texts were to be treated in strophes and which not, he recommended a close study of the complete songs of Franz Schubert, whose acute artistic sense he said was evident even in his most unassuming songs. "There is no song by Schubert from which one cannot learn something". . . .

Although in the beginning Brahms recommended to me that for the time being I should write short songs, irrespective of whether they be strophic or not, he allowed me full freedom. Naturally I chose my texts myself, except that at my request he would lend me collections of poems. In his bedroom there was an armoire that was stuffed full from top to bottom with "lyrics." He knew and read just about everything there was; but he once told me that he had almost never bought a book himself. Into that armoire also disappeared those volumes that were sent to him by the modern poets of the day, always without success. But I often held in my hands the proof that he had read even the most miserable, pitiful scribblings. Once, in one of these volumes, I found a poem that Brahms had marked with signs of his most extreme displeasure: in it, Rückert was arrogantly and contemptuously dismissed. I mentioned this to Brahms, and he said: "I know, a fellow like that abuses Rückert!"

Brahms demanded from a composer, first of all, that he should know his text precisely. He also meant by this, of course, that the construction and meter of the poem should be thoroughly clear to him. Next, he recommended to me that before composing I should carry the poem around with me in my head for a long time and should frequently recite it out loud to myself, paying close attention to everything, especially the declamation. I should also mark the pauses especially and follow these later when I was working. "Just imagine to yourself that Lewinsky[19] were reciting this song," he said once as we were discussing a song with almost no pauses; "here he would certainly stop for a moment."

19

It is particularly pleasurable to observe the way that Brahms knew how to treat these pauses in his songs, how they are often an echo of what precedes them, often a preparation for what follows (*Von ewiger Liebe*); how here, at times, the rhythm undergoes an artistic development and the accompaniment is raised to a factor that has its own independent influence. He placed great importance on these pauses and their treatment, and they are often, in fact, an unmistakable sign that the composer is an artist who creates with freedom and assurance, not a dilettante groping in the dark, influenced by every chance occurence.

Once the song's structure had been examined from all these angles, there followed a consideration of its individual parts. At those points where language inserts punctuation, the musical phrase has cadences; and just as the poet, in his purposeful construction, ties his sentences more or less closely together using commas, semicolons, periods, etc., as his external signs, so the musician, similarly, has at his disposal perfect and imperfect cadences in a variety of forms to indicate the greater or lesser degree of coherence of his musical phrases. The importance of the cadences is immediately evident, for it is through them that both the construction and the proportion of the various parts are determined. Thus Brahms, too, focused my particular attention on them.

Here the main thing was to understand the combination and opposition of the three great factors in music—rhythm, melody, and harmony; to understand, for example, that a cadence that is harmonically and melodically perfect will have a weaker effect if it does not occur simultaneously with the rhythmic cadence; that such an occurrence may, in one instance, be a grievous error, in another an effective means of joining the phrases together; that the weaker cadence must precede the stronger; and finally that the proportion of the various parts must correspond to the text. Sometimes Brahms showed me passages where the cadence was not well motivated rhythmically, and from this circumstance he proved irrefutably that the cadence had been inserted at that point because the imaginative energy had flagged. Often, in such cases, a six-four chord appears, more or less like a rescuing, comfortable armchair into which the exhausted fantasy can collapse prematurely. "Draw a line under every six-four chord and examine closely whether it is in the right place," said Brahms, and from my experience with my own and others' compositions I can say that this rule is a truly fruitful, even a golden one. As excellent as the effect of this chord can be—naturally I am referring only to cadential six-four chords—it is often nothing but the symptom and in its flabbiness the true reflection of a completely lame and exhausted imagination.

The location and form of the cadences is linked in the closest possible manner with the course of the modulation. Here Brahms called for the tightest possible reins and the most extreme consistency. Even in the case of a very long song whose subsidiary phrases were extended and internally consistent, the principal key always had to be clearly articulated and its dominance over the secondary keys maintained by means of clear relationships, so that, so to speak, the sum of all the keys utilized in the piece combined to create an image of the tonic key in its activity. That precisely the lack of clear identification of a key, even the tonic, can serve as an excellent means of expression, is in the nature of the matter. The splendid freedom we sense in Brahms's creative power is rooted in part in his instinctively sure sense of the unified character of the modulation; and the saying that it is only by subordinating himself that man can be truly free finds in him a beautiful confirmation.

How often, when listening to songs, particularly modern songs, must one wonder why a certain song has to end in A-flat major and find no answer except that it began in A-flat major? Here the composer, who appears to move so freely in his modulations, has actually become the slave of an idea whose true meaning he does not seem to grasp. He would be much more consistent in his arbitrariness if he ended in some other key into which he had been led just as his text was coming to its conclusion. For a unified modulation does not in any way preclude the use of even the most distant keys. Quite the contrary, these keys become distant only by virtue of the fact that another key governs; this is what gives them their expressive power. They say something different; they are like the colors of a painting that contrast with the background color and are simultaneously contained and intensified by it.

Among other things, it was in order to help me acquire a reliable sense of the unified character of the modulation that Brahms had me imitate in my own compositions the modulations from Adagio movements of Mozart or Beethoven. "If Beethoven goes from C major to E major, you do the same; that is how I used to do it myself," he told me. With regard to the overall course of the modulation, with the exception of individual divergences, the guiding principle was: The straight path is the best path. In specific instances, too, as he corrected me, I often thought of the saying: "Do you want to wander farther and farther away? Look, the good things are so near." And precisely these nearby, good things—how often they are overlooked because our vision has been obscured by the force of a hastily conceived idea and we have neglected the essential things in favor of inessential ones, so that we can't see the forest for the trees!

After what I have just said it should be clear that Brahms was not one to be impressed by a few "interesting" phrases or by complicated and "atmospheric" accompanimental figures. His eye remained keen. Sometimes he used a drastic but unusually simple means to open my eyes and make me sense quite clearly that under that sumptuous and glittering cloak lay hidden a pitiful, shabby, and undernourished being, which could not possibly show itself naked. Brahms would cover up the upper system of the piano accompaniment with his hand, and pointing to the vocal line and the bass he would say with an expressive smile: "I read only this." Through such a procedure the unnaturalness of the invention was often demonstrated to me *ad ocolos,* as it were; I no longer understood how I could have arrived at such a dreary melody and such boring basses, unless I were to assume that I had actually been captivated by the accompaniment figures. In other words, that I had been unfree. The determining role of the melody and of clearly perceived basses created in good counterpoint were an absolute requirement for him, one that remained in force even when the overall design of the song was at its most artful. Brahms, as I have mentioned, loved to elevate the accompaniment to a fully equal, even independent, element and sometimes to move it canonically in relation to the voice. But one never has the impression that the melody has been invented under the coercion of the canon. The canonic form never develops into the controlling element, but serves, on the contrary, only as a means of increasing the charm of the vocal melody. And the melody will always and unhesitatingly break the form whenever its powerful and sublime flow so dictates. But if, as occasionally happens, only a few poor crumbs from the piano accompaniment are allotted to the vocal part, then Brahms could never permit such concoctions to be dignified by the appellation "song."

On the other hand, Brahms could of course never be satisfied if there was nothing there but a pretty, well-accompanied melody. In one case, when my melody did not seem to him to do justice to the text, he said: "Write yourself another text underneath that." Brahms believed strongly in something that can be briefly characterized as "word expression" [*Wortausdruck*]. Often one will find in his songs remarkable melodic turns of phrase that have evidently been brought about by certain individual words in the text. But far from disturbing the melodic flow, these phrases seem to be essential components of the melody, imparting a particular physiognomy to it. Indeed, they often resemble the kernels of motives from which the whole melody seems to grow. It is instructive, in this context, to study which passages of text Brahms handles this way in his songs, while he passes over others that seem to offer the composer an equal opportunity to indulge in such characteristic turns of phrase. One will then find that here too his keen eye always separated the essential from the inessential. Nor did he ever compose any so-called "mood poems" consisting of nothing but an accumulation of these kinds of word-painting. When the melodic line followed a particular verbal expression too closely, he would criticize it with the words: "Think more of the larger picture!" And with that he hit the nail on the head.

Although Brahms's awesome talent and enormous experience made it self-explanatory, I nevertheless often found it amazing to observe how the creative process of my compositions seemed from the first moment completely transparent to him. The occasions when I learned the most from him were when he would not only point out the mistakes themselves, but also reveal how they had come about. At the same time he was not always pleased if I showed him the same pieces, especially songs, in reworked form. He preferred to have me bring him new songs in which the errors he had inveighed against were avoided. He spoke from his own experience when he said: "It is rare that a piece, once it has been completed, becomes better through revision; usually it gets worse." Then he advised me never to begin the working out of a song before the whole thing had taken definite form as an outline either in my head or on paper. "When ideas come to you, go for a walk; then you will discover that the thing you thought was a complete thought was actually only the beginning of one."

Again and again he would impress upon me that I should mistrust my own ideas. I have often had the experience that precisely those ideas which become rooted in the mind, like an *idee fixe,* are the natural obstacle to free creation, because one falls in love with them and instead of being their master, becomes their slave. "The pen is not only for writing, but also for deleting," Brahms would say. "But take care. Once something has been written down, it is hard to get rid of. But if you have come to the conclusion that it will not do—even if it is good in itself— then don't think about it for long: simply strike it out." How often one attempts to save such a passage and thus ruins the entire thing! Sometimes passages like this also serve to conceal the troublemaking elements whose presence I might have intuited but would not have looked for there at all. When Brahms then subjected these very passages to his candid critique, I was hurt and surprised at first because these passages were my favorites, until I came to see that I hadn't found the troublemaker because I had inadvertently assumed that this particular spot must be allowed to stand under any circumstances. I have had the opportunity to feel the truth of those Brahmsian judgments myself; they are the result of long suffering and unrelenting self-criticism.

What I have just said may seem to be contradicted by the fact that a Brahms manuscript often bears a great many corrections. For example, the Clarinet Trio, op. 114, is very heavily "patched" and pasted over. But these corrections have to do with particular details of the composition. Even a composer as technically secure as Mendelssohn was constantly making changes in his works, sometimes while they were bring printed.

Another obstacle that often stands in the way of the young composer cannot be overcome early enough: learning how to "write" in the first place, that is, to master the technique that is necessary before the composer can even begin to form his ideas freely and put them down on paper. This problem is related to the superficial, thoughtless, and completely wrongheaded method of musical education in which our young people are wont to be instructed, whereby a composer finds himself in the position of having to free himself with great effort from an instrument that he has, up until that point, used only as an expedient for his composing. With an education like the one Mozart, for example, enjoyed, such a method is precluded from the first. Natural talent obviously makes a great difference here, but in this matter even the greatest talent cannot escape the necessity of an appropriate and reasonable education. Even Mozart had to begin by mastering the technique of writing; that he was able to do this while still so young is due not least to his excellent father.

In not a few cases a composer who has already emerged from childhood without having acquired this technique may be held back by a kind of false pride which is fundamentally nothing but vanity, and which Brahms sought to discredit in my eyes by saying: "You must learn how to work. You must write a lot, day after day, and not think that what you are writing always has to be something significant. It is the writing itself that matters in the first place. I don't always want to see it. That's what the stove is there for. You must make many songs before a usable one emerges!" I can state most definitively that Brahms understood the last sentence in the most literal sense, and I can cite a large number of texts which, according to the evidence of his own words, he may have composed, but never published; instead he destroyed them. Perhaps it may be of more general interest if I remark here that Brahms's first violin sonata is the fourth. Three previous ones were suppressed because they did not pass his criticism. . . .

"Writing variations is the smartest thing you can do for the time being," Brahms had told me at the very beginning of my instruction, and so one of the first assignments I brought him was a theme with variations for piano. I had preceded these variations with a poem whose four stanzas had exercised a determining influence on the same number of groups of variations, in the sense that each individual stanza preceded each group as a motto. Brahms was delighted with this notion and told me that he had once carried out the same idea, but nothing had come of it. Then he criticized the excessively large number of variations, which must necessarily detract from the idea. "The less variations, the better; but then they must say everything that is to be said." The variations themselves were much too free for him; for he was very exact when it came to this form. Beginning with the choice of a theme, he recommended the greatest caution. "For only a few themes are suitable." Even though I had succeeded in inventing one that he considered suitable, he advised me that next time it would be better to look for one in Schubert or somewhere else. As a model he named Beethoven's variations, which he said I could not study too closely. Everyone knows nowadays that Brahms himself has scarcely any rivals in this area. But Brahms never, in the whole time during which he was teaching me, referred to one of his own compositions for purposes of instruction. It was as if they did not exist. The anecdote is well-known about the time when Beethoven, confronted by someone who showed him a composition and complained that he himself had committed the criticized error in his own works, said with annoyance: "*I* am permitted to do that; you are *not.*" I am aware that once in a similar situation Brahms told someone—not me, for in such things I was always very circumspect—"Have I ever offered you my compositions as a model?"

Notes

1   The Concerto was performed on 1 January 1888, with Brahms conducting and Joseph Joachim and Robert Hausmann as soloists. The Trio, with Brahms as pianist, was played the following day, 2 January. [Ed.]

2   Fritz August Simrock (1838-1901) was Brahms's publisher, friend, and advisor. He inherited one of Germany's most distinguished music publishing firms, founded in 1790. [Ed.]

3   Klaus Groth (1819-99) was a North German poet and professor in Kiel. He was a friend of Brahms, who composed twelve songs to poems of Groth, including the famous *Regenlied,* op. 59, no. 3. Apart from his relationship to Brahms, Groth is best remembered as the editor of a collection of Low German poetry, *Quickborn* (1852). [Ed.]

4   Julius Spengel (1853-1936), teacher, composer, and pianist, was active in Hamburg. [Ed.]

5   Eusebius Mandyczewski (1857-1929) was a prominent figure in the musical life of Vienna. He was a choral conductor, teacher of counterpoint and composition, and holder of significant official appointments in the areas of music education, scholarship, and concert life. But he is best remembered as archivist of the Gesellschaft der Musikfreunde and as a distinguished musicologist—he edited the first complete edition of the works of Franz Schubert—and scholar. He was a close friend of Brahms and mentor for several generations of musicologists. [Ed.]

6   Jenner refers to an "Austrian Regie-Trabuco," an inferior imitation cigar produced by the state tobacco monopoly. [Trans.]

7   A legendary eating and gathering place in the center of Vienna. It was already well-known in the 1830s and 1840s. Until 1870, the home of the Gesellschaft der Musikfreunde was located directly adjacent to it. [Ed.]

8   Brahms was referring to the inn and coffeehouse on the Petersplatz where Mozart lived from May to December 1781 with Madam Weber, whose daughter Constanze he later married. It was during these months that Mozart wrote the *Abduction from the Seraglio.* The building was demolished in 1896 and replaced by a new one in 1897. [Ed.]

9   Ludwig Rottenberg (1864-1932), composer, conductor, and pianist, was a student of Robert Fuchs and Eusebius Mandyczewski in Vienna. He was the conductor of the amateur orchestra of the Gesellschaft der Musikfreunde from 1888 to 1892. In 1893, at the recommendation of Brahms, he became director of the Frankfurt Opera. He is best known as an accompanist of singers, among them three with whom Brahms was particularly associated: Gustav Walter, Hermine Spies, and Alice Barbi. [Ed.]

10   A park in Vienna adjacent to the Ringstrasse, designed along English garden lines and opened in 1862. The park today contains innumerable monuments to composers, the most significant of which, the Schubert monument, was erected in 1872. [Ed.]

11   The Prater was Brahms's favorite park in Vienna. It was by far the largest park in the city and possessed racing facilities and an amusement park. The Prater was given over to public use in the eighteenth century by Joseph II. It was the site of many annual festivities and celebrations. [Ed.]

12   Max Kalbeck (1850-1921), writer, librettist, poet, and music journalist, was Brahms's biographer. Immensely prolific, Kalbeck was a major figure in the world of Viennese letters, particularly with respect to issues of theatre and music. He also edited and wrote the biography of the great Viennese satirist Daniel Spitzer. It is for this and his immensely detailed, multi-volume Brahms biography that he is best remembered. Kalbeck was not universally liked or trusted and was the victim of Karl Kraus's trenchant satire. Anton Door (1833-1919) was a Viennese pianist and piano teacher. A student of Czerny, Door taught at the conservatory in Vienna from 1869 to 1901. Ignaz Brüll (1846-1907) was a Viennese pianist and composer. Unlike Door, Brüll was self-consciously a virtuoso. He was a close friend of Brahms's and a student of Julius Epstein, who was instrumental in Brahms's initial success in Vienna in 1862. Brüll was also a composer of piano music, operas, and orchestral music. Brahms had little good to say about Brüll's music. [Ed.]

13   There were 100 kreuzer to one florin or gulden. Since in 1889 one florin = ca. $.40 U.S., Brahms's typical meal would have cost between $.28 and $.33 U.S. In comparison, the Hotel Sacher in 1889 charged between one and three florins, or $.40-$1.20, for its *prix fixe* menu. [Ed.]

14   *Robert Schumann's Werke,* Series XIV, Supplement, ed. Johannes Brahms (Leipzig, 1893). [Ed.]

15   Friederich Rückert (1788-1866) was a significant German poet of the first half of the nineteenth century. His poems were set by Schumann, Brahms, and Mahler, among others. [Ed.]

16   Brahms's apartment looked out on and was a short distance from two of nineteenth-century Vienna's most important architectural monuments: Fischer von Erlach's eighteenth-century masterpiece, the Karlskirche, and the Technical University, built in 1815. The building was a fine example of late classical architecture. In 1838 and 1866 it was enlarged. Shortly after Brahms's death in 1897, an extra floor was added. [Ed.]

17   Theodor Storm (1817–88), German poet and prose writer, was a particular favorite of Brahms, who possessed his entire writings. [Ed.]

18   Hermann Allmers (1821–1902), Frisian essayist and novelist, is best known for two books: his *Marschenbuch* (1858) and *Römische Schlendertage* (1859). [Ed.]

19   Josef Lewinsky (1835–1907) was the most famous and respected tragic actor in Vienna during Brahms's lifetime. He was also known for his impressiveness as an orator. He commissioned the five Ophelia songs, WoO 22, from Brahms for his wife, who was due to play the part, in the Schlegel translation of *Hamlet*, at the *Deutsches Landtheater* in Prague. [Ed.]

Alexander von Zemlinsky
and Karl Weigl

Brahms and the Newer Generation: Personal Reminiscences

Translated by Walter Frisch

Alexander von Zemlinsky (1872-1942) was one of the most talented and promising young Viennese composers of the turn of the century. After an auspicious study period at the Vienna Conservatory, he went on to have a distinguished career as a teacher, conductor, and opera composer. Among his pupils were Alma Schindler (later to become Mahler's wife) and Karl Weigl. Zemlinsky was the first and only teacher of Arnold Schoenberg; the two friends also became brothers-in-law when Schoenberg married Zemlinsky's sister Mathilde in 1901. Weigl (1881-1949) was a prominent conservative Viennese composer and teacher, who served as Professor of Theory and Composition at the Vienna Conservatory after World War I. Zemlinsky and Weigl were among the many Jewish artists who fled to the United States with the advent of the Nazis. Neither found here the kind of respect and acclaim they had experienced in Europe in the years before World War II.

These reminiscences appeared in the Viennese journal Musikblätter des Anbruch 4 *(1922), 69-70.*

When I think of the time during which I had the fortune to know Brahms personally—it was during the last two years of his life—I can recall immediately how his music affected me and my colleagues in composition, including Schoenberg. It was fascinating, its influence inescapable, its effect intoxicating. I was still a pupil at the Vienna Conservatory and knew most of Brahms's works thoroughly. I was obsessed by this music. My goal at the time was nothing less than the appropriation and mastery of this wonderful, singular compositional technique.

I was introduced to Brahms at the occasion of a performance of a symphony of mine, which I had composed as a student.[1] Brahms had been invited by my teacher [Johann Nepomuk] Fuchs. Soon thereafter, the Hellmesberger Quartet performed a string quintet of mine, which Brahms also heard.[2] He asked for the score and then invited me to call on him; he did so with a brief and somewhat ironic remark, casually tossed off: "Of course, come if it might interest you to talk to me about it." This cost me a hard struggle: the idea that Brahms would speak to me about my attempts at composition elevated my already powerful respect to the level of anxiety. To talk with Brahms was no easy matter. The question-and-answer was short, gruff, seemingly cold, and often very ironic.

He went through my quintet at the piano with me. At first he would offer corrections gently, looking carefully at this or that spot. He never really offered praise, but would grow more animated, and ever more passionate. And when I timidly sought to justify a passage in the development section which seemed to me to be really successful in a Brahmsian spirit, he opened up the string quintet by Mozart and explained to me the consummate qualities of this "still unsurpassed mastery of form."[3] And it sounded self-evident when he said, "That's how it's done from Bach up to myself." Brahms's ruthless criticism had put me in an extremely despondent mood; but he soon cheered me up again. He asked about my financial situation and offered me a monthly stipend so that I could work fewer hours and devote myself more to composition. Finally he recommended me to his publisher Simrock, who also agreed to issue my first compositions.[4]

From then on my works fell even more than before under the influence of Brahms. I remember how even among my colleagues it was considered particularly praiseworthy to compose in as "Brahmsian" a manner as possible. We were soon notorious in Vienna as the dangerous "Brahmins."

Then came a reaction, of course. With the struggle to find oneself, there was also an emphatic repudiation of Brahms. And there were periods when the reverence and admiration for Brahms metamorphosed into the very opposite. Then this phase of undervaluation gave way to a quiet reassessment and enduring love of Brahms's work. And when today I conduct a symphony by him or play one of his splendid chamber works, then I fall once again under the spell of the memory of that time: each measure becomes a personal experience.

Alexander von Zemlinsky

＊　＊　＊

When in my earliest student years I saw Brahms in person for the first time, I knew very little of his music. But the powerful head, surrounded by snow-white hair and a beard, and at that time not yet drawn by the hand of death, left an indelible impression on me. I experienced for the first time the thrill aroused by being in proximity to an immortal.

It took much time and labor before I could make his work my own. I was accustomed to the sensuous power of Mozart and Schubert and the forcefully blazing rhythms of Beethoven. The language of Brahms seemed to me strange and cold. When I finally succeeded—chiefly through his splendid Lieder and his chamber works—in gaining entry to this world that had previously been closed, he became one of my great teachers.

It is not my task here to say how and how much my works were influenced by him. This much I must say, however: that I owe to him purity of compositional technique and seriousness of thematic work, and not last, a new insight into the masters with whom he himself had studied—Haydn, Mozart, Handel, Bach, and the older vocal composers.

Today, direction and desire lead far away from the paths that Brahms trod with manly seriousness. Yet now as then I remain in awe of the spiritual and ethical loftiness of this great master, for whom his art truly meant more than "a play with sounding forms,"[5] who was like few others relentlessly self-critical and was at once   5
a believer and a savior.

Karl Weigl

Notes

1   The occasion of the meeting was actually the premiere of Zemlinsky's Orchestral Suite at a concert at the Gesellschaft der Musikfreunde on 18 March 1895. Brahms led his own Academic Festival Overture on the same program. The event is described vividly in Max Kalbeck, *Johannes Brahms* (Berlin, 1904–14), IV, 400–01. [Ed.]

2   The String Quintet in D Minor (unpublished), performed on 5 March 1896. [Ed.]

3   Zemlinsky does not specify which Mozart quintet Brahms was examining: most likely the C-Major (K. 515) or G-Minor (K. 516). [Ed.]

4   In a letter to Simrock, Brahms recommended Zemlinsky as "both a person and a talent." See *Johannes Brahms Briefwechsel* (Berlin, 1908–22), IV, 212. The work that stimulated Brahms's letter was the Clarinet Trio in D Minor, op. 3, which had received a third prize at a composition contest at the Wiener Tonkünstlerverein. Simrock published the work in 1897. [Ed.]

5   A reference to the "tönend bewegter Formen" (forms moved in sounding) that lay at the heart of the aesthetic position on music espoused by Eduard Hanslick in his *Vom Musikalisch Schönen* of 1854. [Ed.]

Appendix

211   "Dedicated to Johannes Brahms"
prepared by Walter Frisch

"Dedicated to Johannes Brahms"

Prepared by Walter Frisch

Something of the esteem in which Brahms was held can be seen by the large number of works dedicated to him by other composers. In a small notebook now at the Wiener Stadtbibliothek, Brahms himself kept an ongoing handwritten list (headed "Widmungen") of these titles; the list runs to 78 musical entries, plus 4 books and 1 collection of prints. In his own extensive library, Brahms had copies of most of these works, no doubt sent to him by the authors (see Kurt Hofmann, Die Bibliothek von Johannes Brahms *[Hamburg, 1974], esp. the segment "Johannes Brahms' Musikbibliothek," compiled by Alfred Orel, pp. 139-66, which transcribes Brahms's own catalogue of his music collection.) The following list presents the titles of musical works and other books bearing printed dedications to Brahms. It has been compiled primarily from Brahms's own handwritten list and catalogue, supplemented by further research (which has also turned up several works written in his memory soon after his death). Where possible, each title has been verified independently in printed bibliographic sources. (It was not possible at press time to have consulted Brahms's actual library at the Gesellschaft der Musikfreunde.) Full names, dates of publication, keys, performing forces, and opus numbers have been supplied when locatable (Brahms's own list has few such details). The sequence of musical titles follows principally that of Brahms's own "Widmungen" inventory, which was compiled in the order in which he received the items and thus is essentially chronological. One can reasonably assume that a work for which no date is available was published at a time very close to that of a dated work near it on the list. Some works by the same composer have, however, been grouped together; and some works for which a date of publication was found have been placed nearer other works of that date. Where titles are specific or unique, I have tended to leave them in the original language. Generic titles like "Clavierstücke" or "Quintett" (or even "Romanze") have normally been translated.*

ART

Max Klinger, *Amor und Psyche* [46 prints] (Munich, 1880)

BOOKS

Gustav Wendt [trans.], *Sophocles's Tragödien* (Stuttgart, 1884)

Adalbert Kupferschmied, *Linguistisch-kulturhistorische Skizzen und Bilder aus der deutschen Steiermark* (Karlsruhe, 1888)

Eduard Hanslick, *Musikalisches Skizzenbuch: Neue Kritiken und Schilderungen.* Die Moderne Oper, part 4 (Berlin, 1888)

Title page of Woldemar Bargiel, *Fantasy* no. 3 for piano (1860), dedicated to Brahms.

Hugo Riemann, *Katekismus der Kompositionslehre: Musikalische Formenlehre* (Leipzig, 1889)

Hedwig Kiesenkamp [pseud. L. Rafael], *Ebbe und Fluth: Gedichte* (Leipzig, 1896)

MUSIC

Robert Schumann, *Concert-Allegro mit Introduction,* piano and orchestra, D minor–major, op. 134 (1855)

Clara Schumann, Three Romances, piano, op. 21 (1855)

Robert Schumann, *Des Sängers Fluch* (Uhland), Ballade for soloists, chorus, and orchestra, op. 139 (1858)

Woldemar Bargiel, *Fantasie* no. 3, piano, C minor, op. 19 (1860)

Joseph Joachim, Hungarian Concerto, violin, D minor, op. 11 (1861)

Carl G. P. Grädener, Piano Trio no. 2, E-flat Major, op. 35

Adolf Jensen, *Fantasiestücke,* piano, op. 7

Adolf Jensen, Piano Sonata, F-sharp minor, op. 25

Johann Peter Gotthardt, *Ave Maria,* tenor, men's chorus, organ, op. 39

Johann Peter Gotthardt, 10 Pieces in Dance Form, piano four hands, op. 58

Ferdinand Thierot, Trio, F minor, op. 14

Georg Heinrich Witte, Waltzes, piano four hands, op. 7

Ernst Rudorff, *Fantasie,* piano, G minor, op. 14 (1869)

Max Bruch, Symphony, E-flat major, op. 28 (1870)

R. Schweida, 7 Piano Pieces, op. 7

Karl Reinthaler, *In der Wüste* (Psalm 63), chorus and orchestra, op. 26

Albert Dietrich, Symphony, D minor, op. 20 (1870)

Anna von Dobjansky, Nocturnes, piano, op. 2 (1870)

Hermann Goetz, Piano Quartet, E major, op. 6 (1870)

Louis Bödecker, Variations on a Theme by Schubert, piano, op. 3 (1871)

Julius Otto Grimm, Suite no. 2 in Canonic Form, orchestra, op. 16 (1871)

Josef Rheinberger, 2 *Claviervorträge,* op. 45 (1871)

Franz Wüllner, *Miserere,* double choir and soloists, op. 26

Karl Tausig, arr., Chorale Preludes by Bach (1873)

Julius Stockhausen, Four Songs (1873)

Heinrich Hoffmann, Hungarian Suite, orchestra, op. 16 (1877)

Stefanie Gräfin Wurmbrand, Three Piano Pieces

Karl Goldmark, *Frühlingshymne,* alto, chorus, and orchestra, op. 23 (1875)

Xaver Scharwenka, *Romanzero,* piano, op. 33 (1876)

Theodor Kirchner, Waltzes, piano, op. 23 (1876)

Bernhard Scholz, String Quintet, op. 47 (1878)

J. Carl Eschmann, *Licht und Schatten,* 6 piano pieces, op. 62

Hans Huber, Waltzes, piano four hands, violin, cello, op. 27 (1878)

Otto Dessoff, String Quartet, F major, op. 7 (1878)

Ferdinand Hummel, Suite, piano four hands, op. 17

Vincenz Lachner, 12 Ländler (1879 or 1880)

Georg Henschel, *Serbisches Liederspiel,* op. 32 (1879)

Robert Fuchs, Piano Trio, C major, op. 22 (1879)

Adolf Wallnöfer, *Grenzen der Menschheit* (Goethe), alto or baritone solo, mixed chorus, and orchestra, op. 10 (1879)

Constantin Bürgel, Variations on an Original Theme, piano four hands, op. 30 (1879)

J. Gustav Eduard Stehle, 5 Motets, op. 44

Antonín Dvořák, String Quartet, D minor, op. 34 (1877)

J. C. Gegenbauer, *Transcription de mélodies hongroises,* op. 10

Fran Serafin Vilhar, *Albumblätter*

Karl Nawratil, Piano Trio, E-flat major, op. 9 (1881)

Leander Schlegel, Ballades, piano, op. 2

Philipp Wolfrum, Organ Sonata no. 3, F minor (1883)

Rudolf Bibl, *Klavierstücke in Romanzenton,* op. 45

Algernon B. L. Ashton, *Englische Tänze*, piano four hands, op. 10 (1883)

Eduard Marxsen, 100 Variations on a Folk Song, piano (1883)

Charles Villiers Stanford, *Songs of Old Ireland* (1884)

Heinrich von Herzogenberg, Three String Quartets, op. 42 (1884)

Jean Louis Nicodé, Symphonic Variations, orchestra, C minor, op. 27

Ernst Seyffardt, *Schicksalsgesang* (Geibel), alto solo, mixed chorus, and orchestra, op. 13

Ferruccio Busoni, Six Etudes, piano, op. 16 (1883)

Ferruccio Busoni, *Etude: Tema e Variazioni*, piano, op. 17 (1884)

Richard von Perger, String Quartet, G minor, op. 8 (1886)

Samuel de Lange, Organ Sonata no. 5, C minor, op. 50 (1887)

Fritz Kauffmann, String Quartet, G major, op. 14

Anton Urspruch, *Ave maris stella*, chorus and orchestra, op. 24

Emil Kreuz, Lieder, opp. 1 & 2

Giulio E. A. Alary, String Sextet, op. 35

Anton Rückauf, Piano Quintet, F major, op. 13

Niccolò van Westerhout, Piano Sonata

Richard Barth, Partita, solo violin, op. 10

Johann Strauss, Jr., Waltzes, *Seid umschlungen Millionen*, op. 443 (1892)

Elie-Miriam Delaborde, *Morceau romantique* (Quintet)

Eugen d'Albert, String Quartet, E-flat major, op. 11 (1893)

Josef Suk, Piano Quintet, G minor, op. 8 (1893)

Reinhold Stöckhardt, Three Piano Pieces, op. 10

Walter Rabl, Piano Quartet (with clarinet), op. 1

Vítězslav Novák, *Eclogen*, Four Piano Pieces, op. 11

Julius Röntgen, Ballade on a Norwegian Folk Melody, orchestra, op. 36 (1896)

Karel Bendl, *Rosenlieder*, three-part women's chorus and piano, op. 121

Arthur Hinton, *Weisse Rosen* (Josef Huggenberger), 6 Lieder

Otto Barblan, Passacaglia, organ, op. 6

Hans Schmitt, Brilliant Piano Etudes, op. 65

Eugen Philips, Piano Trio no. 2, D major, op. 28

Heinrich von Herzogenberg, Piano Quartet no. 2, B-flat major, op. 95 (1897)

Marco Anzoletti, Variations on a Theme of Brahms, violin and piano

Carl Reinecke, Sonata no. 3, cello and piano, G major, op. 238. "To the memory of Johannes Brahms" (1898)

Max Reger, Rhapsody, piano, E minor, op. 24, no. 6. "To the memory of Johannes Brahms" (1899)

Max Reger, "Resignation," piano, op. 26, no. 5. "3. April 1897—J. Brahms†" (1899)

Index of Brahms's Works

Index of Names

Adorno, Theodor, 87
Alary, Giulio E. A., 215
Allmers, Hermann, 196, 204 n.18
d'Albert, Eugen, 75, 215
Allgemeiner Deutscher Musikverein: 65, 72, 75
Anzoletti, Marco, 216
Ashton, Algernon, B. L., 215

Bach, C. P. E., 194
Bach, J. S., 5, 72, 93, 110, 123, 154, 194, 206
Barbi, Alice, 31, 203 n.9
Barblan Otto, 216
Bargiel, Woldemar, 110, 119, 212, 213
Barth, Heinrich, 57
Barth, Richard, 177, 215
Bartók, Béla, 73–74
Bechstein, Carl, 59–60
Beckerath, Alwin von, 177
Beethoven, Ludwig van, 5, 27, 28, 34, 35 n.15, 49, 53, 72, 97, 109, 135, 138, 145, 154, 165, 178, 199, 202, 206; Cantata on the Accession of Emperor Leopold II, WoO 88: 167, 168; Cantata on the Death of Emperor Joseph II, WoO 87: 167–68, 182 n.5; *Fidelio*, op. 72: 168; *Missa solemnis*, op. 123: 118; Piano Concerto no. 3, C minor, op. 37: 151–52, 153; Piano Concerto no. 4, G major, op. 58: 118; Piano Concerto no. 5, E-flat major, op. 73 ("Emperor"): 77 n.20, 118; Piano Sonata no. 29, B-flat major, op. 106 ("Hammerklavier"): 105; Scottish Lieder, op. 108: 55; Symphony no. 5, C minor, op. 67: 123; Symphony no. 8, F major, op. 93: 136; Symphony no. 9, D minor, op. 125: 7, 118, 152; Variations on a Waltz by Diabelli, op. 120: 55; Violin Concerto, op. 61: 118, 155

Bendl, Karel, 215
Berger, Ludwig, 110
Berlioz, Hector, 72
Bernstein, Rosa. *See* Neuda-Bernstein, Rosa
Bibl, Rudolf, 214
Billroth, Theodor, 4, 6, 8, 25, 28–29, 32, 46, 65, 66, 145, 163–64, 176, 178–79, 183 n.24
Bismarck, Otto von, 25, 176
Bödecker, Louis, 213
Bösendorfer, Ludwig, 55, 57, 61
Breitkopf & Härtel, 41, 182 n.6
Brendel, Franz, 65, 72, 79, 80, 80 n.b, 103, 105
Broadwood, John, 50
Brodsky, Adolph, 65
Bruch, Max, 213
Bruckner, Anton, 7, 8, 18, 34 n.14, 163
Brüll, Ignaz, 191, 203 n.12
Bülow, Hans von, 59, 60, 66, 75, 80 n.b, 167, 174
Bülow, Marie von, 167, 174
Bürgel, Constantin, 214
Busch, Moritz, 176
Busoni, Ferruccio, 215

Cecilia Society, 183 n.9
Cherubini, Luigi, 134
Chomsky, Noam, 11